ALSO BY LUC DE BRABANDERE

The Forgotten Half of Change: Achieving Greater Creativity Through Changes in Perception

Thinking in New Boxes

THINKING IN
NEW B◻XES

A New Paradigm for Business Creativity

LUC de BRABANDERE AND ALAN INY

RANDOM HOUSE  NEW YORK

Thinking in New Boxes is a work of nonfiction. Some corporate names and identifying details have been changed.

Published in the United States by Random House, an imprint of The Random House Publishing Group, a division of Random House, Inc., New York.

RANDOM HOUSE and the HOUSE colophon are registered trademarks of Random House, Inc.

LIBRARY OF CONGRESS CATALOGING-IN-PUBLICATION DATA
Brabandere, Luc de.
Thinking in new boxes : a new paradigm for business creativity /
Luc de Brabandere and Alan Iny.
pages   cm
Includes bibliographical references and index.
ISBN 978-0-8129-9295-3
eBook ISBN 978-0-679-64436-1
1. Creative ability in business.   2. Creative thinking.   3. New products.
4. Diffusion of innovations.   I. Iny, Alan.   II. Title.
HD53.b7125 2013
658.4'0714—dc23   2013000538

Printed in the United States of America on acid-free paper

www.atrandom.com

9

Book design by Simon M. Sullivan

This book is dedicated to all of our colleagues and clients, who have enabled us to learn about creativity while teaching it, and to our wives, Bernadette and Roberta, who have enabled that to happen.

Contents

□ □

N A SMALL FARM amid gently rolling hills, there was once a playful Labrador retriever named Sartre. Every day Sartre would leap over a fence at the back of the farm to run through the woods and chase squirrels. Eventually, the fence was dismantled, freeing poor Sartre from the burden of having to hop over it every time he wanted to frolic, but Sartre still jumped every time he came to the spot where the barrier had been. He had developed a set of memories and assumptions that made it almost impossible for him to notice the fence was no longer there.

Sartre's behavior was in some ways similar to that of the three main characters in *No Exit*, the famous play by the French existentialist philosopher for whom he was named. Garcin, Estelle, and Inez are prisoners in Hell (a boxlike room) who long to leave the claustrophobic space. Yet in the play's final moments, when the door suddenly flies open and they are free to leave, they stay, terrified to step out into the unknown space beyond.

The dog's mistake may seem comical, and the plight of Jean-Paul Sartre's pathetic characters a bit heavy-handed, yet both of these stories expose profound truths about human nature.

Every day, all of us create countless mental models—or what we will refer to here as "boxes"—in order to make sense of the world. Many of these boxes will help you for a while—as Sartre the dog's fence-jumping tactic did for years. But they can also hold you back and make it hard for you to notice important changes around you. Our brains pull us toward the familiar, so we cling to old boxes that may no longer be relevant. Most of us are averse to risk, and try to confirm existing opinions and deny how rapidly and radically things are changing.

In today's ever more turbulent world, such failures of perception can be costly. Relying on your existing boxes to simplify the infinite unknown is useful, indeed unavoidable, but relying too heavily, or for too long, on any mental model can lead you to miss exciting opportunities. It can prevent you from seeing critical "breaks in the fence" or from achieving success in the abyss of the unknown (which, in essence, is the fate of the characters in Sartre's *No Exit*).

As business strategy consultants with decades of collective experience working with major organizations worldwide, addressing high-stakes challenges that can affect thousands of employees and millions of customers, we have seen that the key distinction between winners and losers, leaders and followers, those who soar in the face of change and those who are defeated by it, comes down to the form of strategic creativity that we refer to as "thinking in new boxes." This process marries pragmatic analysis with the free-flowing generation of ideas. When you think in new boxes, you continuously develop and test hypotheses—including new ways to embrace complexity, navigate uncertainty, and prepare for the disruptions that inevitably await you.

Perhaps you are an entrepreneur introducing a new idea or an architect imagining a dazzling edifice. Or maybe you're an engineer trying to conceptualize a new software program, a politician seeking revolutionary social change, or a manager leading your organization through one of the most perilous economies in modern times. No matter what challenge you face, the creativity process we describe in this book can change how you interpret everything happening around you and how you solve problems. It can improve how you lead your team despite not knowing what lies around the next corner (after all, no one does). You will rediscover the full power of thinking, in all its many dimensions, via our pragmatic system for achieving productive, free-flowing, perspective-expanding, life-enhancing, practical, and sustainable creativity.

Read on, and our system will help you imagine, shape, and then release into the world new designs, strategies, and visions that could help you and your colleagues create the next Post-it note or the next iPad—or at least help you think of business creativity in a completely new way. It will spur you to dream up multiple future scenarios in which you could be doing business, and thus better prepare for whatever the future holds. And it will even guide you toward a more open way of thinking about your life and show you how to ask the right questions, to better enable you to reach all your goals, both personal and professional.

You will learn to think differently, and more effectively—and this will change the way you do business, and the way you live your life. And it will be fun. We promise.

Thinking in New Boxes

New Boxes for a New Reality

□□□□□□□□□□□□□□□□□□□□□□□□□□□□□□□□□□□□□

L ET'S START WITH AN EASY QUESTION: How many colors are there in a rainbow?

Would you say five? Seven? Ten? At some point in your schooling, you were probably told that a rainbow has a fixed number of colors. The common explanation is that the human eye sees just seven colors—red, orange, yellow, green, blue, indigo, and violet—and hence many of us were told as children that there are seven colors in the rainbow. But that's not quite correct—a rainbow is a continuous spectrum of colors, at least according to our models of physics. To cope with complicated ideas such as this (in this case, an infinite number of colors) the mind simplifies, placing the physical reality in a more conveniently sized, manageable "box."*

Boxes can include, among many other things, ideas, approaches, philosophies, tactics, theories, patterns, and strategies. Every human idea can be expressed and/or interpreted through numerous mental models, or "boxes." Your brain constantly uses boxes—and cannot do otherwise—to make it possible for you to cope with and process reality. The world confronts us with an infinite array of people, places, and objects; we use patterns and systems to simplify these, and categories to organize them.

We all have boxes of many different sizes. The smallest type of box would be a grouping of like things—such as "the consumer electronics

---

* Actually, studies have shown that the eye commonly sees only six colors in a rainbow (indigo is generally missing). So our mind's answer of "seven" (because that's what we were told growing up) is even more artificial than we realize—it could have something to do with the cultural significance of seven as a special number.

companies" or "the set of coffee shops in my neighborhood." Examples of slightly bigger boxes include stereotypes or judgments—"our customers love chocolate" or "basketball players are tall." A paradigm is a box so big (for example, "democracy" or "freedom") that sometimes you don't even realize it's still just a box, like being on a boat so big you forget you're at sea. Boxes of other sizes include what we commonly call structures, hypotheses, frameworks, mindsets, frames of reference, and so on.

All of these various boxes help make the world more manageable. Every one of us constantly takes the broad variety of experiences we have and information we observe and reduces them to segments or categories, "boxes" with which we try to make sense of things. But even the most seemingly obvious and widely shared boxes should not be confused with reality: Accounting is always just a snapshot of the past, not an accurate representation of the present; dividing up your customers into market segments is an often-useful distortion that relies upon artificial distinctions and generalizations.

In addition to being simplified, a box is your mind's fuzzy representation of reality. You might have a seemingly solid image of the Google logo in your mind, of primary colors for the six letters. Could you say with certainty which colors appear twice? Your boxes help you make sense of things, but only up to a certain level of detail (in this case, enough to avoid confusion with some other company's logo), and only for a certain period of time. Every box is subject to revision, refinement, and even replacement.

For example, suppose you're eating dinner in a restaurant and a gray-haired man who appears to be in his mid-fifties, dressed in a well-tailored suit, walks in, accompanied by a much younger woman dressed in jeans and a T-shirt. They look vaguely alike, and you immediately decide that they are father and daughter. When they sit down at the table next to you, however, you notice telling attributes, and slowly learn more about them. Perhaps the man presents the young woman with an investment opportunity, and you decide she is a wealthy client of his. Perhaps they hold hands and you decide they are spouses. Or they're trying to distract you while their colleague steals your wallet. Regardless, you cannot avoid settling on an explanation; you cannot avoid building boxes.

The same kind of serial "deciding" occurs all the time in business. Suppose your CEO appoints a new CFO in a surprise announcement that thanks the former CFO for her service and praises her desire to spend more time with her family. You may take this announcement at face value, or you may "decide" there was too much tension between the departing CFO and the CEO. Perhaps later at the water cooler you hear rumors of fiscal impropriety, and a few days later new expense reimbursement regulations are announced, and so you decide the old CFO was padding her expense account. Or perhaps you are told of an emergency board meeting where the CEO was apparently fighting for his job and hence you decide that the CFO was offered up by him as a sacrifice.

When we see news of an airplane crash in Africa or a merger between two companies, we immediately come up with a rationale for how and why these events happen. And as all of these examples show, your interpretation of reality evolves as you gather data. Much as scientists develop working hypotheses that, after investigation, they modify into more definitive "theories," you reshape and refine your boxes based on the new information. When refinement is not enough, for example if some fresh observation is completely incompatible with your existing boxes, a fundamentally different box may be required.

Moreover, relying upon just one box is generally not sufficient. The complexity of the world requires you to constantly juggle multiple theories, models, and strategies. As your "box" describing the couple in the restaurant evolved, you also used and updated other mental models, such as whether the soup was any good, which fork to use for dessert, whether to respond to the waitress honestly when she asked how your meal was, and how much to tip her.

The key difference to be aware of is between the multifaceted and difficult-to-understand world *in front of you* and the ways you perceive, interpret, and simplify it *within you*. Or as we like to put it, people use mental models or boxes within them (such as concepts and stereotypes) to handle the complex, continuously changing, often chaotic reality in front of them.

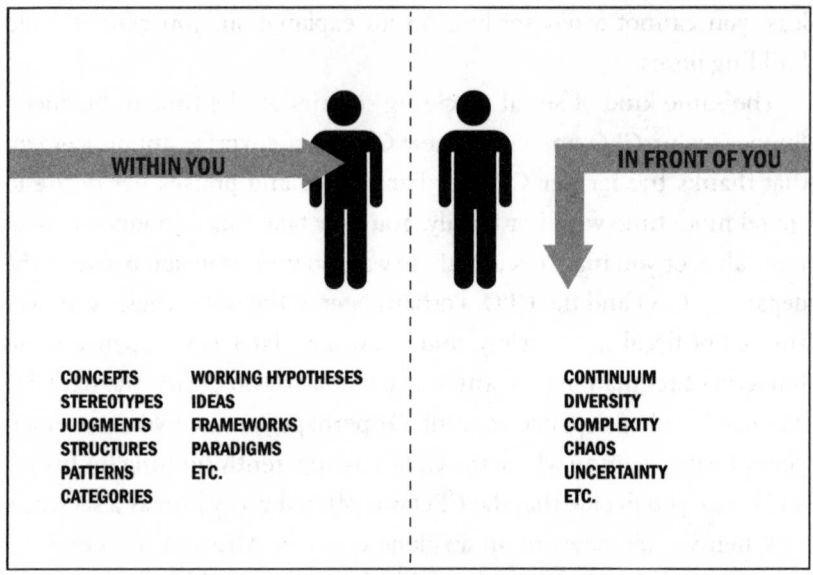

WITHIN YOU		IN FRONT OF YOU
CONCEPTS	WORKING HYPOTHESES	CONTINUUM
STEREOTYPES	IDEAS	DIVERSITY
JUDGMENTS	FRAMEWORKS	COMPLEXITY
STRUCTURES	PARADIGMS	CHAOS
PATTERNS	ETC.	UNCERTAINTY
CATEGORIES		ETC.

To be more creative, and to survive in a world of accelerating change and challenge, we believe you must do more than simply think "outside the box." Rather, you must learn to think in new boxes, which means deliberately (not just subconsciously) creating a range of fresh mental models, and methodically exploring and prioritizing them.

YOU CAN'T THINK WITHOUT BOXES, SO DON'T EVEN TRY

You can't think or make decisions, let alone create new ideas (or recognize a good idea when you see one), without using a range of mental models to simplify things. Most of the time, thinking includes a process of *classification:* Your mind is confronted with reality—a multiplicity of stimuli, elements, and events. To make sense of all these disparate inputs, your mind either relies on preexisting categories that it has already created or, if none of those categories fits the present reality, it generates new ones.

You might think of the mind as a giant cupboard, with compartments and drawers, a place to tidy up the messiness of reality, to sort it all into a much more comprehensible and manageable set of ideas. Each of us creates order by sorting; things with some shared characteristics are put together. Nobody can deal with the many complicated aspects of real life without first placing things in such *boxes,* the raw materials of human thinking and creativity. When you say "my customers" as a salesperson, or "my students" as a teacher, you're using a box to categorize, or to visualize a couple of individual customers or students in your head. In contrast to saying "my children" or "my office," where you can usually be referring to the real thing, the set of customers or students is large enough to make a simplification necessary.

Consider the first pages of the Judeo-Christian Bible. When God placed Adam in the Garden of Eden, God told him he had to be a master of the other animals: "God said, 'Let us make mankind in our image, in our likeness, so that they may rule over the fish in the sea and the birds in the sky, over the livestock and all the wild animals, and over all the creatures that move along the ground.' "[1]

What was the first thing Adam did in order to establish his mastery? He gave names to each species of animal. In essence, Adam was saying: *I am master of the lion because I told him, "You are a lion."* And *I am master of the bear because I told him, "You are a bear."* Names—and words—don't exist anywhere but in our minds, yet people need them in order to deal with reality. By giving names to animals, objects, and the other facets of reality, we draw distinctions, make judgments, create links between things, foster order, exercise control, and, most important, put things into easier-to-understand categories.

Indeed, one of the most primitive forms of a box, and perhaps one of the most important inventions of all time, is the *category.* When Aristotle, in his *Organon,* crafted ten categories (including "quantity" and "location") in an attempt to organize all the possible kinds of things that can be the subject or the predicate of a proposition, he set the stage for the science of logic, which led to more formalized human reasoning.*

---

* Why did Aristotle come up with ten rather than, say, twelve categories? According to the renowned French linguist Emile Benveniste, the reason is simple: In Greek, the verb "to be" can be said in ten different ways: "I am," "I am in France," "I am a man," "I am happy," and so on. Aristotle observed these ten uses of "to be"—these were what were in front of him—and therefore he perceived within himself ten very helpful categories. Had Aristotle hailed from a different part of the world where there were more or

Of course, categories represent just one relatively simple type of box. Thinking also requires many other, more sophisticated mental models, including stereotypes, patterns, systems, rules, assumptions, and paradigms. These various boxes arm us with helpful ways of coping with reality. If you are like most people, you stay a safe distance away from lions because you have already created a "carnivorous feline" box in your mind to identify the beast as a danger. Each time you see an animal that looks like other animals you've seen and categorized, you place that new idea in those previous boxes, and they help guide your reactions, in an instant.

People love to reduce uncertainty. In fact, they desperately *need* to reduce it. They feel woefully uncomfortable not knowing. Boxes are an easy way to simplify, to minimize your anxiety about the world. When you think about a real-life situation or problem, you humanize it: You re-create the world in your image, in your likeness, by using your judgments, assumptions, categories, and other mental models, based on everything that has been "in front of you" until that point. You need these boxes to produce further related ideas—whether complementary or opposing, closely connected or wildly distinct.

In this way, boxes are sketches, your mind's way of simplifying, naming, and framing things—whether it is a starving lion, a crying infant, or a popular uprising in your friend's home country—so that you can determine how best to respond to them.

Thinking "Outside the Box" Is Not Enough

But how can you use boxes to generate new creative ideas and approaches?

At a conventional workshop on creativity or innovation, you are encouraged to "think outside the box." Leaders of such seminars have been imploring people to do this for decades, but there are three basic

---

fewer such usages of the verb "to be," he might have increased or decreased his number of categories accordingly.

problems with this advice: 1) It is very hard to get out of a box, 2) it is tricky to determine *which* of your many boxes to think outside of, and 3) even if you do manage the trick, and get out of a specific box, it often isn't enough—you still need a new one.

Suppose you are an executive at a bank in downtown Chicago and during a corporate workshop, someone asks you to "think outside the box." In that context, "outside the box" doesn't mean outside the bank, but rather outside the way you *perceive* your bank and, perhaps, outside your working hypotheses about banks in general.

In other words, a box is not a tangible thing. Rather, it is a model *in your mind*. And every mental model you create, no matter how brilliant or profitable, will eventually need to be refreshed and replaced, since the world will continue to evolve while your box stays frozen. Our four-legged friend Sartre wisely jumped over the fence that prevented him from exploring the fields behind his farm. But change occurred—the fence was taken down—and his old pattern of leaping over the fence no longer made sense or held any value. He needed to dump his old box and build a new one that no longer included the fence as part of the world in front of him.

What Sartre the dog failed to realize is that mental models can both guide you and set you free. But they can also obscure the truth and hold you back. They trap you in rigid assumptions and well-worn paths of action. They push you toward tired routines and stale conventions. They choke your creativity. They hold you captive.

So why doesn't it work to simply "think outside the box"? One key reason is that it is difficult, often impossible, to do on command. As with Sartre (the dog once again), it often takes time and effort to change one's mental model and come up with effective new ones. And since you always use more than one box to handle any situation, you will have numerous possible theories, hypotheses, or approaches—which means there is never any easy way of determining *which* box you should be trying to think "outside" of. And finally, even if you could isolate just one such box from among all those you have created, you will still struggle to think outside it because the space beyond it is too expansive. There is too much room to roam in the unknown.

THE FIRST "OUTSIDE THE BOX" BOX

The origin of the phrase "thinking outside the box" is uncertain, but it seems to have sprung from the corporate culture of the 1960s and 1970s. It is believed that the phrase first referred to a now-familiar nine-dot puzzle used to provoke creative thought. The challenge is to connect nine dots on a square grid by drawing four straight lines through them without the pen leaving the paper, as shown on page 11.

This at first seems impossible—and it is indeed impossible if the pen never moves outside the grid created by the dots. The only solution is to extend at least one of the lines beyond the boundaries of the grid; hence "outside the box."*²

---

* The identity of the inventor of the nine-dot test is in dispute as well. John Adair, a British academic and expert on leadership, claims to have introduced it into corporate culture in 1969, while management consultant Mike Vance has said that the puzzle stems from the Walt Disney Company corporate offices. The earliest citation of the phrase "outside the box" is in *Aviation Week & Space Technology*'s July 1975 issue. But

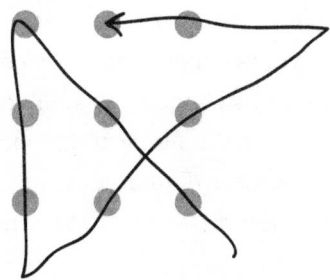

This classic puzzle sparks discussion of two fundamental questions in the old-fashioned model of business creativity. The first is "What sort of boxes are you in?" The second is "How do you think outside them?"

The first question is usually answered by thinking about questions such as: What sort of business am I in? What, exactly, do I spend most of my time doing? What are the skills for which I am rewarded? What assumptions, spoken and unspoken, do I make about the world because of the way my day-to-day activities shape my thinking?

If you are sitting at a conference table surrounded by other automobile executives, one of the most powerful boxes might be "We are an automobile company." If the seats at the table instead contain accountants, the most strongly held box might be "We are an accounting firm."* This model of creativity assumes that if you are an accountant you "think in a certain way" about things. You think *like an accountant*. Conventional theories of creativity urge you to step outside such a box, but the most creative element of that sort of thinking is usually something along the lines of asking, "Are any of our competitors doing anything different, and if so, should we copy them?"

Instead, imagine what would happen if you tried to see an accounting firm in the way people in completely different careers would see it—software engineers, nurses, or sommeliers, for example—if taken away from their own lives and temporarily placed in your shoes. Think-

the concept of unrestricted thinking goes back further. For example, in 1945, the *Oelwein Daily Register* in Iowa defined blue-sky thinking as "Real thinking. Speculation. Pushing out in the blue. Finding out [the facts] was what put me onto the theory of blue-sky thinking."

* This book should not be seen as encouraging "creative accounting."

ing outside *this* box in this way would add an element of difference that could lead to less conventional and more creative thinking. Would the software engineer see accounting as a set of core principles plus a set of add-on "apps"? Would the nurse triage clients based on the severity of their financial issues? This is not the sort of expansive thinking that being encouraged to "think outside the box" automatically spurs you to do.

The issue is not that thinking outside the box is a worthless exercise. It can be an important way to examine business problems, as well as perform other creative tasks. The problem is that while it helps people avoid solutions that are too obvious or conventional, it offers little to no guidance about *where* the best solutions can be found. Just telling someone to avoid conventional thinking is like telling them not to drive on the highway, without giving them any information on which roads to take instead—or whether they should consider flying or going by train.

So rather than asking you to consider how you can connect nine dots using four lines, there is a different sort of question, more emblematic of our "new paradigm" approach, we'd prefer you ponder.

Look at the square below and try to imagine different ways to divide it into four parts that are equal in size.

What are all the different ways in which you can do so?

You might first divide the square by drawing a vertical line and a horizontal line. You could also draw diagonals, or strips:

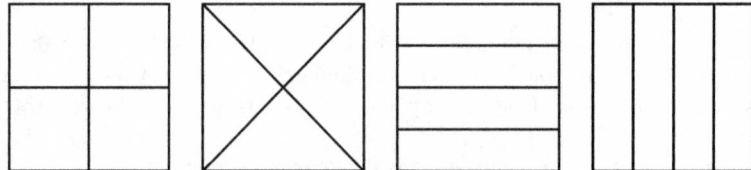

What other options are there? Did you consider other possible shapes?

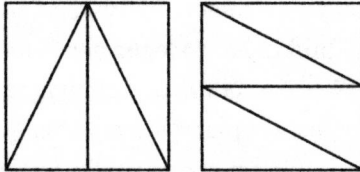

What about creating shapes within the square that are not triangles or rectangles? What about rotating the X, or using lines that aren't straight?

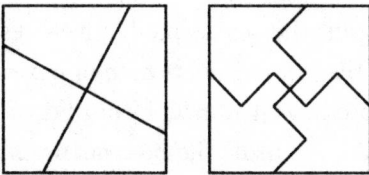

That begins to suggest an infinite number of solutions. And we haven't even tried using curved lines yet:

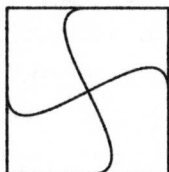

If you think more about it, you'll see that there is an infinite number of ways to divide the square into equal parts. As you develop these various models in your mind, you realize that new horizons are opening, horizons that can never be exhausted. This leap from a few answers to an infinite number of solutions is analogous to the jump from "outside the box" to "new boxes": You come to fundamentally change the way you look at the problem, and to realize the breadth of possibility in front of you.

THE GREAT ESCAPE

Years ago, when we were at a conference in Paris talking to participants at a workshop about "thinking outside the box," someone came up to us afterward and said, "What exactly is this *box* you're talking about?"

The intelligent, inquisitive man who put this question to us understood that we were speaking metaphorically, but he pressed for more answers: "Who builds the box? Can the box be dismantled? Why *should* I try to leave it? How will getting outside the box help me come up with new ideas?"

This man's wise questions prompted us to wonder whether telling people to "think outside the box" is productive—it seemed almost akin to telling them that they are prisoners of their boxes and should escape! In some sense, we are indeed all tied, by our boxes, to a certain view of the world, and thinking outside the box means escaping from at least one tether. But more generally, we realized that asking people to escape a prison will have a chance of working only if people realize that they are, indeed, in some form of prison, and if they understand the specifics of it. They'll need to learn the rules and practices of the ties that bind them to their models, where the vulnerabilities are, and what they need to achieve to discover the gaps in the system and then walk through one of those gaps. Once they are outside that box, they will also have to figure out where to go—and that means finding new boxes instead.

We soon realized that the clever man in Paris played the role of a freedom-seeking prisoner perfectly for us because he had the kind of inquisitive mind and practical creative reasoning that ultimately leads to liberation. Indeed, simply insisting that one should leave the box—or the prison—won't bring freedom. Instead, pondering the nature of the box, questioning why it is there in the first place, striving to understand the strategies and constraints of those controlling it—those are your first steps toward liberty. As we will emphasize throughout this book, *doubt* is the crucial first step toward creativity and liberation.

As the characters in Sartre's *No Exit* found, it is often tremendously difficult for people to realize when they are chained to a model, especially if it is subconscious or so woven into the culture or their expectations that they can no longer see how much it is holding them back. Your current box may be difficult to leave simply because it is familiar and comfortable, and because the boundless space beyond seems perilously uncertain.

We believe the story of creativity is an epic of freedom: You have to be free in order to create, but you must first recognize you are a prisoner in order to break free. And this is true no matter how smart someone is, no matter how well run an organization is—we all become trapped by our boxes over time.

When you ask questions about any box, then, you are also asking questions about yourself and your mental powers: *What kind of box is this?* entails asking yourself, What kind of prisoner am I, and what sort of prison am I in? How can I break out? And once I achieve my freedom, what kind of world will I seek to create?

In other words, you can't get away from your current models until you are conscious of their existence, and start to doubt and investigate them. And it also means creating new ones, and then breaking free from *them* to come up with yet more.

Since your brain needs models or boxes to think, the key to being creative in practical ways, to managing change during these times of such uncertainty, is to first try to understand your existing boxes to a greater degree, and to then attack any situation or issue by developing a *range* of new boxes. You can then carefully choose which box(es) to use, even as you embrace the ambiguity inherent in doing so. It is these new models, these new boxes, these new ways of thinking, that will free you to see not only what is possible but also what you must do to survive and to thrive.

Being inspired to create new boxes may sound difficult—but with the guidelines in this book, and some work, it will become more intuitive, and easier.

TWO

How to Create and Use Boxes

COMPLETE THE FOLLOWING SENTENCE:

An example of a bird is . . .

Now, complete this one:

A bird is an example of . . .

Which of the two exercises seemed easier? If you're like most people, it was quick and easy to come up with examples of birds—pigeon, crow, sparrow, dove . . .

The second sentence was probably marginally more challenging. We suspect you thought a bit and then—after "A bird is an example of . . ."—you might have settled on "an animal." If this is how you completed the sentence, you have nothing to be ashamed of. But we will not congratulate you, either: This answer falls in what is commonly referred to as the "comfort zone," and it does not take full advantage of the creative freedom available to you.

In trying to finish the first sentence, you had no choice but to look for examples of a bird; you didn't have the freedom to take any risks. It was a more automatic mode of thinking; you were stuck in the "bird" box. But for the second sentence, you could have done so many things. You might have said a bird is an example of something that flies, or something people like to look at. You might have said a bird is an example of something covered in feathers, or a symbol of liberty. You might have offered an even more provocative "out there" response: "A bird is an example of something I like to roast and then eat" or "A bird is an example of the perfect thing to have in a cage in my living room." Put another way, you were free to defy your first logical sense and take a risk; you had the chance to build many different boxes.

Those two sentences forced you to think two different ways: When answering the first question, you were thinking *deductively*, whereas in the second case, you were thinking *inductively*. Challenges such as this one help people experience the difference between these two types of thinking—and encourage them to take full advantage of the creative freedom available to them when thinking inductively, rather than simply answering that a bird is an animal.

With deductive thinking, your mind uses a logical process—a basic algorithm, for instance—to solve a problem to which there is just one possible solution (or a limited set of correct solutions, as in the bird example). When you're using deductive reasoning to solve a problem, over time you'll keep on returning to the same solution(s).

What is 500 minus 400? The only answer is 100. What is the speed of light? There's just one correct response: 299,792,458 meters per second (though it can be expressed in various increments, such as 186,282 miles per second). What is an example of a bird? There are many possibilities, but they are all drawn from the same subset of objects you have in your box for "birds"; any answer is either correct or incorrect.

With inductive thinking, by contrast, your mind can go in many different directions. It is free to make new associations, take risks, invent, imagine. The end result can still be logical, but it can be a much more unexpected logic. With inductive thinking, there is always more than first meets the eye. In fact, the eye (as well as the mind) deceives you constantly as it simplifies the world in front of you—sometimes in harmless ways, sometimes not.

When you are confronted with something in the world "in front of you," how do you go about interpreting it? According to logic or your imagination? Using objective or subjective criteria? Put another way, deduction and induction are two different ways of thinking that can help you solve problems.

Induction is when you observe something and use that information to create new models or update existing ones—for example, if you read something inspiring about Peru today and make a decision to take a trip there this fall, or if you conduct a survey of your customers and use it to develop a new segmentation of the market.

Deduction is when you take the models in your mind and use them to act. You have an idea and you apply it to confront and perhaps even change the world. For example, tomorrow you might spend time trying to sort out the logistics of your fall trip to Peru (booking the cheapest possible flight in the first half of October, or seeing if any of your friends know people there), or call an agency to develop customized plans for each of your new segments of customers.

Put simply, deduction uses existing boxes; induction creates new ones. Both types of thinking are critical for practical creativity, though not at the same time, as we will soon see. Both, and a good understanding of both, are essential for thinking in new boxes.

Let's look at how induction and deduction can work together in business. If you are involved in finance in any way, or ever took Accounting 101, you are familiar with double-entry bookkeeping. It is the generally accepted method used in accounting for recording a financial transaction, where every event is credited to one account and debited to another (if you sell something for $10, your cash goes up by $10 and your inventory goes down by $10, say).

The concept of double-entry bookkeeping was codified in the fifteenth century by Friar Luca Pacioli, a collaborator of Leonardo da Vinci, although there were earlier experiments with it. He introduced it by stating that a successful merchant needs three things: sufficient cash or credit, good bookkeepers, and an accounting system that allows him to view his affairs at a glance, which the double-entry system could do since you can quickly see how much is in each account at any time.

In some ways this was more complicated than the single-entry system that came before (where you would, for example, just count the amount of cash you had at the end of the day rather than have separate accounts for assets, liabilities, etc.)—indeed, it was twice the work and hence there was resistance. But the double-entry system enabled a much more solid understanding of profits, equity, and the distinction between capital and income, and established a built-in error-catching system.

Since this inductive leap was made, since this new box was created, the world has changed dramatically. The complexity of accounting has increased markedly in terms of taxes, foreign exchange, trading of securities, and mergers, to name but a few ways. But the fundamental core of the system has not changed. We have built deductively for centuries on the box that was created inductively more than five hundred years ago.[1]

A similar situation exists with regard to complex numbers in mathematics. Before their conception in the sixteenth century, there was no such thing as a square root for a negative number. This meant certain polynomial equations simply couldn't be solved. Once the box of complex or "imaginary" numbers was put in place using induction, with i defined as the square root of -1, centuries' worth of very real applications in engineering, electromagnetism, and quantum physics built deductively upon that breakthrough.

Let's revisit the diagram from earlier so that you can see how your thoughts play in these two spaces, flowing back and forth from one side to the other:

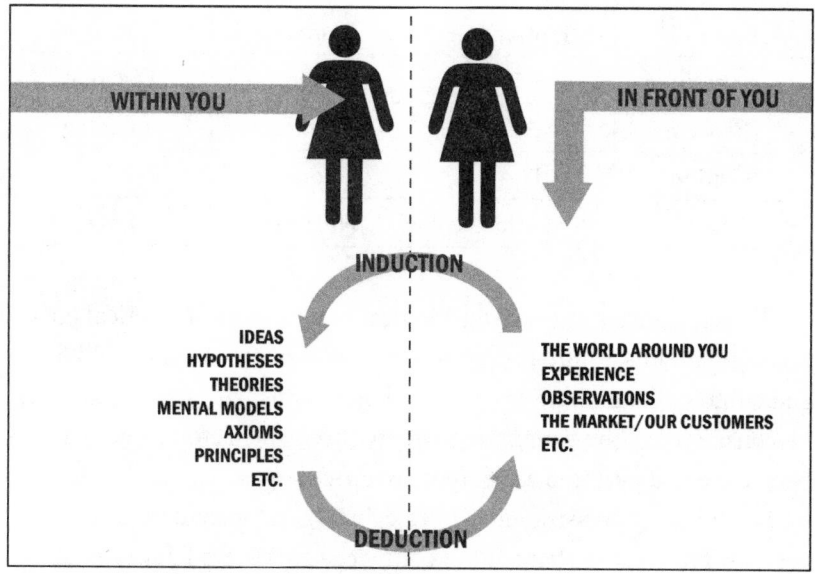

As valued as deductive thinking is throughout Western society, induction is the richer form of thinking. Induction pushes you to ask questions, to challenge rigid rules and tired frameworks, and to take risks that you simply can't take when thinking deductively. Induction always adds something, and offers the best chance of making creative new findings. It is not purely and objectively logical, in part because it is linked with your subconscious, with your subjective experiences, with parameters that are yours and yours alone. No two people are identical in how they will see and interpret what is in front of them, nor are they identical in how they will then use those interpretations to build new models. For almost all of us, induction is underappreciated and underutilized—to understand and embrace it can be a huge advantage in all facets of your life.

Let's try one more exercise. Look at the list of words below, and sort them into various categories:

Digit	Straight line	Diagonal	Addition
Division	Infinite	Curve	Millimeter
Equality	Equation	Side	Point
Circle	Perimeter	Diameter	Area
Pyramid	Subtraction	Limit	Derivative
Twenty-three	Rectangle	Angle	Decimal
Theorem	Pi	Denominator	Percentage
Fraction	Form	Cone	Zero
Volume	Surface	Number	Edge

A quick glance suggests some logical categories: arithmetical operations, synonyms, numbers, geometric shapes. For instance, division and subtraction are both arithmetical operations; surface and area can be considered to be synonyms; twenty-three and zero are both numbers; cone and pyramid are both geometric shapes.

We all have a pressing need to categorize, and if we don't find a way to sort such words or items into existing categories, we'll try to establish new ones, or dump them in a category such as "other" or "miscellaneous."

But if you gave yourself the chance, you might come up with a slightly more sophisticated (and less obvious) category such as opposites (addition as compared with subtraction), or perhaps words with four letters, words with an even number of letters, or words that are the same in English and French. Most people would say these categories are more creative—still, you can then use deduction to drop items into the categories you have created; they are logical and objective, even if it is an "unexpected logic."

Did you consider classifying these words according to their relative beauty? How about words you happen to like? Or perhaps words you think all children should be able to spell by the time they are eight years old? Such categories are more subjective, and they would have been creative in a different way, in an inductive sense.

In any case, it's very hard to look at that list of words and not immediately start to classify, using logic or subjective criteria. Classification is one of the first movements of thought—and the human mind can't work without such boxes. Society constantly rewards you for doing a good job of categorizing information, organizing it in appropriate cognitive storing places, memorizing it, and then regurgitating it whenever you're asked to do so. Many traditional approaches to educating young people—including the rote learning of math facts and the use of standardized multiple-choice tests—place a premium on your capacity to perform such deductive tasks. When presented with the list on page 20, people are consistently unhappy with their categorization because there is no real way of confirming that their answer is correct. It's not as easy as if there were a few mathematical terms, a few colors, and a few cities, say. They are forced to compromise—and this is the way it works most often in real life, too.

But creativity lurks in other questions. Which boxes should you choose? And which names should you give them, according to which criteria?

When you answer questions like that, you are forced to go beyond cookie-cutter, ready-to-use information. This process, in turn, leads you toward an idea, which you eventually accept as a working hypothesis. Then you bring this hypothesis back to the facts with which you are faced, and that is where you will test the idea by confirming, refuting, or modifying it.

EUREKA! AND CARAMBA!

Thinking in new boxes is a discipline that uses both inductive and deductive approaches to 1) gain more control over your current boxes by understanding them clearly as what they are—mental representations of reality; 2) create lots of new boxes to test your assumptions, envision new opportunities, and strengthen your capacity for innovation; and 3) eventually select among these new boxes. It will help you use your mind in the same way as have the most brilliant discoverers, creators, and inventors* in world history, including Franklin, Einstein, and Pasteur; Bach, Beethoven, and Debussy; Edison, Jobs, and Bich.

Bich?

The late Marcel Bich acquired the patent to ballpoint pens following World War II, and founded the storied BIC corporation. He initially envisioned BIC as a stationery company that would specialize in selling low-cost ballpoint pens. From the late 1940s through the early 1970s, BIC's management spent most of its time developing innovations within the "low-cost plastic disposable writing implements" box, varying the number of colors on each pen, putting gold trim on the pens,

---

* We define "create" as coming up with something new that otherwise would not exist, such as a Mozart symphony, a Beatles song, or the design of a new skyscraper. To "discover," in our lexicon, is to uncover for the first time something that already existed, such as a physicist investigating radioactivity or an astronomer seeing a new star. And to "invent" is to uncover for the first time something new (but probably inevitable, unlike a creation), such as a telescope, a compass, or calculus. There is room for debate: For example, is a mathematical theorem an invention, discovery, or creation? Is the Post-it note an invention or creation? In any case, most of the business world, as well as this book, focuses on what we have defined as inventions. For more details, please see Luc de Brabandere, *The Forgotten Half of Change: Achieving Greater Creativity Through Changes in Perception* (Chicago: Dearborn Trade, 2005).

and applying various advertising logos to them. Although its business was healthy, BIC wanted to grow.

One can easily imagine early brainstorming sessions in which various executives suggested the company create different-sized pens, multicolored ones, ones with erasable or invisible ink. But imagine the response when one BIC executive gingerly proposed that the pen company consider making lighters!* The proposal would have seemed preposterous . . . until the other executives *shifted their perception* to see BIC not as a pen manufacturer, but instead as a designer and maker of all manner of disposable, inexpensive plastic items. The key word changed from "writing" to "disposable." Nothing changed in the world in front of them; this was not a new idea, as plastic razors and lighters already existed. But once BIC executives made this mental leap, the company's expansion into other areas probably seemed both logical and obvious. Buoyed by aggressive, sexy advertising, BIC launched its first disposable lighters in 1973 and its first disposable shavers in 1975, eventually becoming the global market leader in branded pocket lighters and achieving the number-two market position worldwide for one-piece shavers. The company's creation of a remarkable new box for itself is now legendary. BIC went on to experiment with all sorts of products, including perfumes, surfboards, and, more recently, inexpensive precharged mobile phones (sold at newsstands, train stations, and airports). Some of these leaps into new areas have been successful, and others less so, but arguably all of these creative efforts are now part of a company culture and strategy that have helped BIC remain a market leader for decades.

BIC's creation of a new valuable box—low-cost disposable *everything*—is a powerful example of what we like to refer to as a *Eureka* moment. When *Eureka* happens, you are in control: You ride ahead of the wave of change, taking advantage of it. You shift your perceptions and strategies in a timely and thoughtful way, and you create the new box.

Eureka moments can entail product or process innovations, like

---

* It may even have been Bich himself. See Laurence Bich, *Le Baron Bich: Un Homme de Pointe* (Paris: Perrin, 2001).

Apple's invention of the iPhone or Toyota's postwar development of its formidable, industry-challenging "lean" manufacturing strategies. They can produce brilliantly imagined service paradigms that swiftly rise to dominate a market, such as the franchise business of Japanese-headquartered Kumon Math and Reader Centers, whose after-school learning centers service more than four million school-aged children each year in forty-seven countries.[2]

Eureka also happens when you create new markets or business models for your company or situation. IKEA noticed that real estate prices and development followed whenever it opened a store, typically in an underdeveloped area outside a major urban center. So to capture some of that value, IKEA in Russia launched a subsidiary to develop entire shopping complexes and lease the space itself. This subsidiary now earns higher profits than the original standalone retail business, and the business model is being exported to more mature markets as well. Another *Eureka* moment was when Sir Fazle Abed created BRAC, the world's biggest citizen sector organization, which today includes more than seven million microfinance group members in Bangladesh alone. Using a novel multifaceted approach to self-empowerment—including early education, healthcare, and microlending services; farming support; and legal aid and business development services—BRAC has helped more than 110 million people in such countries as Uganda, Tanzania, South Sudan, Pakistan, Sierra Leone, Liberia, Sri Lanka, and war-torn Afghanistan. It has shown them how to garner the resources, skills, and self-confidence to rise above poverty.[3]

When *Caramba* happens, by contrast, you've been left behind, watching a rocket ship soar into the heavens without you. You're on the losing side of social, technological, or economic progress. With *Caramba*, others are developing powerful new models and strategies before you do. They are in control; change is happening *to* you (or your business or environment) rather than *through* you. You have to catch up because your perceptions have not shifted fast enough.

Examples of companies that, in our opinion, had a *Caramba* reaction include Blockbuster starting up a video-by-mail business to compete with Netflix and a kiosk business to compete with Redbox; and, CNN, once the leader of 24/7 cable news (which it had essentially invented in a *Eureka* moment years earlier), struggling to regain a leading share of an industry that Fox News, with its subjective "talk radio" type of entertainment, came to dominate.

Even though they may feel very different, *Eureka* and *Caramba* are essentially the same thing from a cognitive perspective—an idea you had been holding on to is instantly replaced with a new one. They are moments of sudden recognition—moments of shock—in the face of revolutionary change (*Caramba!*) or a brilliant new possibility (*Eureka!*).* Both can eventually lead to success (*Eureka* can lead to a brilliant new idea; *Caramba* can spark a fantastic reinvention of your boxes) or failure (not capitalizing on a *Eureka* moment, not recovering from a *Caramba* moment). And so avoiding *Caramba* and achieving *Eureka* is not merely a function of having more or even better ideas. Most *Caramba* moments are not due to a lack of ideas; rather, they are due to the way ideas are processed. They happen when people don't move to a new box in time.

In the summer of 1999, a baby named Noah was unable to breathe shortly following his birth. In a nightmare situation for any parent or parent-to-be, this so-called blue baby was rushed into intensive care to make sure that a sufficient level of oxygen was restored to his bloodstream. His father, a biologist and entrepreneur named Jonathan Rothberg, was incensed: "I was upset," he said, "because we didn't know what was wrong. I was upset for lack of information. . . . Why can't I have complete information on Noah? Why can't I have Noah's genome? Because if I had his genome, we'd know, with the physicians, what to worry about and what not to worry about."[4]

The world presented Rothberg with complex (and insufficient) information on the sequencing of the human genome. It also presented the heartbreak of watching his child struggle with a disorder he believed could have been controlled if DNA sequencing were a standard component of medical practice.

---

* Indeed, humor uses the same effect, too: When you "get" a joke, a change in your mental model occurs in an instant. For example, when Peter Sellers, as Inspector Clouseau in *The Pink Panther Strikes Again* (1976), asks the hotel clerk (Graham Stark) whether his dog bites, and the answer is no, he proceeds to pet the dog at his feet . . . and gets bitten. "I thought you said your dog does not bite," says Clouseau, and the clerk delivers the punch line: "That is not my dog." In an instant, your box changes!

Rothberg would go on to have a *Eureka* moment that ultimately led to profound new research into human DNA sequencing. His moment of inspiration occurred when he was sitting in the waiting room of the hospital where Noah was being treated, and looking at the cover of a magazine with a picture of Intel's Pentium microprocessor.* With that image in front of him, Rothberg came up with the idea—in the classic "lightbulb" way—to try to achieve for DNA sequencing what, in essence, Jack Kilby and Robert Noyce had famously done for the computer industry when they invented the integrated circuit back in the 1950s.[5] Rothberg saw the opportunity to develop a much quicker, more compact, efficient, and affordable way to sequence individual genomes. "If we could do what the computer industry had done [with] personal computers," said Rothberg, "we could in fact sequence individual genomes. That night, my vision was to create a chip to sequence individual and personal genomes."

Confronting the chaotic world in front of him—and the injustice of Noah's suffering—Rothberg imagined a whole new paradigm for DNA sequencing. The idea behind prior DNA sequencing devices—the older box that researchers and biotechnology companies had long been relying upon—entailed *imaging,* that is, using cameras to detect fluorescent dyes attached to the A, C, G, and T bases† in a gene or chromosome.[6] Inspired by Intel's fabled technology, Rothberg came up with the idea of instead using a silicon chip to detect the hydrogen ions produced when a new base is inserted into a strand of DNA.[7] This new approach—*decoding DNA using semiconductors*—represented a whole new box. *Eureka!*

Inductive and deductive thinking both played a key role in Rothberg's creative process. When he noticed the image of a Pentium semiconductor in front of him, he used inductive thinking to apply that to

---

* A microprocessor is a single integrated circuit capable of housing *millions* of transistors. In the years prior to its development, large, clunky computers with much less efficient central processing units could contain only thousands of such transistors. http://en.wikipedia.org/wiki/Microprocessor.
† As a general matter, the process of DNA sequencing involves identifying the order of the "bases" (A, C, G, and T) in a gene or chromosome.

his situation, and to come up with the idea of creating a similar chip that could sequence an individual's genome. It was an inductive leap in the face of ambiguity. He then relied on *deductive* thinking, using all of his existing models pertaining to biotechnology—his years of studying chemical and biomedical engineering, his deep knowledge of biology and genetics, his subsequent experiences researching and developing innovations pertaining specifically to personal genomics—to develop a hypothesis about how he could design that chip and bring it to market.

In our view, Rothberg would not have been able to make such a game-changing shift (from the use of imaging to the use of a semiconductor chip) if he hadn't first carefully identified and probed the boxes that he and others were using to think about genome sequencing. Because he was already keenly aware of the existing paradigms, he was able to see the potential that semiconductors (a long-established technology) could have for sequencing human genomes. Scores of other highly knowledgeable scientists could have made the same creative leap that Rothberg did, but why didn't they? They needed to change their perceptions first—they couldn't imagine an approach to DNA sequencing involving semiconductors while stuck in the "imaging" box.

Soon after coming up with his new ideas, Rothberg founded a company he called "454 Life Sciences," which, within just a few years, published the full genome of legendary DNA scientist James D. Watson as well as that of a Neanderthal.[8] He also created a second company, Ion Torrent, which by 2011 was marketing a DNA sequencer called the "Personal Genome Machine," a device the size of a desktop printer that is now in doctors' offices, clinics, hospitals, and other medical centers everywhere, fulfilling Rothberg's dream of making DNA sequencing an integral (and relatively efficient and affordable) part of everyday medical practice.[9]

Through subsequent innovation, Ion Torrent developed a device that today requires only an hour or so to sequence a sample of DNA, whereas prior machines took many days, or even longer.* Following Ion Tor-

---

* In a tremendous coup, during the summer of 2011, Rothberg and his colleagues published an article in *Nature* magazine announcing the development of an "integrated

rent's acquisition by Life Technologies (the deal was announced for $375 million, but reached $725 million as certain milestones were met) in the fall of 2010,[10] this remarkable innovation is now radically improving the ability of healthcare professionals to diagnose and treat scores of illnesses and medical conditions. It is boosting the quality and duration of millions of human lives the world over.

Rothberg's story is a powerful reminder that relying on the status quo is not a viable option in a changing world. People will either develop new ideas on their own (*Eureka!*) or others will do it for them (*Caramba!*).

Those who want to cope effectively with the increasing volatility in market leadership, with the ubiquity of data points and stimuli that undermine traditional information advantages, and with the accelerated blurring of boundaries in so many fields, cannot put their faith in the way they've always been doing and seeing things. They must embrace the world in all of its contradiction and complexity. To do that requires thinking in new boxes.

THE FIVE-STEP APPROACH TO THINKING IN NEW BOXES

Each step in our five-step framework builds upon the "theory of the box" we explored in chapter 1, and, more broadly, on an understanding of how the human mind actually thinks and reasons. For each step, there are tools and techniques that will move you closer to finding a radical freedom from preexisting beliefs, discover original ways of looking at the world, and then modify those mental models in interesting ways. When the process is done, you will have a clear method for releas-

---

semiconductor device enabling non-optical genome sequencing." This article showed how this new machine was used to sequence the personal genetics of Gordon Moore, the cofounder of Intel, whose famous chip had helped inspire Rothberg's visionary new box in the first place. Jonathan Rothberg et al., "An Integrated Semiconductor Device Enabling Non-optical Genome Sequencing," *Nature* 474 (July 21, 2011), p. 474. See also Nicholas Wade, "Decoding DNA with Semiconductors," *New York Times,* July 20, 2011.

ing your untapped creative power and developing fresh ideas—and fresh perspectives on existing ideas.

We have used this powerful five-step approach with executives from some of the world's largest companies to help them sharpen their vision, sketch alternate futures, and strengthen their firms' capacity to innovate new products, services, and business models. Anyone can use it to question their current repertory of ideas, come up with new ones, and then decide which ones are most worth pursuing.

We will lay out each step in separate "deep dive" chapters (chapters 3–7), but here, in brief, is what you need to know:

Step 1: Doubt Everything

First, we will explore how to *doubt* everything you think you know, and remember that all your ideas, even the most successful, are hypotheses within you—and not set in stone. We will enable you to challenge the boxes that determine how you perceive the world, and think creatively about how you're defining the specific problems you're hoping to solve. Step 1 proposes a variety of approaches to help you understand how the ways you've been pre-wired may be curtailing your ability to develop new perceptions. It encourages you to rediscover inductive thinking and understand the need to step outside your narrow cognitive comfort zone and take risks. Step 1 pushes you to contemplate provocative ways to frame the primary question or issue you're hoping to explore.

Step 2: Probe the Possible

Here you will reexamine the world in front of you with vigor, diligence, and refreshed self-awareness. You will ponder the questions or issues you began to formulate and refine during Step 1. You will identify the essential changes you and your organization believe are most likely to shape not only your firm but also your entire field—and beyond, like BIC—over the next several years. For example, you'll explore who your future clients, customers, or followers could be; what they'll need and want most; what your competitors will be doing to attract and retain their business; and what global waves of transformation, or mega-trends, are expected to occur in different areas of business, culture, technology, and society. By the end of Step 2, you will have established a very clear sense of the issues you want to address and the objectives you hope to accomplish. In essence, Step 2 will help you analyze the world not so that you can determine the right answers, but rather so that you can ask the right *questions*.

Step 3: Diverge

The best way to have a good idea is to have a lot of ideas. Divergence calls upon you to create many new models, concepts, hypotheses, and ways of thinking. It entails a freeing up of the mind and spirit so that even what may seem like foolish or ill-advised boxes are not rejected—yet. We will offer you a plethora of fun, easy-to-implement divergence exercises designed to help you and your team generate many new and exciting ideas.

Step 4: Converge

Here we will switch from the open-minded delight of divergence to the more analytical (and familiar) process of testing your ideas to see which ones you want to move forward with. Convergence is where your ideas transform from a long list into a more select group, and then eventually down to a still smaller number (or even just one idea) that can be implemented to achieve breakthrough results.

Step 5: Reevaluate Relentlessly

In a world of perpetual change, no idea remains good forever. Here we will ask you to stay on top of your boxes to determine when it is time to discard old ones and develop new ones. A fundamental requirement in this step is agility, a penchant for taking thoughtful risks and learning from examined failure. We will guide you through a range of "weak signals"—signs that your current thinking may be nearing obsolescence. We will show you, too, how even the most creative thinkers can become overly attached to the boxes of yesteryear, necessitating a whole new process of "doubt"—and starting all over with Step 1. The key objective of this fifth step, and indeed of the entire cycle, is to help you foster a new kind of creative process that is not only practical but also *sustainable,* enabling you and your organization to remain creative over the long haul.

A Whole New Mindset

There is an infinite number of ways to think in new boxes, whether with a small group of business partners, your colleagues at a Fortune 500 company, or simply a few trusted friends.

Our five-step process can help you build broad core boxes such as a new strategic vision or something like BIC's new "low-cost disposable plastic objects" concept, and then "fill them in" with possibilities (as BIC did with the "smaller" boxes of lighters and razors). It can also enable you to strengthen your boxes, and better prepare for an uncertain future, by developing a variety of scenarios tailored to your situation. After we take you through the five steps, we will discuss some of the many such applications our clients frequently ask us about (chapters 8–9). Applying *Thinking in New Boxes* will give you unfettered and more powerful—yet more pragmatic and sustainable—creativity.

But remember that our five-step approach is just another box! Though we suggest that you go through the steps in sequence, you might on occasion find it helpful to use them in a different order (for example, the first two steps can often be intertwined, as research into trends and customers happens in parallel with your efforts to understand and doubt your existing boxes), and sometimes it's smart to repeat one or more steps (as you'll see, we often encourage people to conduct multiple rounds of divergence and convergence). Sometimes it's beneficial to repeat a step *several* times before moving on. However you use these steps, we are confident you'll find our approach liberating. That said, we are also counting on you to doubt, revise, refine, and adapt to make the process work best for you. We even encourage you to replace it with yet another paradigm if you determine (after a lot of careful thinking) that it is no longer relevant or helpful. Our key point: *Every* box, no matter how useful and brilliant it may be, eventually needs to be revised or replaced.

Whether it's through the five-step process we present here, or your own updated paradigm, we urge you to cultivate the invaluable back-and-forth between deduction and induction, between the world in front of you and the boxes within you, between the most logical and objective analyses and the most far-fetched, subjective, and risk-taking ways of pondering things. We want you to doubt all of your current mental models before you strategize or take action, to embrace ambiguity and let it spur you to ask all the right questions. We invite you to move beyond merely trying to think "outside the box" and instead to think in a multitude of new (mind-expanding, life-altering, or simply refreshing) boxes. The table on page 33 outlines some of the most practical differences between the old paradigm for business creativity and the new one we are proposing.

Toward a new paradigm for business creativity

THINKING OUTSIDE THE BOX	THINKING IN NEW BOXES
First proposed in the 1960s—the world was more predictable, less complex, etc.	Product of the twenty-first century—the world is demonstrably more volatile, with more uncertainty and more possibilities.
Key assumption: The idea we're looking for does not yet exist. Our response: We need new ideas!	Key assumption: There are a lot of ideas already in existence. Our response: How can we change the way we look at them? What new lenses might be useful? With the right question/framing, we can emerge with new ideas—and/or old ideas could suddenly make sense.
How should we do what we do? For example, how can we sell more pens?	First, ask "what should we do?" Then worry about how! Are we a pen company or something else?
There are two main steps to generating new ideas: divergence and convergence (per de Bono, Osborn, etc.).	There are five steps: Begin with doubt, then explore before diverging and converging—and always be open to monitoring.
The process is done on an ad hoc basis and is linear.	The process is a constant loop, especially monitoring and doubting—this makes the result more sustainable.
Generally, the output is a new product or new service.	The output is a new box, a new mental model—products and services, visions and strategies emerge as a result, and they can be made more robust by a set of boxes called scenarios.

"Thinking Outside the Box" compared with "Thinking in New Boxes"

BE CREATIVE

THREE

Doubt Everything

Question What You Think You Know

The beginning of wisdom is found in doubting; by doubting we are led to question, and by questioning we arrive at the truth.*[1]

—Peter Abélard, medieval French philosopher

To have doubted one's own first principles is the mark of a civilized man.[2]

—Oliver Wendell Holmes, Jr.

T HE FIRST STEP toward thinking in new boxes is to doubt absolutely everything: your most fundamental beliefs, your perceptions of reality, and your assumptions about the future. Doubt the rules you're living by, and the ones governing your organization. Doubt that your extant tactics, models, and strategies are the best ones. Above all, doubt that the way you've been going about getting everything done will continue to serve you well over the long run.

This step, which builds on Descartes and his methodological skepticism, encourages you to adopt a whole new mindset. It is a mindset grounded in personal (and sometimes institutional) humility: Creativity is possible only when you are humble about your existing approaches to thinking about things.

---

* We don't entirely agree with "the truth" part, since it is all a question of perception— but the encouragement to doubt is a good thing.

Take a moment to consider the image on page 34. When you look back at that image, what do you think it says? Your immediate reaction is probably that it is imploring you to "be creative." But in the spirit of doubting your first perceptions, consider the possibility that, if the shadowing were removed from the image on page 34, the letters might instead read:

RF GPFATJVF

We are guessing that no matter how thoughtful and imaginative you are, you did not question that the letters (if fully revealed) would spell out anything other than "be creative." And you may not have felt comfortable humbling yourself to acknowledge that you couldn't possibly know the "correct" answer. But as a critical step toward sustainable creativity, we would like to encourage you to try to do both of these things in as committed and consistent a way as possible. Try to question your first impressions and accept that, in many cases, you won't be able to know the "right" or the "best" answer, and certainly not before generating and examining lots of possibilities.

Doubt is important in so many areas of society where change is the only constant. Would your grandparents have predicted people—gay and straight—fighting for gay marriage? How many veterans from a generation ago would have predicted that women would have fought in court for the right to enter combat—and won? Who would have expected reality television to explode as a genre? And shortly after the 9/11 attacks, who would have expected the Tribeca Film Festival to help revitalize downtown Manhattan, turning the area from a war zone into a cultural hub, in reality and in people's perceptions?

Consider us evangelists of doubt and humility. We encourage you to embrace just how difficult it is to "know."

Some of the most renowned innovators of all time have evinced the kind of doubt and humility we are referring to. Even Steve Jobs, who by all accounts had plenty to brag about, told *Wired* magazine in 1996,

"Creativity is just connecting things. When you ask creative people how they did something, they feel a little guilty because they didn't really do it, they just saw something. It seemed obvious to them after a while. That's because they were able to connect experiences they've had and synthesize new things. And the reason they were able to do that was that they've had more experiences or they have thought more about their experiences than other people."[3]

When you have the essential humility with regard to your boxes that Jobs's quote suggests,* and keep your vistas as open as possible—when you continuously probe whether everything you *think or believe* is actually true—you become much more creative. You become much more capable of preparing for inevitable changes, of taking advantage of them rather than losing out to them. Sometimes, as Jobs said, you'll be able to see things you couldn't see as clearly before—things you "knew" but couldn't quite get a handle on previously.

THE SEDUCTION OF THE FAMILIAR

It is usually much harder to change existing ideas than to come up with new ones. This is why, for instance, outsiders in an industry or enterprise are often the ones who have *Eureka* moments—think of Facebook implementing what is now the world's most important social network rather than AOL, or Groupon developing a whole new way of promoting local vendors (at least for a time), rather than traditional purveyors of the so-called yellow pages.

Expressed another way, Step 1 of our process involves acknowledging the seductive comfort of the boxes you're using now. As intelligent and rational as people can be, they are often blind to the automatic responses and assumptions (including misguided or false ones) that they have already baked into the way they perceive and react to people, things, and events. They hear "orchestra conductor" and immediately envision an aging, white, European male. They purchase shampoo in containers

* We never met Steve Jobs and have no opinion on his personal level of humility.

marked "50% Extra Free" and don't quite understand that the price of the item has been carefully netted up (or charged back in some other way) to cover the cost of the "free" additional product.

THE FOSBURY FLOP

At the 1968 Olympic Games in Mexico City, a twenty-one-year-old American named Richard Douglas ("Dick") Fosbury shocked the judges and eighty thousand spectators at a session of track and field by winning a gold medal and setting a new Olympic record with a new back-first jumping technique. This technique revolutionized the high jump and is now widely known as the Fosbury flop.

Until that time, jumpers generally went over the bar either one leg at a time, with a sort of scissors technique similar to how you might jump over a hurdle, or using the straddle technique, facing down and rolling over the bar. Fosbury's revolution was to run at the bar and essentially jump sideways, starting with the outside foot, twisting the body so that the head goes over the bar first. At first appearances, the Fosbury flop looks completely ridiculous. This only made it easier for competitors, journalists, and spectators to stick to their familiar approaches, dismiss Fosbury's method as silly, and ignore his innovation.

How did Fosbury fundamentally change the "high jump" box? He simply wasn't good enough to win any other way, and so he forced himself to experiment, to move away from the conventional wisdom—the only other option would have been to quit the sport. In his own words, "I felt I had to do something different to clear the bar and I tried lifting my hips, which caused my shoulders to go back, and I succeeded. I made a new height, I tried again, and successively I was able to clear six inches higher than my previous best, and that change made me competitive, it kept me in the game, and I converted from sitting on the bar to laying flat on my back."

At the top levels of any sport, improvements are generally measured in fractions of seconds or inches, and so any new approach that enabled an improvement of half a foot clearly deserved serious attention. In the time leading up to the Olympics, which would be his first competition outside the United States, Fosbury honed his approach. "I guess it did look kind of weird at first," he said, "but it felt so natural that, like all good ideas, you just wonder why no one had thought of it before me."*

A journalist from *The Guardian* covering the Olympic trials, where Fosbury barely qualified, was not convinced he had potential and called him "the curiosity of the team." The *Los Angeles Times* wrote that he "goes over the bar like a guy being pushed out of a 30-story window." *Sports Illustrated* said that "he charges up from slightly to the left of center with a gait that may call to mind a two-legged camel" and that having flung himself over the bar back first "he extends himself like a slightly apprehensive man lying back on a chaise longue that's too short for him."

Eventually, in Mexico, the crowd began to notice the unusual technique, with laughter as well as cheers, and Fosbury kept clearing higher and higher bars without any failures. When only two jumpers were left in the competition, the crowd was so engrossed that they essentially ignored the leading marathoner's entrance into the stadium. "Psychologically, I was extremely benefitted by the actions of the crowd," Fosbury said. "I felt their focus, and I was able to channel that attention into a high level of intensity, raising but trying to control my level of excitement." He then cleared 2.24 meters, or 7 feet, 4.25 inches, for gold.

His innovation did not catch on right away—and for Fosbury himself, other than a failed attempt to qualify for the Munich Olympics in 1972, his athletic career was essentially over after Mexico City. But other than 1972's gold medal winner, nobody until today has won an Olympic high jump medal of any sort using a technique other than the Fosbury flop.

To those watching the final in 1968, the Fosbury flop surely seemed

---

* As with many creative endeavors, a couple of people have claimed that they did in fact think of it first, most notably the Canadian future world number one Debbie Brill, who was developing the "Brill bend" at around the same time, and was videotaped using the technique in 1966, according to *The Guardian*. "I was quite shocked when I saw Fosbury jump the first time," she said. "I thought I was the only one doing it."

thoroughly bizarre—that was simply not "how it was done." But today, it is anyone trying a different approach who would be ridiculed—Dick Fosbury found a useful new box that changed the high jump for decades (at least).[4]

Even when people think they are willing to abandon preconceived notions, they bring with them a powerful, unspoken affection for the boxes they're counting on to understand the world. This affection is mostly unconscious: Thinking and behaving based on your tried-and-true methods "feels right" even when you are trying to be radical and new. This phenomenon is hardwired into the human brain: People have a natural bias toward ideas and concepts that confirm, as opposed to contradict, ideas they already believe about the world.* Raising awareness of these wiring issues, and then doubting your current boxes, is the essence of this first step of our creative process.

Google's original aspiration was to build the best search engine ever, and arguably the company eventually achieved that. But in order to enter a new era of growth, Google leaders needed to perceive their company differently. Its official mission was always "to organize the world's information and make it universally accessible and useful," but looking at this differently, beyond the search engine, led to a new "we want to know everything" box, which sparked projects such as Google Earth, Google Book Search, and Google Labs, along with further improvements to the search engine.

Some of your preexisting ideas and concepts may be so entrenched that you may not realize the sway they have over you—or even what they are! Thus another important component of Step 1 is recognizing some of your own boxes, whether deep-rooted assumptions about life or human nature that govern your worldview (such as stereotypes) or preferred ways of dealing with the world that you'll tend to fall into, again and again, without thinking. These could include the approach you rou-

---

* Indeed, this has implications in politics: It is probably better for your brain, and definitely better for the creative process, to spend time reading newspapers and watching news shows where you aren't already well acquainted and in full agreement with the argument being made. A liberal watching Fox News, a Jew watching Al Jazeera, or a conservative reading editorials in *The New York Times* may not enjoy the experience but will surely find perceptions stretched.

tinely take to complete your annual strategic planning, celebrate colleagues' birthdays, or organize weekly meetings at work. They could involve how you resolve conflicts with colleagues or family members, the route you use to drive to work, which sock you put on first, or how you incent and reward good performance at your company. Then, too, much like Sartre the dog jumping over a nonexistent fence, you and your organization may often go "on autopilot" when performing critical functions and pursuing fundamental objectives, even when these responses may be not just ineffective, but harmful.

Doubting what you think you're seeing—and what you think you know—is an indispensable ingredient of our approach to creativity. This includes doubting both the information that you receive and the way you process it. When we work with people and institutions to help them think in new boxes, we ask them to take stock of some of their most deeply held beliefs and assumptions. Then we engage them in several exercises designed to help liberate their minds from the perils of spurious certainty, of holding on too tightly to routine ways of thinking about things. We especially like to help people realize that what they think the "correct" answer to any question is may, in fact, be wrong or just one of many possible answers.

How can people begin to foster doubt, and open their minds? Let's focus on three essential tasks intended to help you do so:

1. *Create a climate of doubt.* How fully are you (and anyone else you may rope into the creative process with you) sensitized to the many ways in which normal cognitive biases are shaping your key mental models and assumptions? How might some of these relatively automatic perceptions—or misperceptions—be deceiving you? Are some of them holding you back from thinking in more open-minded, creative ways?

2. *List (to the extent possible) and then challenge your current boxes.* What are some of the key current models and assumptions you are relying upon? How well are they serving you (and/or your organization)? In what ways can they be challenged, and how should they be revised, enhanced, or replaced?

3. *Carefully frame a set of boxes, issues, or questions to investigate*

further, and the outcomes you're hoping to achieve. Having ana-
lyzed your current strategies, attitudes, constraints, approaches,
or other boxes for their vulnerabilities, what are the most essential
questions or problems that you and/or your organization should
now be trying to address? What can you learn by looking at these
questions or problems from a range of fresh perspectives? How
can you frame (or reframe) them in a way that will enable you to
generate many new ideas and approaches, broaden your vision,
and enhance the overall creative process? How should you move
forward to investigate the world in front of you (Step 2) in relevant, efficient, productive ways? What are the specific outcomes
that you intend to accomplish, and what would constitute "success"?

By addressing these three core sets of questions, you will see that
some of your current views need to be reevaluated—or even overhauled.
You'll have a clearer understanding of the basic issue, or set of issues,
you're hoping to address. You will also end up with more fully formed
ideas regarding the key areas you'll want to investigate during Step 2.*

FIRST, CREATE A CLIMATE OF DOUBT

Fostering a climate of doubt means recognizing that intelligent people
get things wrong regularly—and understanding how these mistakes

---

* One important clarification: We want you to doubt everything, but not so much that
you are paralyzed into inaction. Questioning your existing mental models is about preparing yourself to experiment and take risks. Taken to an extreme, one could become a
leader who didn't trust anyone, who didn't believe any information put in front of them.
That would be a caricature, rather than a recipe for leadership success. The first step of
thinking in new boxes should not lead you only to second-guess your sources of information, become profoundly skeptical about everything, or wax paranoid about whether
everything you've implemented is fundamentally flawed. Rather, it is about increasing
your awareness of how your mind works, and trying to create conditions in your organization and in your life that allow you to imagine new models and new vistas. In other
words, we would encourage you to always doubt . . . but never hesitate.

occur. There is a wide range of unavoidable human tendencies and cognitive biases that cause you to create, and hold on to, mental models that are misleading. When we sit down with a group to begin Step 1, we often do warm-up exercises designed to attune them to the big gaps that frequently exist between the reality in front of them and the perceptions within them.

One of our favorite such Step 1 warm-ups is as follows:

> Imagine that you have a rope going around the circumference of the earth that is touching the ground everywhere it's located. Suppose that you added 3 more meters, or about 10 feet, to its length (perhaps you were worried it was too tight), and then the rope were lifted evenly above the ground across the globe—in your estimation, how high up off the ground would it then be?

Most people assume that by adding only three meters to the rope's length, the rope would not be more than a few millimeters above the earth. Yet the surprising answer is that by lengthening the rope by just three meters, it could then hover almost half a meter off the ground.*

Things are rarely if ever what they first appear to be, and people's first impressions are often distorted, incomplete, or misguided. If you're deciding whether to purchase a certain product, hire a new employee, pursue a new partnership, or launch a new product, your initial reaction will often be flawed. We all tend to formulate our initial ideas based on the ways in which we've always done so. Although this is natural, it's also often very limiting or misleading, and sometimes even dangerous!

For example, one of the authors of this book is of Middle Eastern

---

* Proof: Consider C, the circumference of the rope. $C = 2 \times \pi \times r$. So $r = C / (2 \times \pi)$, or, say, $C / 6.3$. If C increases by 3 m, then the new radius minus the old radius is $(C + 3) / 6.3 - C / 6.3$, which is $3 / 6.3$, or just under half a meter. The trick is to recognize that our instinct of a very minor change is correct—but it's in comparison with the entire radius of the earth, where half a meter is insignificant, not in reference to the height of the rope above the earth. This kind of mathematical brainteaser works very differently in different settings, something we attribute to differences in early childhood math and science education. For example, for several groups we worked with in Korea and Japan, the correct answer seemed completely obvious to everyone immediately.

ancestry, and he was in his twenties and living in New York City on September 11, 2001. Alan quickly learned the importance of shaving regularly in order to avoid being pulled aside and questioned for hours while traveling, based on his appearance. (Being a Canadian Jew didn't really seem to help.) One can argue the merits of this kind of "racial profiling" as a terrorism prevention tool. But one thing is clear: In 2002 and even beyond, if a scruffy-faced Middle Eastern–looking man sat next to you on a plane, particularly if he was wearing casual clothes, carrying a backpack, and looking tired (Alan was a student then, not a consultant), your mind (and even Alan's, if he were in that situation) would automatically develop a different kind of box than if a blond woman were to do so. And the same was unavoidably true for those in authority. Indeed, if there were a young blond woman willing to carry out an attack today, or perhaps a seventy-seven-year-old pale Caucasian male, their odds of "success" would surely be higher than Alan's.

As another example, consider the way in which you attach a value to any given object such as, say, a bicycle. What is the value of a bike?

There is a universal response that has to do with its basic utility: A bike is useful for moving from point A to point B. But much of your personal sense of its value will stem from your own subjective mental models, from criteria that are personal to you. For example, you might attach significant value to a bicycle because you care about sustainability. Or perhaps you hate taking public transportation—the subway platforms in New York City, come summer, often register temperatures over 90 degrees Fahrenheit—and thus love the freedom and efficiency of riding a bike. Or maybe you're a commuter who lives in an area with lots of local traffic—in suburban Los Angeles or downtown Bangkok—such that riding a bike spares you from having to sit in your car for hours each day. In essence, the value of an object depends very much on who is making the judgment, the unique constraints he or she faces, and the specific factors that are most important to that person. Within any organization, determining the value of the whole company, or of some product or other aspect of what the company does, becomes very complex, because it will always depend on whom you ask! People's perceptions about your organization's operations and strategy, about what it needs to do to compete, about the decisions it makes about new products and services and how to develop them, will always vary based on who you are speaking with, the specific words and approach you use to frame the inquiry, your timing, their frame of mind, and their unique window on life.

Global events can provide dramatic examples of different perceptions. In early 2012, the burning of Korans provoked a much stronger reaction in Afghanistan than did the American soldier who went "off the reservation" on a shooting rampage, killing sixteen people including nine children. "How can you compare the dishonoring of the holy Koran with the martyrdom of innocent civilians?" said an incredulous Mullah Khaliq Dad. A typical Westerner might reply, "How can you compare the burning of a book with the murder of innocent children?"[5]

Our key message: Your pre-wired ways of thinking about things—what behavioral scientists often refer to as "heuristics"—will often cause you to cling too fiercely to one way of seeing or doing things.

As part of Step 1, we often show our clients optical illusions, which can become excellent opportunities for reflection on how your brain can hold you back in this way.

Consider this image:

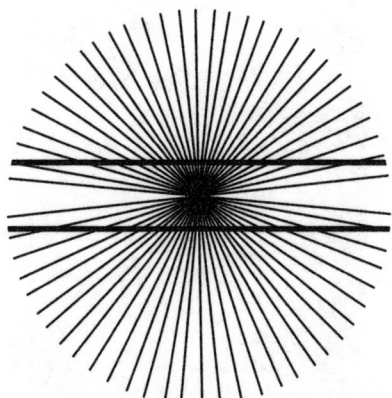

What do you see? Many people perceive the two horizontal black lines as being bent or "warped," although they're perfectly flat and parallel to each other. The eyes and mind will often play tricks on you, and it is important not to always trust your initial, knee-jerk reactions. Sometimes you will see things that just aren't there (or fail to see things that are present). Other times you'll see just one possible explanation or solution when there are many. And in still other cases, you will *know* the truth (for example, you might fully comprehend that the two horizontal lines in the figure on page 45 are parallel either because you trust us or you've compared them using a ruler) yet you find it impossible to compel your brain to see the two lines in that way. You'll fail because the part of your brain that tells you they're straight cannot "override" the part of your brain that perceives them as curved.

If you are not vigilant about acknowledging the many ways your mind can cause you to misinterpret information, you will be stuck in your old (and not necessarily best or "correct") ways of seeing and doing things. This sort of rigidity, in the context of our careers and working life, and especially as leaders in business, government, society, and other contexts, can really impede us.

The human brain has many marvelous attributes—it is complex, it is evolving. But it is also lazy! It regularly goes on "automatic," processing information in the easiest or most convenient way possible. Look, for instance, at this picture:*

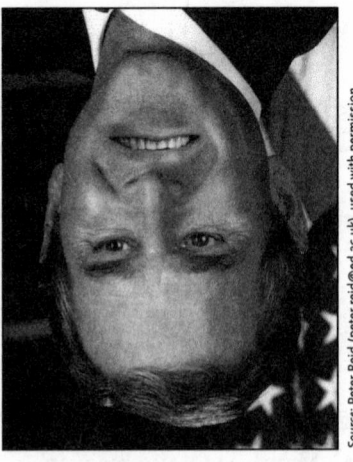

Source: Peter Reid (peter.reid@ed.ac.uk), used with permission

---

* A range of other perception-stretching images from the same source is at http://www .scifun.ed.ac.uk/pages/about_us/shows_senses-vision.html.

When we ask people what they see when regarding this image, most will immediately reply "an upside-down picture of George W. Bush smiling" and move on to something else. But turn the picture upside down and you'll probably develop quite another interpretation.* Some people will not be "fooled" by this image—they'll understand that the image, when flipped, will have a different impact. But they still won't be able to eliminate the initial impression: Each time they glance at the image, they'll see George W. Bush's big, toothy grin.

Research confirms that people tend to opt for the simplest interpretation, to develop the simplest possible box. This tendency is consistent with the principle of Occam's razor, named for a fourteenth-century English logician, which states that the simplest solution should generally be assumed to be the most plausible one (until the evidence proves otherwise). In many contexts, this propensity to simplify is a wonderful gift, and why people often perform better than machines. IBM has tried for generations through Deep Blue and Watson to simulate the human mind's ability to simplify and take action based on such cognition, but we doubt any machine will ever be able to truly induce, that is, to create a new box.†

Still, you can inadvertently injure yourself with Occam's razor! To think in new boxes, you must be aware of how, when, and why people rely too much on simple deductions, to see one "right" way of doing things rather than all of the many possible answers. In the business world, notice the way people tend to jump to conclusions based on insufficient information, to judge people without getting the full picture, and to make impulsive decisions based on their relatively narrow set of experiences. Step 1 teaches you to dive much deeper, to stay mindful of how your mind can betray you and how hard it can be to override this natural tendency. It encourages you to solicit lots of ideas and perspec-

* Note this has nothing to do with politics—we've seen this done for Barack Obama and Margaret Thatcher as well.
† Our rationale for this is that a truly perfect induction would take an infinite amount of time—even the machine cannot take every element of the world into account. The perfect deduction on a given issue, by contrast, is perfectly doable and something machines already help with in numerous ways.

tives so that you can embrace the complexity in front of you and develop several potential approaches.

As you try now to release your mind from the "way you've always done and thought about things," consider one further puzzle. Suppose that this equation is spelled out using matchsticks:

$$XI + I = X$$

What is the smallest number of matchsticks you would have to move to make it mathematically correct?

Most people would eventually say "one" and be quite proud of arriving at such a low number. And indeed, that can be achieved by moving the first I to the other side of the first X, or by turning the equal sign into a "does not equal" sign. But an even better answer is zero—as with the image of George W. Bush, just turn the problem upside down and it will be correct. When confronted with this type of problem, you might suspect or "know" that it's intended to be a trick, especially in the context of this section of the book. And whether or not you stopped at "one" or made it to "zero," it is precisely this practice—of *doubting* that what you *think* is the case is, in fact, the case—that is the start of thinking in new boxes. Recognizing complexity, detecting paradoxes, and routinely questioning the widely accepted "reality" are all critical to the process.

There's a famous painting by the Belgian surrealist painter Magritte of an old-fashioned smoking pipe. Inscribed below the image is the phrase in French "Ceci n'est pas une pipe," meaning, "This is not a pipe." We're not surrealists, but Magritte seems to be telling us, "Yes, I know that you think you see a pipe here. But in fact, you're looking at an image of a pipe. It's not the real thing." You can almost see viewers flipping back and forth between the ambiguity of what's *in front of them* (a celebrated painting), and then what's *within them* (models such as the set of all previous pipes they've seen, their knowledge of art, and so on) to translate it, to interpret it.

Ultragames: Video Games for the Future

What exactly should you do to cultivate doubt, the first critical step as you embark on the journey toward thinking in new boxes? Let's imagine that you are an executive at Ultragames, a hypothetical company that has been in the business of developing video games for decades.* The company was founded in 1987 by two long-haired friends who played together in a punk rock band and made their own games while at college in Charlotte, North Carolina, writing code late into the night in the basement of their ranch house on a dusty forgotten street a few blocks beyond the campus. For historical context, 1987 was the year *The Simpsons* first appeared and the band Nirvana first performed. Ronald Reagan was president, Alan Greenspan became chairman of the Federal Reserve Board, and the Dow Jones Industrial Average passed 2,000 for the first time. By today's standards, Ultragames developed relatively conventional, simple games to start—forms of solitaire, mazes, colliding objects, and a game called SuperFly, which contains elements of what are known today as Tetris and Minesweeper.

As these early games proved popular, Ultragames hired additional programmers and a sales team, and began producing a series of very popular sports-related video games, including Formula2 Auto Racing, Ultra Netball, and Ultra Field Hockey. With these established products and compelling marketing to support them, the company's successes grew, and it moved into adventure games as well, including its bestselling The Zone franchise, where players go from level to level to achieve a set of ever more daring and challenging quests. Ultragames has so far managed to "survive" its own business success. It has adapted and updated its games as the relevant technologies have evolved—for example moving from floppy disks to CDs and then online platforms over time—and thus emerged as a major success story for the local community in Charlotte.

* This is a composite story based on experiences that we have had advising a wide range of companies, with inspiration from various third-party articles and real-life companies as well.

As an executive leading the company forward, you currently feel there is no need for "doubt," especially if revenues and profits at Ultragames are still keeping your shareholders very happy. But you see a cliff approaching: Social media and mobile games set up as "apps" on smartphones are creating a disruption that is beginning to affect your customer base. These new games are being created by start-ups, in an area where your team has limited experience, and are appealing to customers more and more every day—indeed, you have become something of a heavy iPhone or Android user yourself. You feel that these platforms can be ignored only at your peril; and so, in order to ensure additional revenues, you could automatically decide to imitate these new start-ups, jumping immediately into the mobile world, offering games for free, and entering the advertising sales market. Alternatively, you might opt to enhance the differentiating aspects of your product— the feeling of adventure, and the higher-quality video and audio experience—and thereby help the company convince customers that "with Ultragames, you get what you pay for." But none of these normative impulses is likely to protect you from *Caramba*. None will help free you up to think in new boxes. Regardless of your situation and the changes happening in your world, you'll likely be blind to the best solutions—you won't know the most creative *and* practical approach to take—if you haven't first asked a lot of questions and thought through a range of alternatives. And this, if you hope to make Ultragames what Atari was in the 1970s, what Nintendo was in the 1990s, or what Sony was in the 2000s, requires cultivating a climate of doubt.

To Foster a Climate of Doubt, You Need to Understand How the Mind Creates Boxes, and Some of the Biases That Challenge You

It's normal to trust your "common sense," to rely upon your thoughtful perceptions, your sense of what is or is not possible. Whether you're an entrepreneur, a midlevel executive, or a CEO, whether you're an engineer or an architect, a scientist or an artist, you are a human being with your own values, preferences, past experiences, and working hypotheses about everything. When confronted by situations entailing lots of moving parts, you use heuristics—literally "ways of finding"—to make decisions both small and large. Some simple examples include analyzing a situation applying a "rule of thumb," using your "common sense," or drawing a picture to represent a person, place, or thing.* Of course, if you didn't have such heuristics at your disposal, you wouldn't be able to make any decisions requiring inductive thinking—you wouldn't be able to choose a restaurant for dinner or decide what kind of car to purchase, because such decisions, if they're going to serve you well, really can't be made using some absolutely clear, predefined, objective rule-set. Even if you could come up with such a rule-set that worked well for you, it would probably not be of much help to other people, since it would be subjective, and thus distinct from the one that would reflect other people's various values, preferences, and requirements.†

Granted, certain problem-solving situations—calculating the distance from one place to another, the determination of a city's population, the measuring of various compounds to create a pharmaceutical elixir—require one or more rigorous algorithms. In contrast to a heuristic, an algorithm is tied to deduction: It is a formula. Think of a scientific experiment, a recipe, or the rules of accounting. As long as all the ingredients are the same and each step of the instructions is clear, an algorithm will build upon existing models to deductively produce the same outcome every time.

But in so many situations in which you have to make a decision, many of the factors are subjective, vague, and rife with uncertainty, and so there will be no logical, computer-like way of making the call. Instead, your decision will turn on the facts at hand but also on all kinds of heuristics: your intuitions; long-held beliefs, values, and assumptions; subjective estimates of risk; as well as your personal biases, some of them conscious (such as your sense of what is fair) and others that are largely subconscious. Induction and deduction are intertwined: You will inductively make a new mental model for any particular decision, by deductively using several of your existing models. As consultants, we're particularly keen on helping people learn to detect those cognitive biases that are subconscious yet constantly shape your thinking, like

---

* Think about how you react when you lose your wallet or keys—each of us has a specific personal "way of finding."

† Indeed, it could be said that it wouldn't be rational for you to be 100 percent rational.

the inexorable pull of a gravitational field. As a tremendous amount of research by behavioral economists, social psychologists, and others now shows, such cognitive biases mean that you routinely make mistakes based on normal, built-in cognitive factors rather than because you've weighed all the evidence and made a deliberate, rational decision. The good news is that these cognitive biases can be tamed, to a certain extent, if you become sensitive to them before they sabotage you. And this is a key component of fostering a climate of doubt.

Try to look out for cognitive biases that stem from both your deductive thinking (for instance, when you're trying to apply specific guidelines, rules, or algorithms) and from your inductive thinking (when you're relying on heuristics), as follows.

Biases in Deduction Mode: Making Mistakes Even When There Is a Good Answer

Sometimes you get things wrong even when you're thinking deductively and there is a correct answer. For starters, people routinely misapply logical rules such as "modus ponens," erring, for instance, by assuming that "if P then Q" always also means "Q therefore P."[6] All of us would agree, for example, that "if it rains, then the road will be wet." But this does not automatically imply that just because the road is wet, it has rained (someone may have been watering a garden, or a dog walker may have just allowed several dogs to relieve themselves). In business this happens all the time. Can you imagine a company winning a big contract, and the CEO or head of sales triumphantly telling her team "this proves that we're better than our competitors" or "this proves that our approach was the best one"? And yet even if the oversimplified statement "if we're the best, we'll win the contract" were completely solid, winning the contract doesn't automatically mean "we're the best." We could be the cheapest, or there could be political reasons, or maybe no other firm wanted it . . .

People constantly make errors in logic and often either misunderstand or ignore relatively basic mathematical concepts or laws of probability. But beyond purely logical mistakes, however, and into the realm of biases and fallacies, sociologist James Henslin has shown that people, harboring the so-called illusion of control, will tend to throw dice more vigorously when asked to try to roll a six, and more gently when asked to try to roll a one. They erroneously believe that by exerting more energy, they can change the outcome of a dice roll![7] Other researchers have established that an individual's level of belief in global warming varies based on the weather in their local community.[8]*

People also tend to make mistakes based on the "conjunction fallacy," that is, they improperly determine that specific conditions are more probable than a single, more general one.

Consider this next example:

> My daughter is studying philosophy, and in her spare time she volunteers for Greenpeace and works at a women's shelter. Do you think there's a higher chance that twenty years from now she'll be working in a bank, or that she'll be working in a bank and engaged in a feminist association?

Research by renowned behavioral scientists Amos Tversky and Daniel Kahneman (upon whose work the above illustration is based)[9] shows that most people are more likely to say the latter (she'll be working in a bank and engaged in a feminist association) even though the former (she'll be working in a bank), based on simple rules of probability, is obviously more likely to be the case.

In a business setting, how do your perceptions play out when you meet someone new and learn the person has a degree in engineering from MIT? Or when you meet someone who majored in classics at Oxford, or a CEO who didn't finish college? How does this affect what you think of their work?

Mistakes stemming from the conjunction fallacy are also said to entail the "representativeness heuristic," through which people evaluate probabilities based on the extent to which one factor (wetness) is representative of another one (rain), that is, by the extent to which the first

* In an even more extreme skew, Jane Risen and Clayton Cutcher showed in the *Journal of Personality and Social Psychology* (January 20, 2011) that asking people their beliefs about global warming in a hot room versus a normal room, or outdoors in the sun versus inside, skewed their beliefs.

thing resembles the second. Sometimes people rely on this heuristic to invite false inferences.

Consider the following three statements: "All cars have four wheels. The Toyota Corolla has four wheels. Therefore the Toyota Corolla is a car." Most people would agree that the reasoning is correct, since the third statement is clearly true. However, the logic they might rely upon is flawed. The following three sentences apply the same logic: "All flowers need water. My dog needs water. Therefore my dog is a flower." People tend to accept such logic when the conclusion fits their current knowledge base.

Consider this example:

> Jack looks at Helen, Helen looks at Charlie. Jack is married but Charlie is not. Is there a married person looking at an unmarried person? Would you respond: 1) yes, 2) no, or 3) not enough information?

Most people reply "not enough information" since they don't know whether Helen is married. Yet, whether or not Helen is married, the answer is yes—either Helen is married (in which case she, a married person, is looking at Charlie, who is unmarried) or she isn't (in which case Jack, a married person, is looking at her).

Another celebrated example of a similar phenomenon is the so-called Monty Hall problem, named after the original host of the television game show *Let's Make a Deal*. First developed by a statistician, the problem was made popular by columnist and inveterate puzzle solver Marilyn vos Savant, who published it in her "Ask Marilyn" column in *Parade* magazine in 1990. We've paraphrased it:

> Imagine you're a contestant on a game show, and you're given the opportunity to choose from among three doors: Behind one door is a car; behind the others, there are goats. Suppose that you select door #1 (and assume that door is not opened). Now, imagine that the host, who is fully aware as to where the goats and car are located, opens another door, perhaps #3, which reveals a goat. The host then asks you, "Would you like to pick door #2?" Would it be

beneficial for you to change which door you choose, or stick to your original choice?[10]

In her column, vos Savant explained that contestants should always change their minds—that is, should always doubt—and select the other door. Although the car is initially equally likely to be behind each door, a contestant who picks door #1 and sticks to his or her first choice has a 1-in-3 chance of winning the car whereas one who first selects door #1 but decides to switch has a 2-in-3 chance. Put another way, contestants who change their selection of doors double their chances of winning the car.

Even scientists and mathematicians have solved this problem incorrectly (and, when it was first published, debated it vigorously), but it has since been proven by others. In one simple proof, California-based statistician Matthew Carlton reasoned that deciding to change your decision leads to losing if and only if you initially pick the car, which will occur with a probability of 1 in 3, so if you switch, you'll have a probability of winning of 2 in 3.[11]*

Another interesting distortion is people's perception of randomness. Studies show that if you ask people to draw thirty Xs randomly on a piece of paper, they will tend to organize them more systematically than what randomness would really dictate (for example, by putting the same number of Xs in each quadrant of the page). From our perspective, the implications of this particular sort of mistake are profound: Hard as you may try to anticipate uncertainty and the randomness of future events, opportunities, and hazards, you will probably *underestimate* just how chaotic and unpredictable these things truly are and can become. You need to actively doubt the way you think about what could happen tomorrow, because the amount of chaos and uncertainty at play is (on average) more than you expect.

All of these examples demonstrate the importance of doubt and can

---

* The newer television game show *Deal or No Deal* takes this concept to an extreme—there is no opportunity to switch the case that the player has chosen to keep (each case contains the hidden amount of a money prize), but the entire premise of the show takes advantage of contestants' inability to understand and act upon the Monty Hall problem.

help you realize that even when you try to use your most rational, deductive skill sets, you are still prone to biases and errors.

Biases in Induction Mode: Making Mistakes When There Isn't a "Good" Answer (or When There Are Many)

Cognitive biases can also lead to errors when we're in induction mode, that is, when we're trying to solve a problem, or approach an issue, to which there are multiple possible answers or solutions (or perhaps no good answer). Although there are countless such biases always in play, two prominent ones include those connected to "availability" and to so-called anchoring.

An example: Why does Google's success lead many people to invest in companies developing leading-edge technology? Why do published listings of the "best songs of all time" skew toward ones written within the last three decades? These are two classic examples of the pull of the *availability* bias—where you go wrong by basing your decisions on the data that's easy to get, or memorable.

Likewise, consider people's tendency to *anchor* decisions based on what is top of mind. To take a simple example: If you ask someone the population of Venezuela, the answer you'll get is likely to vary widely. But if you first asked, "Does Venezuela have more or fewer than twenty million people?" the answer to the second question will be closer to twenty million, regardless of whether the person answered "more" or "fewer."[12]

Look at the following set and ask yourself which company doesn't belong:

Goldman Sachs / Deutsche Bank / American Express / Pfizer

Write your answer down. Then take a moment to consider this set:

American Express / Pfizer / Goldman Sachs / Deutsche Bank

Which company should be left out in this case?
Of course, both sets of words include the same companies. But when

people see the first set of words, where Pfizer is named last, they tend to see the category as "financial services companies" or companies with two-word names, and drop Pfizer. When they see the second list, they are more likely to respond, "U.S. companies," and drop Deutsche Bank. The human mind builds a box after pondering only the first three data points, anchoring its decision earlier than it should. People are remarkably susceptible to this sort of mistake. Previous year's sales figures, previous financial results—how often do you make present estimates and future forecasts using prior data points? Or jump to conclusions in the opening minutes—or seconds—of someone's presentation? Or before they even start! Sometimes in tragic proportions, the familiarity of these numbers, or the leaps we make before having all the information, can prevent the mind from appreciating the critical impact of new events or situations as well as the degree of variation that can be seen over time.

Suppose you are told there is a rule for producing sets of three numbers, and the set 2, 4, 6 fits the rule. How would you determine what the rule is, and provide other sets of numbers that fit the rule?

Almost everyone will immediately say that the rule is about subsequent increasing even numbers, and so another set is: 8, 10, 12 or 20, 22, 24. Although this rush to judgment—that is, wherein you say to yourself, "I should continue along my first hypothesis, the pattern of even numbers based on the factor 2"—is normal, it leads you to overlook the full range of possible answers. The rule could be only about increasing numbers (so 3, 5, 7 could work), or only about even numbers (so 6, 4, 2 would be a good answer, too). It could be about any set of three numbers where the third is the sum of the first two, or the middle number is the average of the other two. Or the rule could be something as narrow and arbitrary as "any three numbers other than 43."[13]

Our point is this: The best way to find the answer (and to come up with solutions for many other such problems that you might face) is to *generate a range of possibilities* and test them rather than merely try to confirm your first hypothesis. In the case of the present problem, that means you'll be less effective if you immediately try to propose rules or sets of numbers that fit than you will be if you first posit and then test alternative hypotheses; for example, first confirm whether the numbers need to be increasing (by asking, for instance, if 6, 4, 2 would work), whether they need to be even (by trying out, say, 11, 13, 15), and then continue testing various approaches until you come up with the answer or answers you believe are the best. But people's bias is to confirm, not to refute; they want to prove themselves right.

Along similar lines, studies have been done analyzing the annual reports published by companies and how they communicate their respective twelve-month results, whether favorable or disappointing. These studies have shown that when the company in question had good news to report, the CEO's introductory note would often take credit for the success by saying things such as "Here at Tech Co., we accomplished this, and we pulled off that." However, if the company had bad news to report, the CEO frequently attributed it to external factors such as rising oil prices, climate change, earthquakes, or political revolutions.[14] (Imagine if the CEO were instead to write an introductory letter that said, "The news for our company is good because we were just lucky" or "The news for our company is very bad because we really failed to do our jobs as well as we could this year.") In some cases, one can properly interpret this behavioral phenomenon as merely that of a CEO being savvy about corporate communication. But in many other instances, CEOs and the organizations they lead may unwittingly distort how they interpret positive as opposed to negative outcomes, seeing the former as anchored in who they are (what some experts refer to as the bias of "self-attribution") or in their successes, and seeing the latter as aberrant and attributable to external factors.[15] Doubt is even more important when this begins to happen, and it's not just CEOs who are at risk: Not only do we jump to conclusions early in a presentation, but we then spend the remainder of it trying to prove ourselves right!

Risk aversion is another powerful form of cognitive bias that often holds people back from seeing and pursuing new opportunities.

Imagine that it's winter, you're walking in the forest, and you see a frozen pond with one hundred people skating on it. Now, imagine if you walked by the same frozen pond but saw nobody, or just one person skating on it. Would you be more likely to go skating on the pond in the first case, or in the second one?

If you're like most everyone else, you would probably be much more reluctant in the second case even if the ice were more frozen and solid than in the first scenario. The presence of more people will tend to make you feel better about the risks, but you're not necessarily any safer in that instance (in fact, for any given pond, you're necessarily less safe since the weight of additional people increases the odds that the ice will break). People often make similar misjudgments in a business context. They miscalculate risks, spend too much time trying to benchmark them in futile, time-wasting ways, or simply fail to take risks that would have rewarded them. Much like taking the leap to skate alone on a frozen pond *before* you "know" it's safe, it's often better to be the first one to act upon a breakthrough idea than to wait until you feel as though you're obviating risk by simply joining the crowd.

Biases can also change the way you perceive the value or impact of something. For instance, research on so-called mental accounting (much of it first conducted by University of Chicago economist Richard Thaler) suggests that you will probably value something that you own—say, a diamond ring—more than if you didn't own that same object. This is known colloquially as the "endowment effect."[16] By contrast, much research shows a strong aversion to loss, such that, for example, stock investors will often "chase a loss," holding on to shares of a company whose stock price is clearly plummeting below the price at which they acquired it, rather than selling off their shares and having to recognize and cope with the loss.[17]

There is now a rich body of literature on behavioral economics exploring the plethora of cognitive biases that lead us to err when making financial, business, or other decisions. When we consult with organizations yearning to create new boxes, we don't review all of these various biases in an exhaustive way. In fact, no expert and no book could do that—the science is still evolving, and there are way too many such biases that have already been identified to cover them in one document. Our objective is instead to sensitize people to the range of ways in which these biases can affect their judgment, so they can detect and transcend them in a smart, resilient, and timely way.

We hope that you'll begin to wonder which of your assumptions, and your organization's assumptions, are the most dubious, and which of your rules most merit reexamination. Doubt that your long-accepted values and objectives are serving you well, and consider ways in which you may be fooling yourself. Look at mistakes that were made, and what can be learned from them. When you rejected possibilities, did you do so because they were bad ideas or because of biases? Explore ways to change the ways you see and do things—in what ways are you and your colleagues holding yourselves back?

SECOND, ENUMERATE AND CHALLENGE YOUR CURRENT RULES, ASSUMPTIONS, PARADIGMS, AND OTHER BOXES

Having created a climate of doubt, it is now a good moment to begin to identify some of the most important mental models you are currently using in connection with your enterprise or situation; after all, you can't easily change how you're dealing with an issue or challenge in front of you if you haven't first identified the ideas and beliefs you're presently harboring about it "within you." It is absolutely critical to remember that these existing boxes or mental models are in fact just that—models. The aptly named statistician George Box said "all models are wrong, but some are useful."[18] Practically, your boxes are not "right" or "wrong"; rather, they are just more or less useful. They are "working hypotheses," inductive leaps you take that may hold value for a while, but only until another one comes along that is more pertinent and effective.

One approach we find helpful when trying to identify an individual's current boxes, or the boxes shared across an organization, is to conduct a "beliefs audit." By interviewing (or conducting a survey among) your fellow leaders and colleagues, you can probe their thoughts and opinions about the situation at your organization as of today. You can ask them about what they see as your organization's sources of advantage, its key values and objectives, and the changes and challenges it may soon be facing in the business environment. You can try to ferret out how open your colleagues really are to effecting change and to embracing new ideas for the future, and find out which boxes are broadly shared, and which are more individual. If possible, find an outside person—a friend or a colleague from an area different than that of you and your colleagues—to do a lot of the investigating and interviewing. This will help make people feel comfortable sharing their genuine feelings and observations, and will help reveal not just their more obvious, superficial beliefs and assumptions but also those that may be more subconscious or repressed.

We recently conducted a beliefs audit for a major European energy company. The idea was that before helping its leaders develop an ambitious new vision for the company's future, we would work with them to clarify the essential identity and objectives of the organization, based on the current boxes that individual executives were using. As part of this process, we interviewed a broad range of the company's top management and assessed each person's thoughts on the current sources of competitive advantage for the company, key risks in the business environment, the company's most fundamental philosophies and commitments, where people were (and should be) spending their time, and ideas for the future. The information gathered during the audit was critical when the company's executives launched into Step 2 of the process to investigate the needs and desires of customers, and then when they subsequently moved into the divergence and convergence processes (Steps 3 and 4) to come up with ideas for the company's new strategic outlook.

We circulated a summary of the beliefs audit findings in a "this is what we heard from you" format, and executives quickly realized that they were spending much too much time and money investigating issues pertaining to dwindling sources of crude oil, and not nearly enough educating their customers about some of the remarkable innovations the company had recently developed relating to alternative energy sources. They also realized that several of their top leaders had long been so intent on maintaining the company's short-term profitability that they hadn't allocated enough cash to the company's five-year research and development program, creating a tremendous competitive risk. It was also useful to understand where there was consensus, and where there were key areas of disagreement among the leaders. For instance, there was clear agreement on the organization's need to delve deeper into renewable sources of energy, but no consensus as to why, with some believing there would be a solid financial return, and others believing that although it was the right thing to do, it would never provide any tangible benefit. Through all of this, we were able to develop a much more detailed view of the strengths and vulnerabilities the company had to take into account, and of the values—including commitments to innovation, sustainability, integrity, and client-focused solutions—that its leaders felt the organization would have to honor in order to fulfill its evolving vision.

A beliefs audit can also be wonderfully helpful in assessing the personal boxes you're using to run a committee at your children's school, raise money for your charity, or handle the ups and downs of your personal relationships.

In conducting a beliefs audit, you can come up with all sorts of questions designed to uncover the core ideas, assumptions, and values; the fears, hopes, and dreams about the future; the current strategies and strategic visions—or "boxes"—of the relevant people involved in your business or situation, collectively and individually. Doing so can be particularly useful because organizations often struggle to come up with one or more new boxes when they cannot coherently state their present ones. Either formally, or informally, you can also sit down together and try to answer some of the following questions, all of which are designed to get you talking about your current boxes:

- What are some of the key assumptions inherent in your day-to-day activities? The established "rules" under which you or your organization generally operates? What core values are a "given"?
- What are some of your own personal beliefs about your organization and what makes it perform effectively at present? In what areas does your organization not devote enough time and resources? In what areas is there too much focus?
- What has your organization *never* feared that you believe could destroy it over the next five years? What has your organization *always* feared that could become its greatest asset over that same time period?

- How would you "sell" someone on working at your company?
- What boxes are you using when you think about the market for your products or services? What is your organization's competitive space, and are there ways it might be redefined?
- What models do you use to think about your customers? Do you think of them as valuable stakeholders, a nuisance to be managed, or in some other way?
- If you or your organization didn't exist, what difference would it make to the world? What would be missing?

These are only sample questions—you should develop others based on the unique identity and current needs of your organization or situation.

A beliefs audit should produce a compendium not only of relatively obvious guidelines and assumptions, but also of profound insights into your organization's most prominent and widely held boxes. Digging deep is critical. For example, in a consulting firm like The Boston Consulting Group (BCG), where we work, there are formal rules for our consultants (for example, maintaining clients' confidentiality, not engaging in insider trading) but also some informal, largely unspoken ones (for example, we treat our assistants and other colleagues with unflagging respect; we think twice before sending "all-staff" emails). But going deeper, there are also clear mental models about what people at our firm value and the ways in which they value those things. We have a deep commitment to pro bono work that makes a difference in the world, but we can only do so much of it because we are a business at our core. We might as a result think harder about which pro bono projects to invest in than about which paid engagements to accept. Similarly, we will unavoidably look at projects that provide the opportunity to build long-term, mutually beneficial relationships with clients differently from "one-off" projects, no matter how interesting those one-offs might be. And there are further levels and categories of rules and variations in how people tend to see them: rules that are visible to our clients and those invisible to them, rules that are conscious and others that are subconscious, codified rules and rules that emerge without any codification. In each case, if we and our colleagues at BCG were trying to build a new box for our consulting company—such as a new marketing paradigm or a new approach to measuring the professional performance of our consultants—it would be valuable to explore these various existing rules and assumptions in depth, before making changes.

Once you've conducted your own beliefs audit, you can analyze which of your mental models seem the most significant, and how effectively and successfully you believe these models serve you and/or your organization. Use the climate of doubt that you have developed to reexamine them in a range of different ways, asking questions that are existential and that challenge your working hypotheses, poking and prodding at them from different directions.

Suppose that after receiving disappointing third-quarter results as an executive at Ultragames (our hypothetical video game development company), and after observing a continued barrage of media and consumer attention focused on smartphone-based games (an area you are not active in), you decide to complete a beliefs audit to learn more about which of your firm's existing boxes might benefit from reconsideration or revision. As part of your audit you conduct interviews among all of your top executives as well as some of the programmers, sales staff, and others working in the company's daily operations. You ask them a range of existential questions ("In your perception, what, really, is a 'game'?") as well as on-the-ground ones ("Which of our competitors do you believe is most likely to eat into our market share in California over the next five years?").

Once you collect the data, you organize the output of the Ultragames audit into a list of: *assumptions* (such as "Video games don't harm the brain," "Video games should reflect the latest video and audio technologies," and "Our The Zone and Formula2 franchises, among others, will continue to be very popular as long as we keep coming up with new editions every two years"), *constraints* (such as "We need to keep targeting our current core customers: teenage boys and men in their twenties" and "We are not big enough to sustain sales of our existing game franchises while also launching more than one or two new games per year"), and *values* (such as "We refuse to include graphic violence, sexuality, or profanity in our games"). You also emerge with some higher-level *themes* reflecting the general ethos of Ultragames as an organization. Your colleagues, for example, report that they routinely see Ultragames as being a company all about "entertainment," "adventure," and "reliable diversion."

Even if you decide that some or many of these mental models need not be questioned or changed, *identifying* them so that you're aware of what they are is critical. As you begin to review them, you decide that one or more seem ripe for discussion and likely revision. For example, you begin to question whether your core customers really are still those teenage boys and men in their twenties—perhaps middle-aged single and divorced women, or retired male senior citizens, or precocious urban toddlers are getting bitten by the video game bug. Following the beliefs audit, some of your colleagues also challenge the long-held assumption that your customers will stay happy if you simply renew your biggest game franchises every two years—perhaps consumers' needs, desires, and dreams are changing more fundamentally, or more quickly. And you question whether your customers are going to remain interested in video games at all: Perhaps their underlying need is actually entertainment, and they are starting to meet that need in other ways. Today's video game consumers want to be entertained through multiple virtual worlds: waging war in outer space, competing with ballet dancers from Diaghilev's Ballets Russes in early-twentieth-century St. Petersburg, or racing against Julia Child to finish preparing and baking the perfect cheese soufflé against the backdrop of her original Cambridge, Massachusetts, kitchen. Or instead of entertainment as the core, it occurs to you that you have long been thinking about Ultragames as a video game company when in reality you are a growing social network. Maybe longtime fans of The Zone want to know one another, and trade stories online or over an interactive network accessed through their televisions, along the lines of Xbox Live, and meet in person at GameStop outlets or at the annual Burning Man festival in Nevada.

Based on these preliminary conversations during Step 1, you can now begin to focus on the boxes that seem the most urgent to your organization (this word *seem* is deliberate—beware of your own biases, always doubt!). As an executive at Ultragames, you might decide, "The values and themes informing our company seem muddled and some of them seem outdated and possibly irrelevant. We really need to rethink our overall strategic vision and the themes informing it." Or you might claim, "We need to do a lot of work to understand what sorts of games our customers are after and what we're capable of; our core assumptions about our franchises might need to evolve. Let's explore some of the trends that are likely to be most influential in our world over the next several years, and what they could mean for our product mix." Or maybe you'll begin to wonder who your core customers will be five years from now. "What will teenage boys and young men be like—and perhaps we should explore the desires of girls and women to learn what entertainment experiences they crave and how those might fit with our expertise."

Granted, whether you're pondering the hypothetical Ultragames or your own real-life situation, it's impossible to create an inventory of *all* of your and your colleagues' mental models (indeed, you and they hold an infinite number at any given time). But by taking time together to discuss some of the most influential ones currently informing key areas of your organization—and the deeper questions and issues that they raise or illuminate—you'll then be well poised to *doubt* them in many meaningful, helpful, and valuable new ways.

THIRD, CAREFULLY FRAME A SET OF QUESTIONS OR ISSUES TO INVESTIGATE FURTHER, AND THE OUTCOMES YOU'RE HOPING TO ACHIEVE

Now that you have begun taking a hard look at some of your most important existing beliefs, assumptions, and approaches—and considered the extent to which they might be causing you to think about things in misguided or erroneous ways—we would encourage you, in this final part of Step 1, to start to consider what issues at your organization you think most need to be further addressed. What are those "ways we've always thought about things" that could most benefit from reconsideration and/or reinvention? What are the essential questions or problems that you and/or your organization are the most eager to investigate? What specific outcomes are you hoping to achieve? What kind of new box or boxes do you want to create?

Sometimes you are in a situation, or working for an organization, where it is clear that change is afoot, and that it's time to start asking some big questions about your fundamental beliefs and perceptions. Can you imagine being an executive at the national postal service of a Western country during the first decade of the twenty-first century? France's national postal service, La Poste, traced its origins back to sixteenth-century horse-driven royal couriers, but like the U.S. Postal Service and so many others, its revenues were in a serious decline with the advent of email, social networks, and online bill payments, not to mention keener competition from the likes of FedEx, DHL, and UPS. When we worked with executives at La Poste in 2006, the first step—doubt—was critical, because the organization wasn't sure in which direction to move forward, and how to bring together tens of thousands of employees. We explored deeply entrenched mental models regarding the organization's basic identity, who its main competitors were, and what its customers and other key stakeholders needed and wanted most. La Poste was indeed unique in terms of its ubiquity across France and the frequency with which mail deliverers and others "touched" each customer. But we began to challenge the concept of who the customers really were (beyond just saying "everyone in the country"), whether physical post offices and delivery were really meeting customer needs sufficiently, and what trends around globalization, the aging population, soaring virtual communities, and growing individual mobility might mean for them.

Imagine some of the ways in which, as an executive at Ultragames, you would choose to frame your company's most pressing issues and specific goals. When you began Step 1, you and your colleagues sensed that what was most important would be to build your expertise in the mobile arena and expand your most successful games to be relevant there. It seemed easy and logical to simply say Ultragames "delivers

video games to a range of customers, via fantastic market-tested franchises, starting with teenage boys and young men" and thus decide that
you and your team should focus on extending both your existing product lines and new releases into the sphere of iPhones and BlackBerrys
and other mobile devices, coming up with new and exciting games designed for all major smartphones, raising the bar on the level of interaction and entertainment those devices can deliver.

But beware: This line of investigation could lead you merely to create
"more of the same" rather than design truly brilliant new boxes. In fact,
your most urgent current struggle should be to overcome your colleagues'
entrenched view that "we are a video game company with fantastic ever-
green product franchises." It is more important, as you think about moving into Step 2, to develop a better understanding of your consumers—
their most pressing needs and wishes, how they think, what they fanta-
size about and long for, and what mental models they're using to judge
and respond to your current offerings—and look more closely at the tactics and strategies of your company's fiercest competitors.

Alternatively, you may need to rethink your company's entire identity and purpose. Is now the time to come up with a radical new vision
for Ultragames?

As you begin to zero in on the issues or questions that seem the most
paramount, and the new kinds of boxes you would like to create, continue to doubt! Doubt that the question you initially thought was the
most critical is, in fact, the right one. Doubt that you've framed it appropriately. Doubt that your way of looking at it, or expressing what it is,
is definitely the best way.

Above all, what can you learn by looking at this question or problem
from a range of diverse perspectives? How can you delineate the question or problem you're eager to solve in a way that will enable you to
generate many new ideas and approaches, open up your range of vision,
and enhance the overall creative process? How can you build inductive
thinking into the process ("a bird is an example of . . ."), rather than
using only deduction ("an example of a bird is . . .")? And what kinds of
new creative outcomes are you hoping to accomplish? What sorts of new
boxes are you after?

To address these questions in this third and final phase of Step 1, you must use exercises that will enable you to think more inductively, and pry open the prison door that will otherwise leave you trapped inside a tired old cell of gray irrelevance. One such exercise entails trying to take on the perspective of other people or institutions. For example, as an executive at Ultragames, ask yourself: How would the CEO of my company's key competitor, Video Games Galore (VGG), look at our business and the issues we're currently facing? That wouldn't be much of a stretch, since she probably thinks about Ultragames all the time. How about trying to think about Ultragames as if you were the COO of Nickelodeon? What if you were the head of a mobile phone manufacturer such as Samsung, or the chief innovation officer at Google? The head coach of the Dallas Cowboys? President of the American Federation of Teachers?

We recently encouraged leaders at a major global airline to take the perspective of Michael O'Leary, the wildly successful CEO of Ryanair, who has become well-known for doubting current models, bucking convention, and introducing successful new consumer-friendly tactics. For United, Air France, and other mainstream airlines, the basic ruleset, for decades, has included such things as offering worldwide routes using a varied fleet of planes, selling tickets via travel agents, and using major airports near big cities. But it is these very rules that have made it hard for mainstream airlines to successfully compete with airlines like Ryanair.

Ryanair moved the sales channel away from travel agents by creating an innovative online ticketless approach so that passengers merely have to present their passports and a booking reference in order to be given a seat. It decided to employ only one type of plane, and thereby reportedly scored huge discounts from Boeing, along with a simpler approach to maintenance and scheduling, since mechanics needed to be trained for only one plane type and the stocking of spare parts was much simpler, too. Ryanair chose to operate only short and medium-haul flights, indicative of a new box with regard to the competition, that of "our competition is the bus and train companies, not just the traditional airlines." Ryanair relies primarily upon secondary but less convenient airports, and offers open seating. The mainline carriers have now copied Ryanair's strategy of charging for bags and in-flight meals, and other such "unbundling" tactics.*

But at its core, the "invention" of Ryanair as an enterprise—and new box—required fundamental changes to several of the most established "rules" of the airline business. For example, O'Leary stated that he would like to allow even more passengers to fit onto Ryanair's aircraft for every flight by removing the last ten rows of seats on each plane and replacing them with an area where additional passengers could stand, holding on to a handrail during the flight.[19]

With Ryanair's example and O'Leary's specific perspective in mind, how could you reformulate the central questions and issues for Ultragames, as an example? You might be inspired to wonder, who, *really*, are our customers, and what are their core needs? What activities can we bring online—or onto mobile phones—that previously were not done there? What products or services can we unbundle and sell separately? How would O'Leary, with his boldly irreverent and imaginative mind, define "entertainment" and what would he think of our games and our company structure? Or simply, "If Michael O'Leary were our chief executive, let's consider the kinds of questions he would ask to help us radically reconsider our entire business model and outlook."

A second helpful inductive exercise entails pondering extreme "what if" hypotheticals. For instance:

- What if a major global economic depression occurred when China, following a massive accounting scandal, was forced to restate its GDP for the past five years?
- What if a large swath of Americans abandoned their mobile phones and returned to using landlines, after research proved conclusively that there was a 12 percent higher risk of brain tumors among heavy cellphone users?

---

* Indeed, Ryanair is often called a "low-cost" airline. But that is a consequence of all these other, more specific changed rules.

- What if your competitor VGG suddenly offered three of its top products for free for six months in a bid to gain market share?
- Or what if VGG partnered with mobile phone manufacturers to de-
velop a proprietary device optimized for their games alone?
- What if gas prices doubled?
- What if customers helped create the games themselves through some
form of wiki?
- What if a disgruntled programmer put a hidden virus into one of your
top sellers?
- What if climate change provoked an ever-increasing and ever-more-
damaging number of hurricanes in the United States and across
Africa, Europe, and Asia?

In these situations, certain key assumptions, constraints, values, and
other boxes may suddenly no longer make sense. You might come to
wonder: Is Ultragames a bit too in love with its most popular games
aimed at its traditional customers? To answer that question, you should
learn a great deal more about heavy mobile users—where they shop,
who they talk to online, what they read, who and what they love—and
create a new line of games aimed specifically at them. You could work
to understand more about what "entertainment" really means for these
groups of customers—what would appeal to a twenty-five-year-old
iPhone aficionado working at her first job in Silver City, New Mexico—
and explore ways to meet those needs building on Ultragames' existing
expertise. These lines of inquiry could lead you, during Step 2, to pursue a deep-dive analysis into customers' needs and wants by conducting surveys among mobile phone users and video game players to
determine the range of their perceptions, both positive and negative,
about Ultragames and VGG, among others. They could also make you
explore how your competitors price their offerings, and where they feel
they are suffering failure—and finding success. During Step 2 you
might be prompted to explore what "entertainment" really means today,
in an era of shorter attention spans and more customized products. You
might discover that for young people it means "five minutes without
Mom or Dad bugging me to do my homework or clean my room"

whereas for parents it might mean "five minutes when I can feel like a kid again." Or that it means "finally feeling like I'm a winner."

A third exercise to try is to look back at your beliefs audit and shift your conversation to one of your organization's current boxes that, on the surface, seems less important to your future decisions. Rather than focusing on your assumption that "we will continue to succeed with our existing franchises targeting our primary market segments as long as we keep the games fresh," you could reexamine your firm's core belief that "we do not include graphic violence, sexuality, or profanity in our games." Should this be reevaluated? It might spark a provocative debate among your colleagues, but perhaps the norms around these issues have sufficiently changed since 1987 to make this a discussion worth having. That discussion could lead to a reaffirmation of most of those essential values, but a shift in relation to profanity (allowing some words but not others), or to a realization that what your games need isn't profanity but rather more current kid-friendly language rich in emoticons and text-style abbreviations (LOL). Or instead, the resulting conversation could lead to a refreshed branding campaign highlighting this box, which had previously been noted only in passing. You could target concerned parents ("No filtering software required! The safe game company for your children!"). Eventually this could even lead to Ultragames licensing its brand to other companies looking for a "clean" image. Looking at the problem from this new perspective, you'd decide that Step 2 should focus most on learning about who else operates in this "clean" space across different industries: Who is the Ultragames of children's clothing retailers? Of the big cosmetics companies? Of the giants in college test preparation? You could also explore what the most important desires of your target gamers' parents are in this regard. And how would the gamers themselves react?

At La Poste, we provoked our clients by asking them to consider what it would mean if the organization ceased entirely to exist by 2020. How could this come to be? Some participants imagined a further extension of the trend toward e-communication, while others suggested that a single EuroMail or GlobalMail service would have taken over. In a bid to shatter preconceived notions, we tasked the group to imagine what would happen if instead of promising not to open anyone's mail, La Poste began promoting a service that would make the opposite promise: "Let us open all your mail for you." Perhaps this would be useful for frequent travelers. Georges Lefebvre, the second-most-senior manager at La Poste, recalled our effort during this first phase of work and said "we were thrown off balance—we had to ask ourselves existential questions over and over again."

A fourth inductive exercise entails imagining what might occur if your organization were to become closely affiliated or merged with an entirely distinct enterprise, or immersed in a radically different sort of world. Imagine if Ultragames were part of a chain of sporting goods stores such as Eastern Mountain Sports, or that there were game consoles in the lobby of every Hilton hotel. Consider a partnership with Bed Bath & Beyond, or KFC. Or how officers of the FBI or CIA would engage with customers who play your games. Or imagine if Ultragames embarked on a joint venture with Disney, Shell Oil, or a West Virginia coal mining company.

These combinations could suggest many new avenues to explore. Perhaps a partnership with Hilton would lead to mini game arcades next to the business center in every Hilton hotel and resort across the globe, and one with Disney based on a shared "clean" focus would lead to your games being featured in all their theme parks and films. Or maybe you would develop a game featuring miners underground and their day-to-day activities that is a smashing success. More expansively, this joint venture exercise can inspire broader changes regarding how you think about your business. It could be that the idea of collaborating with Disney would cause your earlier notion that "in reality, we may be less of a video game company and more of an entertainment one" to gain traction, along with the "clean" focus. Then the key question you'd want to begin to answer during Step 2 would be: "How can we redefine how the world perceives Ultragames and what we do?" In that event, you could perform a competitive analysis studying not only what other video game companies are currently doing but also the business models and product offerings of entertainment companies and "clean" companies. You could also study trends pertaining to personalization, e-communication technologies, demographics, education, and the like, to help you think about the extent to which Ultragames truly is a broad entertainment company and, as such, how it should change its current boxes, and what it could potentially achieve over the next decade by doing so.

All these exercises stretch your thinking, nudging you to ask inductive questions and think about the future in an open-ended way. They are related to some exercises you might use in Step 3, Divergence, to generate new ideas. But for now, they help you shape the issues you plan to address throughout the rest of your ongoing creative process. They put you in a better position to know where to look for relevant information and findings as you turn to Step 2 and set your keen investigative gaze upon the world in front of you.

FOUR

Probe the Possible

□□□□□□□□□□□□□□□□□□□□□□□□□□□□□□□□□□□□□□

Investigate the World in Front of You

I N THE SECOND STEP toward thinking in new boxes, we invite you to become the Magellan of the uncharted seas of the world in front of you. If the first step is to doubt everything, identify existing boxes, and examine how cognitive biases may be distorting your perceptions, Step 2 asks you to use this new sense of awareness to investigate the world in front of you with heightened focus and sensitivity. Step 2 involves firsthand research and exploration. Freed as much as possible from the inaccurate, biased sextants of the past, you will now be able to navigate stormy waters of the unknown more boldly and to notice details you might previously have missed.

Moreover, having taken great care during Step 1 to formulate and sharpen your central inquiry, you'll now be able to look for information and insights in a much more self-aware and constructive way. You'll have specific helpful ideas regarding where you want to begin looking, even if you won't know exactly what you're going to find when you get there.

Intense observation may seem like a hindrance on the path toward creativity. Surely the greatest geniuses of the past simply let their minds roam free and then spontaneously conjured up many amazing ideas, harvesting the best?

But as you have probably gathered by now, we believe that this some-what glamorized concept of creativity is incorrect—or, rather, incom-plete. Of course there are times (and they will feel terrific) when a brilliant idea pops out of your subconscious, but most creative thinkers ponder a problem using all of the faculties of their minds, letting it steep in the unconscious, before this happens. Step 2's call for thorough research is a way to make sure this steeping will be productive, by pre-paring you for it.

Creative thinkers who do not seek knowledge are too prone to com-ing up with "pie in the sky" notions that are difficult to implement and do not offer real value. An inventor rarely creates a novel patentable in-vention before first rigorously examining the existing "art" (and, very likely, failing many times). An investor is highly unlikely to come up with an intentional out-of-consensus position on a company's stock without first being aware of the consensus one. A playwright without any literary knowledge or training is highly unlikely to become the next Edward Albee or Eugène Ionesco.

Indeed, we would submit that few if any of the great *Eureka* moments in the history of business—from Philo Farnsworth's de-velopment of one of the earliest television sets to Microsoft's launch of the Windows operating system—occurred until these innovative business leaders had first soaked in as much information as pos-sible about the big things that were already happening, and soon to happen, in their fields. Steve Jobs and his colleagues at Apple did not invent the mouse, MP3 player, mobile phone, or tablet computer. And yet the dramatic improvements they made by understanding the world in front of them, and by connecting existing possibilities from different domains (and making them user-friendly), have changed the world.

To be clear: *Fully* understanding the world, in all of its complexity, is impossible. Thus, although Step 2 primarily entails collecting and as-sessing lots of relevant information, we believe that sustaining the doubt you nurtured in Step 1 remains critical. Step 2 is not fundamen-tally about "understanding" but about *seeking* to understand. It is less about asking, "How much can I learn about my subject matter" as it is about asking, "Am I posing the best questions possible? Am I pondering my current answers with sufficient doubt? What ideas and out-looks am I clinging to that no longer make sense? How can I change them to make more creativity possible?"

THREE SPHERES OF INVESTIGATION

As you begin Step 2, you'll want to focus on the questions or issues formulated during Step 1 and determine what areas of research would likely be the most instructive—and the most inspiring. For purposes of simplicity, we generally envisage three basic possible spheres for your investigation: the broad global environment; your industry, or the field or area relevant to your situation; and your particular company, team, or organization, or other personal context. These three concentric spheres can be visualized as follows:

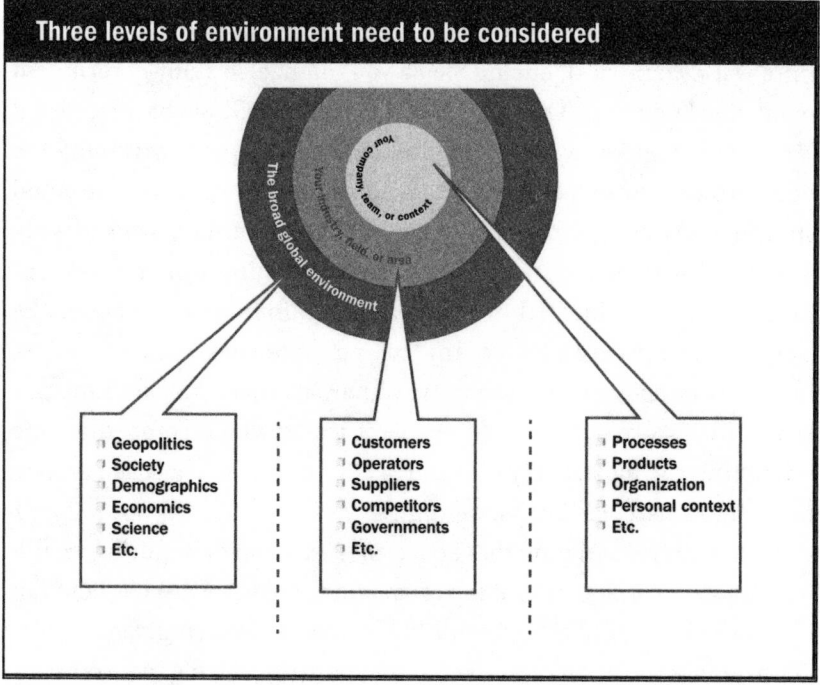

For efficiency's sake, we will focus in this chapter on three specific sample areas of inquiry that cut across these spheres:

First, *consumer insight* involves making a deep dive into the minds of your customers or end users—or your audience or followers—to understand as much as you can about why, where, when, and how they choose to acquire your goods, services, or other offerings (and why other potential customers don't).

Second, *competitive intelligence* entails doing your utmost (within legal and ethical boundaries) to understand your competitors and your potential future competitors, to see if they perceive the world and your business or enterprise differently than you do.

Third, exploring *megatrends* involves identifying and examining key societal, economic, political, and technological trends that may soon influence you, your workplace or organization, and the world in significant ways.

These three domains, while by far the most common we encounter, are not meant to be exhaustive. If you were involved in international development and microfinance (and, say, were trying to develop new rule-sets pertaining to how loans were granted to indigent people in third-world countries), during Step 2 you might also study government regulation and policy. Or if you were focused on selling pharmaceutical products to support a specific subset of cancer patients, mapping the networks of "key opinion leader" doctors and scientists who treat and study that disease (perhaps based on "who has published, worked with, or studied with whom") might help you determine which physicians might be most influential in the broader community and therefore be worth targeting. A snack company looking for the next great snack idea might also undertake a network-type analysis, this time of all the patents in the space—this would enable it to see which competitors are innovating the most, and in what areas (for example, chocolate properties, chemicals, coloring, packaging).

Still, while recognizing that Step 2 may lead you to inquiries regarding all sorts of topics and subtopics, the three areas we discuss here can help you understand all different kinds of situations in greater depth. For example, as an executive at Ultragames (the video game company we met in the previous chapter), you could study these three areas to seek further insights into the issues you decided to investigate after completing Step 1. Let's assume that you and your colleagues determined that as committed as Ultragames should be to the broad boxes of "video games" and "entertainment," you want to boost annual revenues by moving into new areas, developing a range of new service or product offerings. Over the last several years, your collective thinking had been to stay the course by refreshing your core franchise games periodically while targeting the same essential customer demographic (teenage boys and young men) and updating the technology as it evolved. But seeing that your profits have recently been flat—and realizing that over the next few years, your customers will probably develop new expectations and aspirations (and your competitors in the mobile space might fulfill them more quickly or efficiently than you)—you are now eager to try to develop new boxes, or at a minimum, to "fill in" your established boxes of "video games" and "entertainment" with lots of exciting—and, you hope, lucrative—new strategies and ideas, that is, new "smaller" boxes that fit within your existing "bigger" ones. By seeking consumer insights, gathering competitive intelligence, and exploring megatrends, you hope to gather data, and develop thoughtful interpretations of the data that you can subsequently use to generate reams of such new concepts and possibilities.

But remember: The key to Step 2 isn't to be exhaustive in your research. Instead it's to relentlessly reexamine how your *perceptions* about what you're learning are changing. How are your insights and findings revising what you always thought to be true or "the way things have always been"?

Consumer Insight

A fundamental way to probe the future of your enterprise is to develop a deep knowledge of the people who purchase or experience your organization's goods, services, or other offerings. You might start by asking who your customers* *really* are—there can be merit to getting a better

---

* Whether those end users are retail businesses acquiring the kitchen tables you manufacture, the dental services you offer, or the light shows you produce on stages across the world, we'll refer to them here as your "customers" or as "consumers."

understanding of existing customers, potential customers, and groups of people or entities that are *not* currently (or even ever likely to be) your customers.

What are some of the different ways you might categorize your customers, dividing them into various market segments and into yet smaller subcategories within those segments? How does each group relate in its own unique ways to your product or offering? Are customers within these different segments satisfying distinct needs when purchasing it? What specific factors drive their decisions to use your products or services? What are some nontraditional or unexpected ways you might look at these different sets of customers? For instance, are *committed* ongoing customers buying your products for reasons that are very different (perhaps even opposite) from those of *impulse* buyers? What products or services do most of your customers currently not realize that, as a matter of fact, they actually really need?

Engaging in in-depth customer investigation—*consumer insight*—can help you redefine your mission in lifesaving ways. The goal is to better understand their minds. Customers do not always say what they're thinking or even know what they're actually doing when they make purchasing decisions. If you can disarm their defenses and most rational thinking, you can get to the heart of what they're buying, and how and why they're deciding to do so.

One way to do this is through toe-to-toe, in situ observations of your customers, direct personal interaction (or sometimes secret "two-way mirror" observations) with them, and what we term "shop-alongs" and "closet tear-downs" (you go piece by piece through the closets in their homes to see what they've purchased).* Try to demonstrate the specific psychological factors that are at play as they make each decision to acquire one of your products or pay for your services. You will want to strive to understand all the various benefits your products bring your customers—from the technical benefits (what the product actually

---

* A wide range of approaches is possible to suit a given organization's needs and budget, ranging from a handful of in-person interviews to a statistically significant sample from multiple consumer segments.

does, what features it offers), to the experiential or functional benefits (what experience your brand provides to your customers), to the emotional benefits (how your products make your customers feel).

Striving to understand how your customers (and those folks who are not *yet* your customers) perceive your products is also profoundly helpful. Is a particular brand within your organization's product category considered "luxury," "reliable," "inspiring," "good value"? Do your customers view a brand differently depending on when and where they encounter it or buy it? Do they buy your products for one reason some of the time and for other reasons at other times? What are their consumption patterns, and on which occasions do they feel best about their decision to buy the product? All of these issues should be investigated through dialogue but also through observation. Perhaps the stated reason they give for buying your product is not the "real" one. Perhaps there are subterranean forces, intentional or unwitting, that are behind the decision to commit to your products.

There are many approaches you can use to try to map your customers' thinking, both conscious and subconscious. Consumer diaries will help you to understand their purchasing decisions, but to dig even deeper, you can meet with consumers and have them draw images or create collages representing the products or services they would like you to provide them with (or improvements in existing such products or services). You can have them walk you through the ways they use your product, or ask them to react to hypothetical new products or combinations of services. The idea is to try to help remove some of their defenses so that they will reveal some of the true forces behind their buying decisions.

You can also get tremendous insight by asking people from other groups who are familiar with your customers for their opinions about them. Talk with the cleaning staff at your restaurant, hotel, or office. Ask the cashiers who see customers at your shoe, clothing, or electronics stores. Track the February air traffic from the cold northeastern United States to warmer climates, to better understand the behavior and purchasing patterns of the people likely to use your ferry services in the U.S. Virgin Islands.

And, much as you did during Step 1, keep on asking yourself lots of intense "what if" sorts of questions tied to your customers and their needs, for example:

• What would your customers do if you or your business disappeared?
• What would they do if you doubled your fees or prices?
• What could you do to get customers to use your products or services as often and routinely as they do toothbrushes or toilet paper?

Imagine a company that had an inviting, bright yellow sofa in every sales office . . . that no employee was ever allowed to sit on! This is just what happened with one of our clients, the Jungheinrich Group, after an exercise in consumer insight that led it to change the way it viewed not just its products or customer relationships but its entire mission.

The Jungheinrich Group is a Hamburg-based company that manufactures forklifts—a business in which one would expect customer motivation to be relatively straightforward. For years, our client had believed that what drew customers to the company was the power and reliability of its equipment. This company invested little in customer service, spending the lion's share of its revenues in engineering, advertising, and maintaining competitive prices. The basic strategy: Build really good, reliable forklifts and then compete on price. Our client's strategy relied on the assumption that forklift buyers make their purchasing decisions based on these two criteria alone.

However, following an examination of its current boxes as part of Step 1, Jungheinrich decided to focus on its overall sales and marketing strategy, and then organized focus groups during which executives of the company went into a deep investigation of what the company's customers actually (and potentially) wanted. These executives were taken off guard by what they learned. Their customers revealed that one of their top priorities was to be made comfortable, and treated really well. In one exercise, one very intuitive head of manufacturing created a simple drawing of himself lying down on a comfortable couch in his office, relaxing because everything was under control. The image suggested that if something went wrong with a forklift (which would be rare), it could be diagnosed remotely and fixed quickly, without much effort from him.

The entire Jungheinrich team realized that this drawing was invaluable, and quickly decided to make customer service a number-one priority, spending time and money lavishing attention on their customers and making the very industrial and dry procedure of buying forklifts a pleasant, even luxurious experience. Rather than spending almost all of their time and technical thinking on how they could raise the horsepower of their machines, they concentrated on making the client experience warmer, more personal, and more attentive. And as part of this, they put sofas that were the company's signature bright yellow in each sales office as a reminder of the brand promise. They decided that no Jungheinrich employee would be allowed to sit on these sofas, but that customers would be encouraged to do so. The R&D group put substantial new focus on increasing the ability of the company's technicians to diagnose problems remotely. And the sales team determined that it would stress to customers that "your success is our success," which also became the theme of a new ad campaign. This new vision of enhanced customer service led to dramatically increased profits in subsequent years.

As stressed previously, maintaining Step 1's mandate of *doubt* is key to obtaining useful consumer insight during Step 2. Organizations often cling to the reasons that they believe motivate consumer decision-making. It is hard to accept—as the executives at Jungheinrich ultimately did—that their preconceived notions regarding what their customers cared about most, or were actually experiencing vis-à-vis their products, were insufficient or just wrong. Sometimes years of opportunity can suddenly appear to have been compromised because of improper assumptions—because a heuristic inside the minds of an organization's decision makers was leading them down a relatively unhelpful or inappropriate road. As a cognitive matter, sometimes it might feel easier to avoid—or even subconsciously undermine—the consumer insight process if it will help you and your team escape uncomfortable conclusions. Yet only if you are fully aware of such hidden biases and emotional pitfalls, staying fully engaged in consumer insight, and willing to accept its conclusions, will you be freed to begin creating all sorts of visionary new strategies, paradigms, and approaches.

In the past decade, for example, McDonald's has made significant changes to its menu to align with customers' expressed desires for more health food options, including offering salads (2003), removing trans fats (2008), and including apple slices in Happy Meals (2011). This enabled it to increase market share from 42 percent to 50 percent while Burger King, which stayed focused on its traditional menu choices in the face of a changing marketplace, went from 17 percent to 12 percent and lost the number-two position to Wendy's during that time, before finally adding salads to its own menus in 2012.[1] More globally, McDonald's and other leading fast-food restaurants conduct consumer insight surveys and interviews in countries around the world, and customize their menus to local tastes to a significant degree as a result.

There are many examples in the grocery aisle as well. Esselunga was founded in Milan in 1957 as Italy's first grocery store chain. It thrived and grew by perceiving changes in consumer needs—for example, it was among the first to understand time constraints that working women were beginning to experience, and so it offered 70 percent fewer specific products, wider aisles, and more checkout clerks. The result for customers was a shopping experience that was 40 percent faster and more pleasant; the result for Esselunga was growth double that of its main competitors from 2000 through 2010, with profits 50 percent higher than some.

As consumer needs evolve, however, you have to keep on top of them: Whole Foods struggled at the beginning of the 2008 recession because customers were seeing the company's stores primarily as places for premium products. To adapt, the company started offering "Whole Deals" and promoting low-cost recipes and its private-label 365 brand, along with discounts on bulk purchases, to achieve more of a "value" perception as well.

Another example is Trader Joe's: It has created a unique grocery story, with only 10–15 percent of the number of products of a typical

U.S. grocery store, and one-third of the square footage per store. Eighty-five percent of the products it sells are private label, which is three to four times the usual proportion. The result has been double-digit growth for more than fifteen years and very high sales productivity compared with other retailers. The key for Trader Joe's was to understand the importance of the market segment interested in inexpensive and convenient access to health and specialty products, so-called low-income PhDs—and of course to maintain a lean operating model simultaneously.

As an executive at Ultragames, suppose that you have conducted a survey of some of your company's frequent gamers, who were identified via online message boards or previous purchases, and enticed to share their sense of what they like about your products, what features they'd hope to see changed or added, and what would make them choose to play more games in general, and Ultragames' specifically. You and your colleagues had long assumed that most of your customers were teenage boys or young men, had limited disposable income, and used your games to pass the time and compete with their friends. But this preliminary survey suggested to you that a surprising number of your gamers are older, and a surprising proportion is female. Your sample was not statistically significant, but you then verified via third-party data that the average gamer is now 37 years old, with 82 percent over 18 and 29 percent over 50—and that 42 percent are women, with women over 18 being one of the fastest-growing demographics.[2] This seemed to fit with the emerging "mobile technology" demographic, but not with the traditional "gamer" demographic that your team had long been presuming to serve; your own biases had led you to "see" your customers very differently than they actually are. You were stuck in an old box whenever you thought about your customers! Your perception of Ultragames' typical consumer could shift from one almost exclusively focused on "restless kid" to one that also includes segments such as "ambitious mama" or "aging gracefully."

You follow up on this survey by observing and interviewing some of your gamers as they play various Ultragames products. You learn about when and why they play (for some it becomes a habit in the evening, to decompress after work, while for others it is a way to get away from it all whenever time permits, or to relieve stress after the kids go to bed). You understand that in addition to some of these functional and practical benefits, many of your gamers would love to become part of a community, to connect with people who are like them, but they don't feel safe trying to meet up in the "real world." Others are uninterested in that form of social connection but are loyal to Ultragames because of the reputation for avoiding violence, profanity, and sexual content—it even allows them to share their games and screen names with their children. Still other users rely on Ultragames as a safe starting place for nightly online excursions that subsequently bring them into other arenas: checking stock portfolios, searching for medical or other information, shopping, or arranging for travel and leisure activities, even looking for love.

In a subsequent survey designed to understand the different segments of your customers, you confirm that while a significant segment of teenage boys remains, their parents are also a key segment, while two more relatively affluent segments are customers over fifty and young professionals (of both genders). While you understand the teenage boy segment well, you learn that a significant majority of all other segments are happy for Ultragames to maintain its "safe" focus and would be willing to pay up to double the current prices for that to be maintained and promoted further. One memorable customer comment from a mother who enjoyed Ultragames products herself but also allowed her children to do so: "It's getting harder and harder to find ways to keep my kids entertained and happy in ways that I approve of, let alone for us to all be entertained by the same thing. So if you can provide that for me, cost is not the most important thing; you'll have my gratitude and loyalty."

During Step 3's call for divergence, these insights will lead you to come up with all sorts of new ideas. You might have begun Step 2 thinking that Step 3 would be about asking, "How can we move into the mobile space and remain a top-quality game company?" Or even going beyond video games into entertainment, "How can we best target our long-standing core customers and their entertainment needs?" These are not bad questions—but they are not game-changing "new box" questions, either. You can now shift your thinking to decide that your Step 3 divergence session should instead focus on appealing to parents, or some combination of the newly revealed segments, for example, "How can we make Ultragames the company of choice for families who are looking for a single-source entertainment provider?" or "How can Ultragames make soccer moms everywhere thrilled with their daily lives?"

Competitive Intelligence

Step 2 will also help reshape your thinking about your competitors. Do you even know if those people or organizations that you place in the box of "competitors" consider themselves to be in the same business as you? Do you have a sense for the unstated, whether secret or subconscious, factors guiding their strategy? Are there people or organizations you don't even think about right now as "competitors" who may soon overtake your customers?

It's easy to err when thinking about who your true competitors are and what sets them apart from you (and you apart from them). Consider, for a moment, PepsiCo and the Coca-Cola Company. Do you see these two companies as competitors? How many times have you been to a restaurant and had a server indicate to you that the restaurant carries either Pepsi or Coke, but not both? If you consider these two companies to be competitors, though, you're only partially correct. It is true that in markets around the world, they compete in selling their respective carbonated and noncarbonated beverages—for example, Pepsi, Tropicana, Gatorade, and Aquafina versus Coke, Minute Maid, Powerade, and Dasani. In reality, though, while Pepsi is perhaps Coke's primary competitor, Coke is not PepsiCo's primary competitor. Beyond beverages, PepsiCo owns and operates the global Frito-Lay and Quaker brands, along with a portfolio of foods that also includes dairy and hummus. Revenues from PepsiCo's food business account for nearly 50 percent of its more than $65 billion in annual revenues, while Coke's $47 billion in revenues is essentially from drinks alone. As a result,

PepsiCo is focused on winning in a broader range of strategic areas affecting its many brands. Ask top executives at PepsiCo and they'll emphasize that as one of the leading consumer product companies in the world, its mission is to captivate consumers with the world's most loved and best-tasting convenient foods as well as beverages.[3]

Much like gathering consumer insight, developing competitive intelligence entails trying to transcend preconceived notions. Perhaps there are things you believe about your most obvious competitors— they have inferior (or unbeatable) products; they are poorly (or very impressively) managed; they are ruthless, or they are vulnerable; they will always be bigger and stronger, they will always be smaller and more nimble—that may affect the way you view them. Rather than staying locked in these sorts of perspectives, we believe it can be much more interesting, and much more fruitful, to view the competition with the curiosity and open-mindedness that someone completely new to the industry—or a child—might bring!

Ask yourself questions such as, What are some unexpected, unconventional ways I could define my competitors and identify others who could be included in the competitive set? (Or, put differently, What could my customers substitute for what they currently purchase from me?)

If you change the framework you use to identify who your organization is, its mission and vision—and what you see as its core products and services—how would this alter the identity of its competitors? What competitive space can you define that would make its market share five times smaller? What would make it five times greater? Imagine that in seven years your main competitor were an entirely different organization in some entirely distinct industry—for example, you provide information technology services and your competitor is suddenly Hertz; you manufacture and distribute pet food and your competitor is soon Costco; or you own dairy farms across New England and somehow Staples, the office supply store, becomes your leading competitor—how could this have happened and what would those circumstances mean for your organization?

As you begin to consider such questions (and are forced to think more inductively), we suspect you'll begin to see that your future competition could very well come from unexpected directions and players.

As an executive at Ultragames, how could you redefine your firm's competitive space? Rather than merely providing video game services for young males, the company could be seen as providing education and entertainment services for a wide range of groups. Imagine if the company's main competitor, five years from now, was not Video Games Galore, but Cineplex movie theaters, or Major League Baseball . . . How could this have happened? How could these radically changed perspectives on "the competition" help you "fill in" the boxes of video games and entertainment with new product and service ideas appealing to families?

Now, instead imagine that you are an executive at a major camera manufacturer and you're trying to determine the competitive landscape for your company. Who is likely to come up with the next winning idea in photography? Who will invent the next big thing and then innovate the leading products and services? Let's get even more specific: Who do you think would be likely to come up with a new theory pertaining to how light is captured by a camera? And who might use that to create a camera that could take a picture that you could then focus or refocus (on the camera or later on your laptop) depending on which part of the picture you wanted to emphasize? Imagine, too, that these same "shoot now, focus later" images could subsequently be viewed and printed in both 2-D and 3-D formats. Who would you think not only developed the theory behind this new photographic approach but is now marketing these game-changing cameras? Would you guess Canon or Nikon? Kodak? Sony? The correct answer is Lytro, a small, privately held California-based firm. Lytro's revolutionary approach to imaging is based on the pioneering work of scientists at Stanford, and the company is already marketing and selling its category-busting Light Field Camera to enthusiastic early reviews.[4]*

Put simply, an important part of Step 2 is realizing that your competitors may not be who you think they are, largely because the people and organizations most likely to come up with new ideas are often not those with the most experience or the most obvious credentials.

---

* Of course, by the time this book is published, Lytro could be well-known. Keeping up with the constant flow of change is not easy.

Why is this so? As we will remind you throughout your journey with us, if you stay stuck in the prison of your existing boxes, you will struggle to invent breakthrough ideas (and to notice existing "good" ideas right in front of you). And it is often outsiders like Lytro—organizations that are less burdened by existing mental models of "how we do things"—that end up pursuing big new ideas that, in turn, lead to winning innovations. Compared with organizations that may be larger or more established, these outsiders are often better equipped to challenge widely held perspectives and look at things in new ways.

Consider Amazon.com. When Amazon began as an Internet retailer, bookstores were the first organizations to see Amazon as a major threat. But once Amazon diversified into online music sales, it wasn't hard to predict that it would eventually sell virtually all product categories. It would not have been a stretch to imagine that Amazon would soon be editing, producing, and distributing its own original literary properties and underselling the major trade publishers (who may still be relying upon a relatively narrow paradigm regarding who their true competitors are). So many powerful companies did not think much about Amazon because they mistakenly believed it was not in their business.

The key to accurate competitive intelligence is to concentrate on how your competitors describe themselves. But you'll then want to take things a layer deeper. Try to understand their current strategies and missions (not necessarily those they describe on their websites and in their annual reports). What do you see as their *actual* strengths and their *real* identities? Consider what they are especially good at, or what other businesses they could conceivably move into. Some other areas you might consider:

- What sort of improvements could they make to their businesses that would help them perform more efficiently?
- What are some of the ways in which they could compete with you that you have not yet sufficiently explored or acknowledged?
- Beyond simply providing their goods or services more cheaply, what major innovations in customer service, distribution, product innovation, or design might your competitors make? How would you react to these changes?

• Who are your competitors' major partners, and who might they acquire or be acquired by? What would some of those changes mean to you?

Most important, how can you address these critical questions with fresh eyes, free (or as free as you can manage) from your own boxes, such as considerations linked to your organization's history, limitations on its resources and competencies, or other such assumed constraints?

You might even engage in a process like consumer insight—yet focus on how customers (yours or theirs) relate to your *competitors'* products. What does this reveal about both the competitive advantage and the unstated mission and strategy of your competition?

Surveying the customer base of Ultragames, you learned, first, that the "safety" angle was appealing to a wide range of parents, and second, that they feel comfortable knowing their teens and other kids are being entertained by Ultragames, at least in comparison with their kids' experiences when playing VGG's more violent games or watching provocative television shows. But many survey respondents offered a key, third insight: They would still prefer their kids engage in some less sedentary activity. What might this imply about future game development? Perhaps this was the kind of thinking that led Nintendo to develop the Wii, a game console with a wide range of active games. What could this mean for Ultragames, and how could it link up with the trends around mobile technology? Would a joint venture with a manufacturer of exercise treadmills be in store? One with a global health club chain? What might product development gurus at Nike advise Ultragames to do?

Introduction to Megatrends: An Aside About Prospective Thinking

As you launch into investigating your customers and competition, and especially as you begin to think about the megatrends likely to be affecting you, your organization, your industry, and the planet, let us arm you with another vital tool. We would like to help you take advantage of the distinction between predictive thinking, in which you're *trying* to determine what exactly will happen, and prospective thinking, in which you're 1) using your imagination to ask all sorts of questions about what could happen and 2) constantly striving to envision and then act upon *numerous* possible futures. Prospective thinking means taking a more expansive, long-term view of things, staying open to all sorts of possibilities, and doing your best to stay fully aware of what is happening both within and outside your organization or your immediate environment. Both forms of thinking are useful, but we'll shine a light on prospective thinking throughout this book, especially when it comes to identifying megatrends and using them to develop a special kind of box called "scenarios" (as we'll show in chapter 9).

Senegal-born industrialist Gaston Berger,* a noted pioneer of the prospective approach, once said, "If you're driving on a road that you know really well in pitch darkness, you'll only need a lantern. But if you're driving down a road in unfamiliar territory, you're going to need powerful headlights." Prospective thinking is about using high-power headlights to navigate and *prepare* for many possible futures—often in unfamiliar territory—rather than using a lantern to try to predict just one possible future. Prospective thinking is about anticipating long-term changes, including highly disruptive ones (some known, and others entirely unknown), and responding to them early. Prospective thinking—which relies a lot on induction—is at the heart of practical creativity. It's about acting rather than waiting.

When you use predictive thinking, by contrast, you're usually foreseeing events that are considered to be highly likely. It can work well if 1) you are very familiar with the parameters of events likely to occur relatively soon; 2) those parameters are fairly constant, stable, and easy to measure; and 3) you're able to use established algorithms to make decisions about short-term outcomes. Predictive thinking prioritizes your deductive mind. An example might be the way in which traffic control experts at airports are able to decide when to ground planes and when to allow them to fly. Long-term weather patterns are not easy to anticipate but meteorologists can predict short-term hour-by-hour weather with relative accuracy and thus traffic control officers can use

---

* Wikipedia describes Berger as a "futurist," a "philosopher," and an "industrialist," an interesting combination.

predictive thinking to ascertain when, over the next few hours, it's likely to be safe for airplanes to land and take off.

This chart contrasts predictive and prospective thinking:

	Predictive Thinking	Prospective Thinking
Mindset	Forecasting, "We expect . . ."	Preparing, "But what if . . ."
Goal	Reduce or even discard uncertainty, fight ambiguity	Live with uncertainty, embrace ambiguity, plan for set of contingencies
Level of uncertainty	Average	High
Method	Extrapolating from present and past	Open, imaginative
Approach	Categorical, assumes continuity	Global, systemic, anticipates disruptive events
Information inputs	Quantitative, objective, known	Qualitative (whether quantifiable or not), subjective, known or unknown
Relationships	Static, stable structures	Dynamic, evolving structures
Technique	Established quantitative models (economics, mathematics, data)	Developing scenarios using qualitative approaches (often building on megatrends)
Evaluation method	Numbers	Criteria
Attitude toward the future	Passive or reactive (the future will be)	Proactive and creative (we create or shape the future)
Way of thinking	Generally deduction	Greater use of induction

Prospective thinking can help you to answer two key questions as a decision maker: "What might or could happen?" and "What should I do about it?"

In the context of Step 2, such thinking can help you better understand what events might happen that would make your current boxes no longer effective—and what you and your organization need to do to better prepare for such events. You can then explore these possible events to inform the ideas, approaches, strategies, and other new boxes that you will begin to generate during Step 3 divergence.

Using this "many things could happen" mindset, and remaining cognizant of Step 1's imperative to stay on top of all the ways your biases can trip up your best thinking, we now encourage you to explore some of the powerful trends that could have significant multiyear influence over you and your ambitions.

Being Smart About Megatrends

Building on the "prospective" outlook that Gaston Berger and others introduced nearly half a century ago, we believe that a third powerful approach to probing the world in front of you entails identifying and investigating *megatrends*. A megatrend is a large social, economic, political, environmental, or technological change highly likely to have major impact across a wide range of areas. Megatrends will affect your company, your customers, your competition—as well as your family, your neighbors, and your community. Examples of megatrends include the rise of alternative energy sources, which are expected to meet 8 percent of the world's dramatically increasing energy needs by 2030 versus 6 percent of a smaller base in 2010, driven largely by wind and solar,[5] the rise of rapidly developing markets like Brazil and China, and increasing connectivity through the Internet and mobile technology.

Megatrends are not fads. In spite of what she may think, Lady Gaga does not qualify as a megatrend; however, the rising tendency of consumers to purchase music and many other forms of entertainment from the Internet does. Broad economic shifts, whether long recessions, labor shortages, or the rise or fall of different industries or sectors of the economy, are megatrends; quarterly stock market gyrations and products that do very well this season are not.

As a starting point, concentrate on megatrends you believe will likely 1) play out over a relatively long period of time (for example, five to ten years, though different industries could have longer or shorter relevant time frames), 2) have a strong and wide-reaching potential impact, and 3) open up a range of strategic responses on your part.

You'll first want to come up with a broad set of megatrends—long lists are readily available from various sources. But then you'll need to take on the deeper challenge of distilling your list. Which trends will be the key vectors for shaping your future? What are some of the seemingly irrelevant trends you can think of that could end up being surprisingly critical?

One megatrend we have extensively studied is the growing urbanization of our planet. In 1950, about 29 percent of people lived in cities, yet, in 2000, about 47 percent did.[6] What are the consequences of this process, and critically, what are the second- and third-order implications? Clearly the influx of people into cities, one that experts expect to continue to about 70 percent of the population in 2050,[7] will require substantial new infrastructure and new construction. Different building materials will be in demand compared with what might be purchased if people stayed away from cities. Consumer buying power will be more highly concentrated, and this might have a substantial impact on the strategy of consumer product companies. As we passed a point in 2009 when more than half the planet's population lived in cities, new solutions had begun to emerge for urban vehicles, urban public transport, and even urban agriculture. Mayors may come to have more power than national leaders.

In what ways are these and other trends salient or relevant to your business and what you do? Even if all megatrends will have some impact, some will clearly be more germane than others. How can you direct yourself and your team toward the most critical megatrends?

Start by thinking about trends within the three data levels we introduced earlier: 1) the world in general (trends, for instance, regarding demographics, global economics, and technology), 2) your industry (those pertaining to such issues as sustainability or corporate responsibility, outsourcing, regulatory changes, pricing models, the consolidation/concentration of several businesses within the same industry), and 3) your organization (for example, trends involving such matters as labor relations, shortages or influxes of cash, new investment opportunities, operations, productivity and cost reduction, and innovations in information technology).

For example, ponder one of the classic sources of megatrends: demographics. Long-term, predictable changes in the makeup of our society—such as the aging of the American and Western European population—can be seen coming years before consequences begin to manifest themselves. As you consider different regions or markets, you can examine how the makeup of their population has changed and is expected to change further. You can explore whether the population is growing, and, if so, at what rate. You can understand how the balance between men and women, old and young, or different ethnic makeups is changing.

Another good source for megatrends comes from the rivalry between countries and regions. In part, this is also driven by demographics. As one region rises in population, wealth, or industry, the entire pattern of consumer behavior in the region may drastically change, with implications for trade, transport, and other areas.

Major changes in consumer behavior qualify as megatrends, but only when the changes are evidence of a fundamental shift, as opposed to a fad. And when true consumer trends actually do shift, that can be enormously significant. The digitization of almost all forms of media—and the changing way consumers purchase and consume it—has been transformational. Combine this with a second megatrend (customers personalizing their technology) and a third (a heightened consumer passion for design) and you have identified several of the key drivers that make Apple one of the most valuable companies in history.

Technology-related megatrends often evolve very quickly. The rise in nanotechnology, the boom in mobile networks, the invention of more efficient electric cars—all qualify as megatrends. While individual advances cannot always be predicted, broader changes can be tracked. For instance, through technological advances, we will either mitigate climate change or fail to do so and have to live with its consequences.

In light of some of these megatrends, as an Ultragames executive trying to come up with fresh revenue-generating ideas that comport with the company's boxes of entertainment and family, consider the following:

• How might the world's changing demographics affect your outlook? The world's aging population? What about the rise of rapidly developing economies worldwide, starting with India?
• Is Ultragames being as inventive as it might be when it comes to the digitization of media and the personalization of technology?
• What about the importance of design and user interfaces?

- How creative, intelligent, and effective is the marketing and selling process that Ultragames uses to sell its products?
- What about the design of the games and the packaging used to promote them? Is Ultragames achieving in the imagery of the games and the intuitiveness of getting started what Steve Jobs achieved for the iPhone? Is it using the same visual imaginativeness in the marketing of its video games that Oliviers & Company is using to make its Provence olive oils and tapenades (and skin care products) everyday purchases for families shopping in malls across America?
- What megatrends could offer the next wave of growth? Where will the greatest risks emerge?

Take a moment to think about what megatrends are most relevant to you, and use induction to imagine some astonishing ways in which what *looks* like an entirely unrelated—or low-priority—trend could suddenly have major significance for you, your organization, or your industry at large. Can you combine two or more megatrends to imagine a new vision, strategy, or approach for your organization? Can you make a list of the likely implications, over the next five to ten years, of one of the megatrends that you see as the most critical to your future?

You might also try to imagine that the complete *opposite* of these potential implications came to pass over these years. How do you think this could have happened?

Trying to Be Deductive: Prioritizing and Culling Helpful Insights from Megatrends

When individuals and organizations begin the megatrend process, rather than asking questions designed to provoke expansive inductive thinking, they often approach the topic either through a sense of instinct ("Ah yes, this trend seems like it is something we need to keep track of") or, as is more often the case, deductive logic ("These trends have been most relevant for us for the past five years, so we should continue to track them"). We have attended workshops where people suggest individual megatrends that they believe are critical and everyone else quickly announces whether they agree or disagree with each par-

ticular one. This can be very useful, but also limiting: It restricts ob-
servers to the most obvious megatrends—and sometimes these are the
trends most closely related to the boxes, biases, and perceptions these
people were trying to expunge during Step 1.

To avoid such rushes to judgment, it can be helpful to start with a
broad list and winnow down your list of trends carefully. Begin with
a large number of megatrends that cut across multiple categories and
then, by applying more subjective criteria, narrow your list to include
what you and your team believe may be the most high-impact and likely
trends—and thus seemingly the most urgent ones. You will also want
to work diligently to identify highly *unlikely* trends that, improbable as
they may seem, could have a tremendous impact if they came to be.
And when prioritizing, we find it helpful to include not only the clearly
high-impact ones, but also the ones where there is a low level of consensus about the likely impact.

One recent effort we were involved in included using megatrends to
develop a range of scenarios for what the auto industry could look like
fifteen years in the future. After studying significant amounts of new
and existing research collected from consulting companies, automotive
industry associations, and a variety of other sources, we worked together to identify forty-two potentially relevant megatrends. We then
organized these into six categories: demographic trends (for example,
stagnation of population in developed countries, urbanization), regulatory trends (for example, environmental pressure, plant closure re-
strictions), technology trends (for example, alternative energy sources,
wireless communications), economic trends (for example, strong GDP
growth in developing countries, increase of income gap), consumer
trends (for example, brand affinity, demand for green products), and
other trends (for example, war for talent, world instability).

Next, we introduced a more subjective component into our analysis,
asking the auto industry executives in the room to rate these trends to
assess their relative "disruptive" potential. Specifically, we asked them to
rate each trend on a scale from 1 to 10 in terms of not only 1) the possible
impact of the trend on the industry and 2) the level of certainty of its occurring in their view, but also 3) the readiness of the industry for the
trend. The exhibit on page 99 shows how we displayed the results of these

rankings, with impact shown on the horizontal axis, readiness shown on the vertical axis, and certainty reflected in the size of the bubbles.

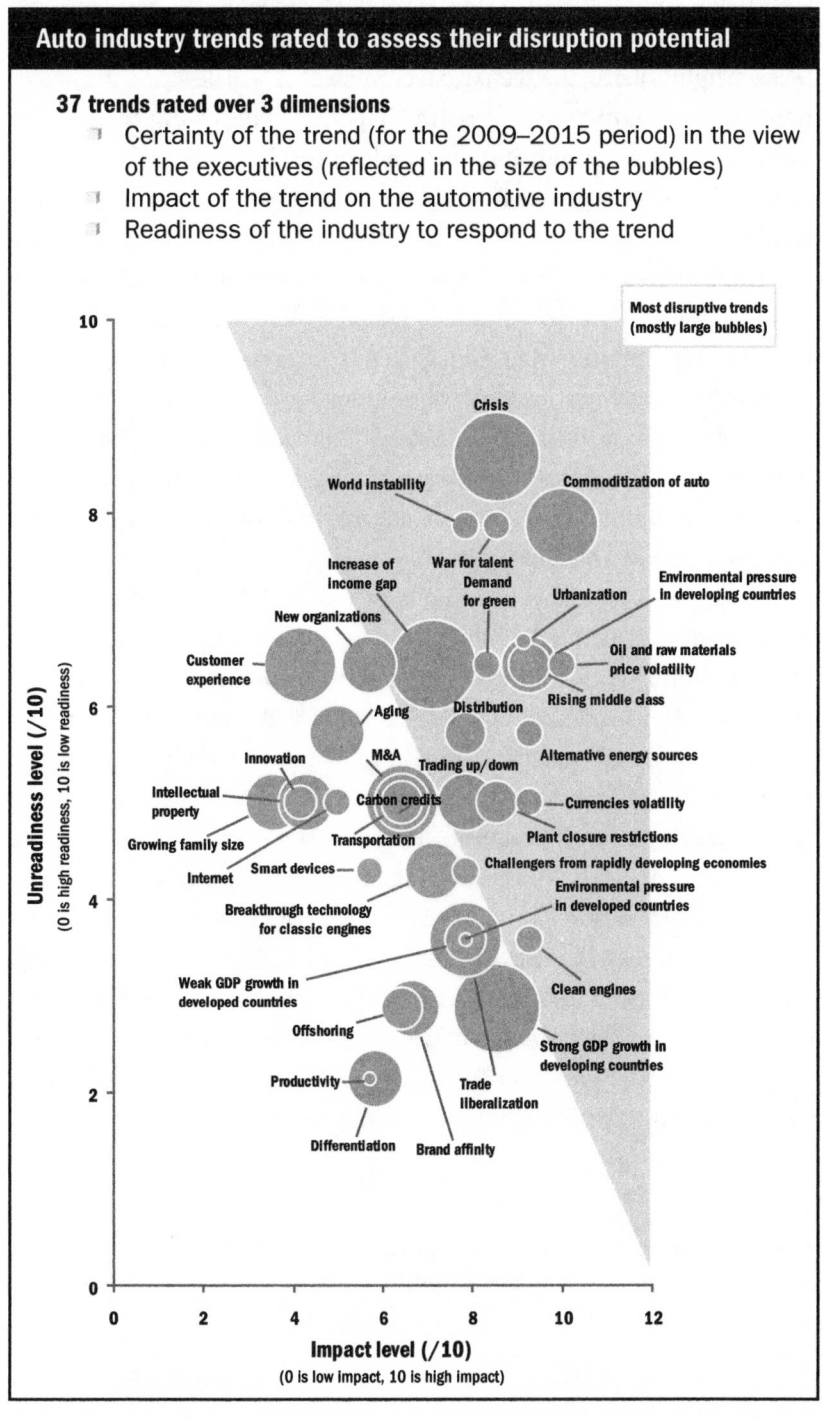

Auto industry trends rated to assess their disruption potential

37 trends rated over 3 dimensions
- Certainty of the trend (for the 2009–2015 period) in the view of the executives (reflected in the size of the bubbles)
- Impact of the trend on the automotive industry
- Readiness of the industry to respond to the trend

Following this exercise, our clients selected fourteen key trends as the most potentially disruptive; in essence, a selection of the largest bubbles closest to the top-right corner of the exhibit on page 99, ensuring at least one to three from each of the six categories. They subsequently used these insights, using the scenario techniques we will describe in chapter 9, to generate numerous fascinating hypotheses regarding the possible impact of each key trend, and the trends in combination.

Still, as illuminating as it might be to develop long, carefully categorized lists of megatrends that might affect your future, and as helpful as it can be to winnow down those lists to home in on what appear to be the most relevant and important trends, the more vital work lies in how you ultimately *interpret* these megatrends, that is, whether you rely on them in relatively perfunctory ways, ignoring those that don't fit with your current boxes, or whether instead you're able to think about them more inductively to question your existing assumptions, paradigms, strategies, and other boxes and, of course, to develop lots of new valuable perspectives and approaches.

For example, in 2001, two giants of the bookselling industry were confronted with the digitization of various forms of media and increasing competition from online retailers, most notably Amazon.com. And they reacted in fundamentally different ways: Borders outsourced online sales to Amazon and focused on growing its store base quickly. It diversified into CDs and DVDs as those industries (music and movies) were starting to go digital, and moved into e-readers in 2010, three years after Amazon's Kindle was launched. The end result was bankruptcy in 2011, to the dismay of many lovers of brick-and-mortar bookstores. By contrast, Barnes & Noble launched its Nook e-reader in 2008 and diversified into toys and games. While B&N is still facing serious challenges from Amazon and in 2013 announced plans to close almost 30 percent of its stores over the next decade as a result, Nook alone is valued around $1.7 billion, which is a massive help.*

---

* At the time of this writing, B&N was planning to spin off Nook as a separate company, which, we hope, will not lead the bookstore division down the same path as Borders.

Inductive Approaches to Speculating on "Extraordinary Futures"

We recently worked with top executives from AGC Glass Europe, a company that manufactures quality glass (for windows and smartphone screens, among other uses), to develop a long list of megatrends. Much as we had done with leaders from the auto industry, we then worked with AGC to come up with a shorter list of megatrends that we thought could be most relevant. Again, we used criteria such as "level of likely impact" and "level of preparedness" to rank the various trends. Prioritization was important because it helped sensitize these executives to what could very well turn out to be critical trends and thus to deepen their knowledge in key areas.

But prioritization of information is just one way people can analyze the relative importance of various megatrends, so we then took further steps to stretch these executives' thinking about the trends they were pondering. For example, we asked them to pick a megatrend that was very low on their prioritization list, that is, one that they thought was thoroughly *unlikely* to be relevant. They ended up selecting the organic food movement. We then asked them to pretend that a boom in organic food turned out to be the key driver for the glass industry.

Why and how, we asked them, did this happen? One executive suggested that the rise in organic and local food led to a massive demand for greenhouses, thus stimulating the glass market; another built upon that idea to suggest that the R&D team in 2013 had developed a brand-new sort of glass for greenhouses that helped plants grow more effectively, upending the value chain for local, organic food.

Can you think of some other possible ways that a quality glass manufacturer could begin serving the needs of a booming organic food movement?

Indeed, later in our Step 2 conversations, these executives were able to see how such an unlikely trend could take on great relevance. They began to think about new products in light of the growth in organic foods (ideas that they might ponder further during Step 3 divergence), but, more important, they began to question things once again, to challenge their perceptions of what the future might hold.

Applying more inductive approaches has the advantage of revealing not only less obvious megatrends but also some possibilities that no one would normally suggest could be relevant without some prospective thinking. Indeed, induction can help you to come up with numerous examples of what we will call "wild cards": *unexpected,* dramatic events with huge potential impact, whose explanations tend to proliferate only in retrospect.* A tsunami. The collapse of the euro. The discovery of a human colony on Jupiter.

For instance, one of the more surprising political events in recent European history was the failure of elected officials in Belgium to form a government. After an election that took place in June 2010, where no party had a clear majority—in part because of divisions between the two main ethnic groups in Belgium, the Walloons and the Flemish—the leader of the winning party went on television and essentially refused to run the country. The country set a historic record for being a democracy without a government for the longest time (541 days), beating even post–Saddam Hussein Iraq. Yet this extraordinary event could in theory have been predicted by those schooled in Belgian culture and history. Those observing life in Belgium might have spotted the rising division within the country and the gradual, growing weakness of its political system—not to mention the statements made by the leader in question during the campaign.[8] It all seems obvious—in retrospect.

To identify such wild cards, we urge you to avoid posing questions that have direct, quantifiable answers. If you asked people, "What is the probability that no one will use toothbrushes five years from now?" the answers would range from 0 to 100 percent. Asking instead, "Suppose people everywhere could simply bite into a device that cleaned and massaged their teeth and gums perfectly in just ten seconds—how did this happen?" leads to more creative possibilities. If everyone in the world were to shift to this new technology, they would have to

---

* This is also commonly known as a "black swan," the term popularized recently by Nassim Nicholas Taleb in *Fooled by Randomness* and *The Black Swan* (Random House, 2005 and 2007, respectively).

be reacting to one or more megatrends—what could those trends possibly be?

Suppose that by 2020, air travel is down 95 percent from today's levels. How could this have happened, building on our knowledge of trends and exploration of wild cards? Some possibilities: an increase in airborne ash because of more and more volcanic explosions—certainly not inconceivable. An increase in the cost of jet fuel, such that flying is only for the richest few. New high-speed transoceanic boats that travel more quickly and more safely than jets. New videoconferencing hologram-like technology. The collapse of the global economy and free trade . . .

What would some of these possibilities mean for you as an executive at Ultragames? For instance, imagine how new videoconferencing technologies that are vivid and powerfully effective (think Skype in 3-D) could change the routines of each segment of your customers. Many of them would travel less, taking fewer flights, and thus purchase fewer games for use when airborne with time to kill. But surely Ultragames could be at the cutting edge in terms of linking games into Skype and other new "virtual realities"—a game to practice taking the SAT or MCAT in an actual exam room, another to experience a first date with someone you just "met" on eHarmony. The question is what you should do *today* to be prepared for this set of new possibilities tomorrow.

What about the trend of women's increased purchasing power and higher wages—you could develop your understanding of this surge in the "female economy" and help Ultragames address this emerging market segment. Or the rise in healthcare spending as a proportion of the economy—what could this mean to Ultragames? Your games could have a role in developing new high-tech medical devices, diagnosing conditions by plugging in symptoms, or finding cures for elusive illnesses and medical conditions such as multiple sclerosis or Lou Gehrig's disease.

Let us indulge you in another similarly expansive approach to thinking about megatrends and "wild card" possibilities. Consider a trend relevant to many people today: sustainable energy use. You might respond in a conventional linear fashion, without fundamentally changing any boxes, listing the various ways in which governments and businesses might react to this trend by becoming "greener" and using less energy. But what if, five years from now, the government imposed a personal quota on energy consumption? How did that happen? Perhaps it was caused by a dramatic rise in worries about "peak oil," or maybe climate change and natural disasters accelerated, causing huge problems, or some unanticipated negative consequence of the use of fossil fuels was discovered.

Now, consider the *opposite* scenario: Suppose that five years from now, there is no scarcity of energy. How could this have happened? Did the world discover a boundless new source of energy? Was there a major scientific advance in, say, the development of solar power?

Coming up with "extraordinary futures"—and then thinking about what trends and events could have led to them (or to their opposite)—can often help you see "wild cards" you wouldn't otherwise be likely to identify, and really move in the direction of new boxes.

Look for "Boiling Frogs"

Even as you seek out "wild cards," be aware of much more insidious, slow-moving, unexpected changes—what are commonly known as "boiling frogs." These are evolving situations that, curiously, are often too slow or subtle for most people to see. Like the proverbial frog in the pot that doesn't realize the water is heating up until it is too late, we sometimes fail to notice profound change that threatens us. Some real-world examples include a lack of response to climate change, people staying in abusive relationships, or libertarians' views about the slow erosion of civil rights.*9 And behind many failed businesses or crises in a company, you'll see a slow erosion of market share, or a gradual buildup of some other problem.

---

* It is also important to point out here that biologists today tend to believe that the frog actually would jump out of the pot—but this is still a generally accepted metaphor. See http://www.fastcompany.com/26455/next-time-what-say-we-boil-consultant.

Warning: "Elephants in the Room!"

Sometimes, too, people fail to see events or trends that are neither "wild cards" nor "boiling frogs," but rather are the proverbial elephant in the room. These are things everyone is aware of—but they don't get the attention they deserve because they are taken for granted, feared, or (consciously or subconsciously) ignored. We were recently holding a discussion with city planners about their "2040 plan" in a country that became part of the Arab Spring phenomenon shortly thereafter. Together, we came up with a rather comprehensive list of seemingly relevant trends to consider. But when we asked about the possibility of regime change, we were told rather clearly that that particular topic was off the table. In this case perhaps the city planners were simply unable to imagine it—or were fearful of the consequences of discussing it. Another reason this sometimes happens is that those in the room won't be directly impacted, given the time horizon and their incentives (for example, executives who don't expect to be around for more than a couple of years). The recent award of the Nobel Peace Prize to the European Union exposed an interesting generational difference: For those born after a certain moment, "peace in Europe" seemed to be taken for granted, while for older people who remembered the "elephant" of World War II, peace in Europe represented a fundamental shift. Whatever the reason, an elephant in the room—something that is big and conspicuous, yet hard for people to accept and act upon—is ignored at your own risk.

Making Sense of Your List of Trends to Think Prospectively

Once you have come up with your "wild cards"—as well as a few "boiling frogs" and "elephants in the room"—combine them with your list of trends and spend some time pondering how you could exploit them. Ask yourself,

• Which of these would be the most disruptive?
• For which ones are we least ready?
• Which ones are right in front of us, yet we are hesitant to admit they're there?

- What about our competitors—why are they ready for some more than others?
- How do these future events, whether likely or unlikely, influence the kinds of new ideas we want to generate during Step 3 divergence?
- How do they change our central line of inquiry?

Posing such open-ended questions to maximize prospective thinking, when combined with divergence and convergence during Steps 3 and 4, will help you articulate lots of new and highly desirable boxes that you and your organization can explore, implement, and monetize.

Decades ago, the Dutch giant Philips identified several megatrends that it needed to address, including the steady rise in healthcare costs, and the fact that the population in developed countries was inexorably shifting such that the proportion of older and elderly people was becoming more dominant. Executives at Philips decided to open a new line of business, building on their expertise in electronics: In addition to being a giant multinational electronics company, Philips would become known as the expert on home healthcare solutions. This allowed Philips to specialize and gain traction in consumers' minds in what has become an increasingly competitive business. This was a wise decision in retrospect—Philips's Home Healthcare Solutions unit has become a billion-dollar business[10]—yet, looking at the same set of data regarding trends and the company's areas of expertise, Philips at the time could have chosen to focus on different trends and decided to instead become the "sustainability company," much as General Electric elected to become known for "Ecomagination," or build on its expertise in televisions to focus on mobile-device screens, as Samsung has done to a degree.

If you were among the largest food companies in the United States, how would you deal with trends such as energy price fluctuations and sustainability, which would be impacting you in numerous ways, ranging from fulfilling customer desires to be "green" to limiting packaging and transportation costs? Kraft Foods has created a refrigerated storage facility in a natural limestone cave near Springfield, Missouri, that uses 65 percent less energy than conventional storage sites. The large size and central location help the company save 180,000 gallons of fuel and one million miles of truck travel annually. General Mills began burning leftover oat hulls from the oats used to make Cheerios and other products, and this now produces 90 percent of the steam used to heat its plant in Fridley, Minnesota. This saves money and cuts the plant's carbon footprint by 20 percent.[11]

In sum, identifying megatrends is just one part of the challenge—deciding how to respond to them is the rest of it. You can be most effective in winning the future by thinking creatively about what the consequences of each trend could be, and then developing all sorts of possible ways to react.

PUTTING IT ALL TOGETHER

Let us take a closer look at Philips: It is a company that claims to be driven by "meaningful innovation"—this means understanding trends, customer insight, and competitive intelligence, and then figuring out how the company can meet market needs. The company is large enough that sometimes what's learned in one of its business units helps in another; for example, the things it has learned from stereo systems about acoustics have helped with vacuum cleaners as well (specifically, how to make the noise loud enough that people think the cleaner is sufficiently strong, but not so loud as to drive customers crazy).

Consider Philips's AirFloss product, introduced in 2011. The main premise behind the product is that a huge number of people know they should floss regularly, but don't. Why might this be? Consumer research suggests that it's not about awareness—people generally know they should floss. The main reason they don't seems to be that flossing is too difficult, and so Philips saw an opportunity in making it easier. The specific question executives there came up with was "How can we find a way to clean between teeth in an easy way?" The word *floss* was not a part of this key question, to avoid bias, and it was also not about cleaning between teeth more effectively or more quickly. It was deliberately and explicitly about *ease* of use.

This challenge did not immediately go to Philips's "development department," which takes new ideas through the innovation phases, but rather to the "innovation research department," which is a group of scientists in Eindhoven, the Netherlands, who were charged with coming up with a breakthrough technology to meet the challenge. They developed and tested a wide range of concepts (think gas, light, lasers, water pressure, physics, and the like) and eventually emerged with the AirFloss. It looks vaguely like an electric toothbrush, and indeed builds upon the electric toothbrushes that Philips was already selling, but it has a small reservoir that can be filled with water or mouthwash that is propelled through the gaps in your teeth. At first glance it might look like some of the existing "oral irrigators" on the market, but customer research showed that for many, those didn't meet the "easy" criteria. Some of them used two pints of water for each flossing, which made things messy and a bit unwieldy. AirFloss uses much less water, and in focus groups seemed much more pleasant and easy to use, getting people to adhere to a flossing-type regimen at much higher rates than any other product. The "oral irrigator" segment was essentially reinvented, and grew by 50 percent following a sensational introduction of the Air-Floss at the major industry trade show in Cologne, Germany. As one Philips executive put it to us, "How much innovation is there in oral care? We stole the show!"[12]

The road to the Airfryer, another product launched recently by Philips, began by looking at how people consume, and their lifestyle habits. Obesity rates were rising in most Western countries, and there was an increasing movement by some segments toward healthy foods. But kids still loved the taste of french fries and other fried foods. So the challenge was to provide the taste and flavor of fried food in a much healthier way, that is, with much less oil and fat, as a solution primarily for parents who wanted food for their families that was healthy and tasty at the same time. Not only was there a gap seen in this market, but sales of traditional fryers were stagnant or declining in a wide range of markets. The Airfryer uses patented technology relating to rapidly circulating hot air, and no oil (or very little, depending on user preferences), to meet this challenge.

After identifying this challenging "healthy *and* delicious" new box based on customer insight, executives at Philips embarked on a very deliberate search of the competitive marketplace. During that process, they were approached by a small company that had invented the technical architecture required for the Airfryer, in a device small enough to fit on a kitchen counter. Philips acquired the technology after determining that this product might help meet the identified market gap. This was of course possible only by thoughtfully challenging the executives' existing perspectives using doubt, questioning whether they could get there alone as quickly as they wanted to, and then methodically exploring the world around them. The Airfryer is now sold in more than eighty countries, with ambitious sales targets achieved years ahead of plans.*[13]

Moving Toward Divergence

The key outcome you'll want to achieve by the end of Step 2 is to identify the most significant question(s) you hope to address through Step 3 divergence. What is the exciting new destination you hope to reach? What kinds of new boxes will help you get there? Albert Einstein is reported to have said, "If I were given one hour to save the planet, I would spend fifty-nine minutes defining the problem and one minute resolving it."[14] That may be extreme, but the importance of using an effective question cannot be overstated.

Of course there is no single "correct" question—but a useful question will be one that meets all of these criteria:

---

* The marketing of the Airfryer was also a new box for Philips that helped the broader "healthy and delicious" box succeed. Philips's executives conducted a series of very market-specific launches, with local resonance as a key theme to attract consumers. Philips also sold the product through more unconventional channels, such as home shopping and social media. "The biggest problem has been keeping up with demand," said a Philips executive.

- *It should build on existing mental models or areas you have explored with a "hook" of some sort . . . while still challenging you to explore new horizons.* That is, it must be somehow tied to something of relevance to your current boxes; it cannot be completely "out there" in every way— but it should also be somehow provocative or surprising.
- *It should be vivid/visual in some way.* That is, not just "how do we grow" or "we need to cut costs thirty percent," but something more memorable and colorful. It often helps to include a character in some way. For example, if the goal is to improve marketing at the bank building on trends relating to mobile technology, with the target customer segment of professional women in their twenties, instead of asking specifically about *that*, ask, "How do we persuade a twenty-five-year-old female accountant in Los Angeles to make our bank's mobile app her most-used app of the year?"
- *It should be limited and constrained in some way, so as to allow you to focus your thinking.* You are surely aware by now that we insist on a specific question, and would never just say "everything is on the table," or only "think outside the box." And so rather than asking "What should our strategy for entering the mortgage market be?" your question could be more along the lines of "How can we create a mortgage offering that appeals to the twenty-five-year-old accountant in Los Angeles while remaining profitable?"
- *It should be clear and understandable to someone coming in fresh.* If an outsider joined your conversation, a question like "How can we build on our existing brand proposition for our desired customers while hitting our profit targets?" would not be as clear as the examples above.

By using prospective approaches to investigate the world, you can generate rich customer insights, competitive intelligence, and megatrends "within you." These, in turn, can help you, once again, to see and understand things "in front of you" in new, illuminating ways. We'll explore the trajectory in the next two chapters; as you move between induction and deduction, and ponder the insights you're gathering, you'll generate lots of new concepts, paradigms, strategies, and other such boxes (Step 3) and then decide which ones to pursue (Step 4). The following diagram shows this interplay between Step 2 and Steps 3 and 4:

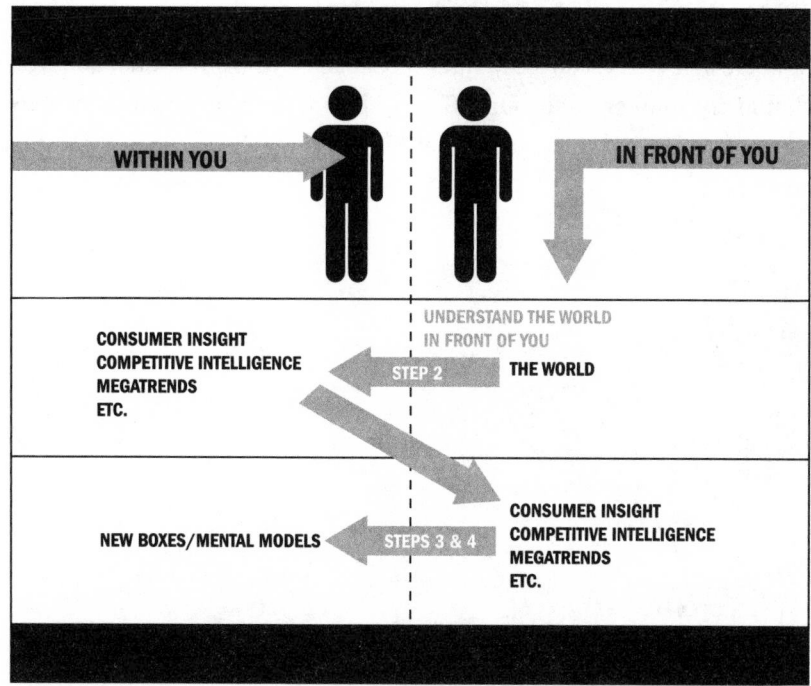

Now that you have taken a closer look at the world in front of you—and thought deeply about what your observations might mean for you and your organization—it is time to allow yourself to engage in some improvisation and play. During Step 3 (divergence), you will let your mind run free and give birth to a plethora of possibilities.

As a leader of Ultragames, what kinds of questions should you be asking right now, building on the criteria listed previously? You know your "family customers" are willing to pay more for safety and age appropriateness, to guarantee a positive and entertaining experience for their children. You've explored the competitive landscape and given serious thought to the possibility that organizations outside of the obvious set (that is, KFC or Major League Baseball rather than just VGG) could introduce game-changing new boxes and innovations. And you've looked not only at relatively conspicuous megatrends (such as urbanization, the aging population, and the growth in digitization) but also at much less expected ones (potential for less travel due to virtual reality, rise in healthcare spending, increased purchasing power of women). How do these observations shape your thinking about the company? What new creative valves do they open? What is the central question you should try to answer through Step 3 divergence? What kinds of new boxes do you need to create? What kinds of new boxes do you *want* to create?

FIVE

Diverge

□ □

The way to get good ideas is to get lots of ideas and throw the bad ones away.

—LINUS PAULING, two-time Nobel Prize winner

N 1992, NASA launched a program that had among its key objectives to "demonstrate a low-cost entry and landing system."[1] Specifically, the goal was to allow for a gentle touchdown of an unmanned craft on Mars, without leaving trace amounts of foreign chemicals that would later make it difficult to analyze the composition of the rocks and soil. So officials were considering a radical new approach: allowing the Mars Pathfinder, armed with a parachute and a rocket braking system as well as multilayered fabric air bags, to bounce a few times on Mars rather than worrying about a single "proper" landing (that is, the way most every plane appears to land today, or the way the Apollo 11 module first landed on the moon).

In 1997 the Pathfinder landed successfully on Mars using this new, controversial approach: airbags.[2] Its first bounce was 15.7 meters (51 feet) high, and there were at least fifteen more bounces before it settled down. NASA's engineers had shifted their perspective from "the spacecraft is fragile" to the new box of "the planet is fragile" and the outcome was a classic example of *Eureka*.

And yet what must it have been like to participate in that first meeting at NASA when someone suggested they could try airbags and a bouncing spacecraft to help achieve a soft landing, rather than retro-rockets? Chances are the suggestion was not met with an immediate chorus of "Great idea!"[3]

"Bounce?" you can imagine people asking. "Are you *kidding* me?"

Officials at NASA must have had to deal with many such skeptical "convergent" thinkers who did not feel immediately comfortable with the airbag proposal. And yet the advocates overcame their colleagues' feelings of discomfort and were able to create a new, exciting box.

Learning how to suspend and transcend just this sort of profound discomfort—so that you can stretch yourself to see new perspectives and generate lots of original and hopefully daring new ideas—is the essence of divergence. You simply have to "go with it" for a while, toler-ating all kinds of new concepts and proposals (including ones that seem absurd or even abhorrent) until it's time to clamp down and decide how to proceed. During divergence, you'll open yourself up to a range of new ways of thinking about things. You'll put forth numerous hypotheses and create a wide variety of new models, paradigms, concepts, and strategies.

Divergence is the time to take full advantage of your freedom and to show your undeniable courage as a creator. It requires the prolific pro-duction of new ideas—and new ways of looking at old ideas—and, in many instances, shrewd departures from convention and even bold acts of rebellion as you suggest audacious new boxes and shifts of percep-tion.

The pioneering work of Finnish software engineer and hacker Linus Torvalds and others in the free-software movement (including legend-ary MIT professor Richard Stallman) offers a dazzling example of di-vergence. Developers of computer software programs long adhered to legal and industry standards calling upon them to create proprietary source code and to rely on operating system environments that were fully privatized. Developers and others generally had to pay licensing fees (and cope with rigid technological standards and constraints) when creating and using software compatible with these "closed" operating system environments. "Only the source can write code," was the con-ventional assumption.

But in the early 1990s, advocates for "free and open-source software" (later referred to simply as the open-source community)—evincing quintessential divergent thinking—rebelled against these assumptions. In October 1991, Torvalds released his free-for-everyone Linux operating system, which works on numerous platforms (such as mobile phones, tablet computers, and personal computers) and today runs the ten fastest supercomputers on the planet. The Linux approach—allowing free, unfettered access to a very high-level operating system environment—represented a radical new box.

Many established businesses in the software and hardware industries were initially hesitant to endorse a paradigm for software development that seemed to challenge basic notions of copyright and customary business practices pertaining to the licensing of intellectual property assets. But as consumers and other end users saw the desirability of creating open operating systems, and as business leaders were able to shift their perceptions to see more opportunity than they did risks, an increasing number of influential organizations and individuals began not only to respect but indeed to support the development of Linux. IBM, Dell, Hewlett-Packard, and Oracle, among many others, became involved. The widespread use of Linux has led to an explosion of new software development and the creation of such applications as Mozilla's Firefox Web browser, the free music-listening program Pandora, and the widely used OpenOffice.org office application suite.[4] Today, the official website for the White House—www.whitehouse.gov—uses Drupal, an open-source content management system that runs exclusively on the Linux operating system.

Divergence is about not only permitting but actively encouraging the expression of diverse and sometimes wildly opposing ideas, beliefs, opinions, and visions, including those that are unpopular, unattractive, or unconventional, even those that seem misguided, reactionary, or downright absurd.

But, as we cannot stress enough, you should always begin divergence armed with a carefully framed question that you will then, instead, work to answer. You will thus arrive for the idea-generation process rigorously prepared. You'll be the sculptor whose preliminary studies are complete and whose knives are fully sharpened. You'll be the explorer who has relentlessly surveyed the maps and the territory, and is now ready to blaze numerous new trails to reach her ultimate destination. You will not be showing up merely to brainstorm or to try to "think outside the box" about some vague and vast issue. Instead, you will be applying yourself to a carefully circumscribed issue.

This is one of the key ways that "thinking in new boxes" differs from "thinking outside the box": We embrace robust divergence and the profound importance of encouraging free-flowing creativity, but we believe that these things are unlikely to lead to ideas of practical value if you haven't first properly framed and articulated your essential inquiry. Yes, we favor "breaking the rules" and shattering existing assumptions and paradigms. But encouraging people to answer carefully considered questions, to ponder the possible impact of various real and theoretical constraints and variables, and to establish at least *some* boundaries for the range of answers they're about to generate is what will lead you to brilliant new ideas.

What would it take for 60 percent of Americans to set your company's website as their home page? That is an example of a question that is evocative and specific enough to lead to a useful divergence session. In a project to develop a new set of Web-based strategies for Generali, a global insurance company based in Europe, we conducted numerous divergence sessions and used several specific creativity exercises to stimulate a maximum number of ideas. We agreed up front that the key issue was to determine what approaches the company could take to develop and launch an inspired new online presence, but we did not then immediately jump into idea-generation mode. Rather, we reframed the company's core issue by asking such questions as "How can we design and build Generali's website so that everyone chooses it as their home screen?" and "How could my grandmother experience pleasure and pride in discovering Generali online?" This maneuver might seem simple, even simplistic, but we believe that by asking these sorts of reframing questions, we were able to hold much more fruitful divergence sessions than if we had just said, "Let's brainstorm a lot of ideas for improving your website!"

LOW-COST HEART SURGERY

We have already seen examples of different levels of boxes, from the broadest paradigms to the "smaller" ideas used to fill them, from "disposable plastic objects" to razors and lighters. How could divergence apply to a very broad conceptual box like "low cost"? Applying this concept to a wide range of areas has led to numerous creative and innovative ideas over history. For example, we have seen how Ryanair and others changed the status quo in various ways and applied the "low-cost" box to airlines, changing that industry in fundamental ways. What other examples might there be? If we go back in time, Gutenberg's original printing press could be seen as the first low-cost approach to publishing, and since then the concept has made its way into retail (think IKEA, UNIQLO, and Zara), mobile telephony (with cheap disposable telephones), and a wide range of other industries. Even banking and insurance are not immune, with E-Trade and other such online brokerages, or even RHB Bank in Malaysia going for growth by launching an "Easy Bank" targeting new lower-income customers, with branches that look and feel more like a fast-food restaurant than a standard bank branch.

If divergence is about being expansive about possibilities, where else might the low-cost concept be applicable? How about to hospitals? Or even heart surgery? Your first reaction might be "If I had heart trouble, I would want the best medical care that's available; I would never trust my life to a low-cost hospital." Without dwelling on the fact that we also trust our lives to low-cost airlines, let us look at how Dr. Devi Shetty, after his own personal periods of doubt and exploration, brought such a hospital to life.

When Devi Shetty was growing up in India, doctors were seen as gods in his household; his father had survived several diabetic comas thanks to timely medical care. This eventually inspired him to become a doctor and a surgeon, and he was a very successful one—he spent six years in London operating in top medical facilities, and then returned to India, becoming Mother Teresa's personal heart surgeon. Indeed, she became a role model for him, and he realized that many patients who couldn't afford to pay were turning away from the healthcare system completely.

Having seen how surgery was set up in both the West and in India, Dr. Shetty wanted to bring the box of "low-cost heart surgery" to life. He opened a new hospital in Bangalore in 2001 and experimented with business concepts such as economies of scale to keep costs low. His hospital chose less expensive products wherever possible to keep costs down, without compromising the effectiveness of treatment. For example, it purchased the least expensive sutures it could find, while continuing to pay for top-of-the-line GE scanning and diagnostic equipment. At the same time, it got more use out of the equipment, again via economies of scale—it performed many more operations than in a typical U.S. hospital. There are 1,000 patient beds, as compared with the average U.S. heart hospital, which has about 160 beds, and the sheer volume of surgeries performed enabled surgeons to become world-class experts. Surgeons were paid the going rate in India, and worked 60–70 hours a week, doing 2–3 procedures a day, 6 days a week (contrasted with 1–2 procedures a day, 5 days a week in the United States). Surgeons also did not generally have other responsibilities such as teaching. All in all, the average price for heart surgery was brought down to about $2,000, compared with U.S. prices of $20,000–$100,000.

All of that would already constitute a new box enabling many more people to get heart surgery, especially in high-population areas like Bangalore. But $2,000 was still a lot of money for many of them. So Dr. Shetty went further, setting up a special insurance plan whereby individuals would pay $3 per person per year in case they needed surgery. This insurance plan would break even by paying the hospital $1,200 per surgery, and to make up the difference, the hospital charged $2,400 for the surgery (instead of $2,000) to patients not on the plan, and also charged up to $5,000 for special service and room upgrades to those who were interested.

This new box of low-cost complex surgery is economically viable and clearly helpful to the masses; indeed, Dr. Shetty is targeting Americans with a new hospital planned for the Cayman Islands, where the price will be higher than in Bangalore, but still 50 percent lower than in the

United States—a world-class heart facility an hour's flight from Miami will presumably be tempting to some.

The Aravind Eye Care System is taking a similar "assembly line" approach to eye surgery, particularly cataracts. The treatment for cataracts is relatively simple and easy from a surgical perspective, but in developing countries such as India, cataracts are frequently left untreated because of infrastructure challenges and sheer poverty. In 1976, Dr. Govindappa Venkataswamy founded what is now the largest and most productive eye-care facility in the world. From April 2009 through March 2010, more than 2.5 million patients were treated and more than 300,000 surgeries were performed. Today the Aravind Eye Care System encompasses five hospitals with more than two thousand beds, a manufacturing center for ophthalmic products, an international research foundation, and a resource and training center that is revolutionizing hundreds of eye care programs across the developing world.[5]

So let us ask you this: As an executive at Ultragames who has completed Steps 1 and 2 and is ready for divergence, what will be your primary question and quest? How can you continue to reframe your essential line of inquiry to produce a maximum of practical ideas during divergence? Using classic "think outside the box" brainstorming, you might have jumped right into considering "How can we update our core franchises to ensure they remain appealing to teenage boys?" or "How can we move into the mobile space?" But during Step 1's doubt phase, you questioned some of your mental models pertaining to the fundamentals of the company and its target customers. You learned that gamers have gotten older and that an increasing proportion of them are female. You doubted whether Ultragames needed to continue upholding such assumptions as "We never use profanity or graphic violence or sexuality in our games." But when you conducted detailed customer research during the Step 2 exploration phase, you emerged with an understanding of the importance of this "safe" image to a range of wholesome soccer-mom-type customers. Make no mistake about it: These elements of doubt and exploration will now make your divergence phase dramatically more fruitful.

Imagine that your longtime banker, believing in your ambitious creative spirit, now offers Ultragames a $5 million line of credit with an affordable interest rate and generously long payback period, giving you the option of borrowing additional funds to invest in the company's activities over the next several years. This new financing emboldens you to challenge your long-held assumptions around being a video game company primarily targeting young men. And given these key shifts in your thinking, you now decide that your core question for divergence should be "How can we dramatically increase our revenues, by making Ultragames the company of choice for families who are looking for a single-source entertainment provider?"

With this key inquiry in mind, you can begin the process of divergence. We generally envision this process entailing three basic phases: 1) fostering a creative environment—and warming up, 2) conducting the divergence exercises, and 3) editing and "crushing" the multiple new boxes you've generated.

FOSTERING A CREATIVE ENVIRONMENT

Divergence can be done alone, but it generally yields a wider range of results, and hence is most effective, if conducted with other people. There are a lot of ways to make that happen, from a quick ten-minute exercise with a friend, to small informal lunches with a few colleagues, to more formal and lengthy workshops. We suggest you try to enjoy this part of the creative process in a setting that is physically (or at least psychologically) removed from your everyday work environment so that you're freed from the associations and distractions that it may hold for you. We encourage you to go to a place where you will feel at ease, and if others are joining you, a place where they will feel free to share the ideas they come up with regardless of their standing or position within the organization.

At the start of a session, whatever the size and format, you need a clear plan and a good sense of the expectations. If others are involved, this plan should be clear to everyone. A good plan would include a view of how the ideas generated will be captured, and when divergence will shift to convergence. Remember (and remind others as needed) to focus on *quantity* for this phase rather than quality—generate as many ideas as possible. And *everyone* present should participate: If you've roped others into joining you, then you are responsible for helping them transcend their inhibitions and tendency to judge and analyze everything, to allow for divergence to happen in a free and uninterrupted way.

To paraphrase Linus Pauling, the best way to have a good idea is to have *a lot* of ideas. No single idea, at its inception, is inherently born good. Rather, to develop a winning new box, you first need to come up with many ideas and possibilities, and later revise them.

During divergence, no idea—as idiotic or inappropriate as it may seem to anyone—should be immediately rejected. Divergence is the time to give birth to many creative new boxes. If it is a group event, it is critical that the facilitator—whether you or someone else who has been designated to be the neutral, open-minded, inspiring leader and "coach"—create an immediate sense of tolerance and inclusiveness so that no one will feel reluctant to share his or her thoughts and ideas.

One of the key impediments to developing exciting new ideas is the phrase and the attitude summed up as "Yes . . . *but* . . ." The dialogue usually sounds something like this:

> "Hey, boss, I have a great idea for a new approach to tinting the glass we use in the windows we're selling. We can create a new photosensitive system so that the glass becomes darker and darker as the sun goes down and becomes opaque by nightfall . . ."

> "Yes, I guess we could do that, *but* . . . I don't know whether our budget would allow it."

> "Well, I found a budget item in our upcoming fiscal year that is more than sufficient to cover the cost of investigating this new approach."

> "Yes, *but* . . . didn't the automotive division try something like that last year? I don't think the big boss would go for it."

There is a time and place for convergent thinking, for making and acting upon practical decisions. But to ensure that you're giving the divergence phase enough time and room for success, we would encourage you to do your very best during this idea-creation phase to use the supportive and enthusiastic "Yes, *and* . . ." rather than the discouraging and often toxic "Yes, but . . ."

Here's the same dialogue rewritten to reflect the "Yes, *and* . . ." approach:

> "Hey, boss, I have a great idea for a new approach to tinting the glass we use in the windows we're selling. We can create a new photosensitive system so that the glass becomes darker and darker as the sun goes down and becomes opaque by nightfall . . ."

> "Yes, *and* maybe some models could provide both options, so customers could use the photosensitive tinting some days and on other days keep the glass clear."

> "Yes, *and* it could be interesting to develop it with additional options for places like Iceland, where some consumers might want to darken it when it's late at night but still light outside . . ."

"Yes, *and* . . ." helps people build upon one another's ideas.

Don't get us wrong: This is not about being gracious or "politically correct" by affirming every idea tossed your way. Rather, the "Yes, *and* . . ." approach is useful during the divergence phase for a purely logical reason: It forces you to come up with lots of ideas and it helps the initial iteration of an idea be further developed. As Pablo Picasso once said, "An idea is a point of departure and no more. As soon as you elaborate it, it becomes transformed by thought." Sometimes even what may at first seem like a very "good" idea may be impractical and require further iteration and development before it makes sense and becomes valuable. Good ideas emerge because you've first come up with (and eventually discarded) a lot of other, less good ones.

Several years ago, we worked with a major telecom company—let's refer to it here as "Allegro Tel"—that wanted to generate positive publicity by rewarding the company's 100,000th subscriber with a fun and interesting prize. In a lively divergence session, Allegro Tel executives came up with all sorts of ideas: a trip to a warm exotic place, a new household appliance, a new car. But the idea they liked best was that the 100,000th subscriber would be visited at his or her home or office by his or her favorite film star or celebrity. Everyone initially said: "What a *good idea!*" But it didn't take long to realize that implementing this "good" idea would be costly and impractical. How would Allegro Tel get Julia Roberts or Queen Elizabeth to show up at someone's home?

Through additional rounds of divergence and convergence, the group revised the idea: Instead of having the star or celebrity show up, use look-alikes. This ended up being an even more useful idea because it was inherently humorous, cost very little, was practical, and led to terrific "photo ops" and thus an amazingly strong public relations campaign for the company. Imagine the local excitement you'd generate if the gentleman on the right below (whose name is Ilham Anas) rang your doorbell and asked to have coffee with you.

Or imagine the publicity that Allegro Tel would receive if it arranged for the below "Barbra Streisand" to serenade its 100,000th subscriber by showing up at that subscriber's home and belting out "The Way We Were."

Source: http://www.lookalike.com/lookalikes/images/barbra-streisand-so.jpg

This campaign would never have come to fruition if the original idea—of hiring actual celebrities—had been rejected too early in the divergence process.

Divergence is the time to transcend the past, shake free of the rigid standards and customs you've always known, and allow new ideas to flow in an unencumbered way, without criticism or second-guessing. Remember: It's the *number* of ideas you come up with that matters most at this stage. You'll have time to analyze them later!

WARMING UP

Once the ground rules are clear, in terms of the importance of sharing lots of ideas and allowing everyone to participate without having their proposals instantly judged or shot down, you should warm up, just as you would before exercise, so that your imagination can flex its muscles. There are numerous ways to do this, and the best ones depend on the circumstances and any people who may be involved with you—how well they may know one another, the cultural issues at play, how much of a sense of humor they have, and other similar factors that you can address based on your own personal style and sensibility and the intuitions you have about what will be most effective with your team. We often start by asking everyone in the room to introduce themselves in a creative and unusual way, sharing something new about themselves, or perhaps by saying "I'm Bruno and what I love about our company is . . ." or "I'm Carly and two little-known facts about my work here are . . ." In exercises like these, there is an early opportunity to make each person's presence felt, and to ensure that interesting (as opposed to generic) content begins to emerge. So, for instance, if somebody said, "What I love about the company is that it really takes care of us," you would then have the opportunity to ask, "What are some of the ways that the company has recently taken care of you?" Or, "Which of the company's most fundamental values do you think underlie this positive feeling you have?"

It helps to infuse an element of randomness into these introductions, too. For example, you might ask people to participate in the introductions in alphabetical order based on their first names, the months they were born (where you might start with December-born individuals, and work backward—or randomly—through the calendar months), or the states—or nations—where their respective elementary schools were located. You could also ask each person to introduce someone else, or to select the next person to speak. Without some element of randomness, the person who knows he or she is next will stop listening and mentally rehearse an introduction.

An essential goal of these initial warm-ups is to help sensitize everyone once again to the ways in which some of their existing mental models, and especially subconscious biases and "rules," tend to guide and sometimes distort or restrain their thinking.

One warm-up that often works well for groups is a "pop quiz" that can be subtly related to some of the megatrends or key themes that were identified during Step 2, without being too closely tied to the problem at hand. For instance, we recently met with executives from a major

U.S.-based consumer products company who during Step 2 had identi-fied the growing wealth of consumers in rapidly developing economies—like Brazil, India, and China—as an important megatrend. To warm them up prior to a divergence session regarding ways by which they could potentially improve their market share in those countries, we asked a series of multiple-choice questions about these nations. We posed relatively specific questions—such as *What is India's leading ex-port? What is the average income in Brazil? How quickly is China building high-speed rail?*—to stimulate curiosity and encourage everyone to open their minds to a new perspective on the subject. Quizzing people on such factual (that is, purely deductive) matters can help them to re-member just how important it is to doubt that their current outlook on things is necessarily "right" or "the only way," and to engage those peo-ple who may be joining the process for the first time, or who are funda-mentally skeptical about divergence.

One of our favorite "deductive" warm-up questions (for which there is only *one* possible solution) is the following:

> Imagine you had a 20-volume encyclopedia on a shelf with each
> volume 2 inches thick (about 5 centimeters), and the cover an addi-
> tional quarter of an inch thick on each side (about 0.6 centimeters),
> and a worm is crawling from the first page of volume 1 to the last
> page of volume 20. How long is that distance?*

Some people answer 50 inches, that is, (20 volumes × 2" = 40") plus (20 volumes × 2 sides × ¼" = 10") = 50 inches total. Many people say 49.5 inches, since we said first page to last page, and hence the first and last covers can be excluded. But the correct answer is actually 4 inches less, that is 45.5 inches, since page 1 of the first volume is on the right-hand side of that volume, and the last page of volume 20 is on the left-hand side of that volume.

A second example of a warm-up is to explore some open-ended, inductive questions, such as "What if life were found on Mars and the planet was inhabitable by humans?" Some of these questions could

---

* For more warm-up exercises, please go to http://www.thinkinginnewboxes.com.

pertain to your industry (such as "What do you think three of the most-read articles in *Advertising Age* might be in the year 2040?") or to your particular organization (for example, "What are three sales venues where products of the kind we sell have never been sold before, but where we might start marketing ours?"). These could build explicitly on the trends and other research done earlier.

A third sample warm-up is to try to come up with as many short creative answers as possible to an interesting open-ended question. For example, imagine you have an unlimited stock of bricks, and then think about all the many ways you could deplete that stock through various creative uses of the bricks. We encourage people to move beyond the assumptions that 1) the bricks will be used to construct houses or buildings, and 2) the bricks are necessarily rectangular and flat. Participants have suggested using the bricks to create works of contemporary art, heating them up in the oven and then grilling food on them at the dining table, and selling them as all sorts of products: bodybuilding weights, doorstops, ice crushers, bookends, even as crude weapons.[6]

In a more visual exercise, ask people to come up with as many explanations as possible for a picture such as the following:

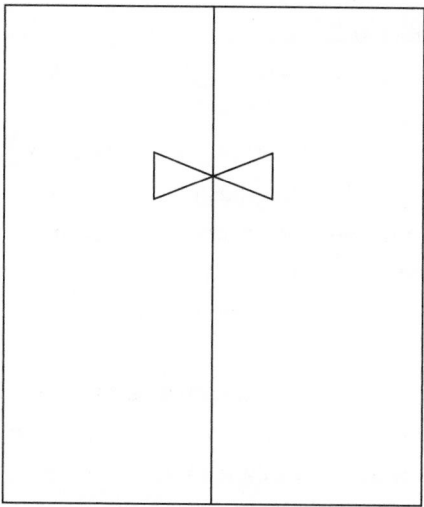

Participants have said they see a man with a bow tie stuck in an elevator, a foghorn on a pole (as seen from the side), or the beak of an albino penguin looking in a mirror.[7]

With these and other such warm-up exercises, everyone involved (again, even if it's just yourself) is forced to use deductive and inductive thinking skills, move beyond obvious and/or conventional ways of thinking, temporarily suspend critical faculties, and free himself or herself to conceive of and develop a multitude of new boxes. The point is for you to embrace a diversity of ideas and possibilities and begin to relate your brainstorming to the megatrends or other key themes or research findings identified during Step 2. You're moving into an idea-generation mode that, free and nonjudgmental as it is and should be, is also informed by all of the preparation that you've done ahead of time. You're moving toward thinking in new boxes.

As you finish warming up, begin focusing on the central issues you'll be addressing. This should involve not just reciting these issues, but exploring them in a way that will help maximize the openness of everyone involved and the imaginativeness that will be applied in responding. You'll want to reformulate and reframe the issues so that they stimulate your creative side.

Rather than saying in a general way, "Today we're going to discuss how to sell our services to government agencies," use a much more specific approach so that anyone faced with that question will feel much more directly challenged. Thus you might ask: "What would you say to the head of Governmental Agency X if by chance you were alone together for thirty seconds in an elevator?"

Or rather than asking, "How can we make our brand of crackers better known?" reframe the same basic issue as "What could we do that would make all supermarket managers want to put our crackers in prominent spots at the end of the aisle?" Or, "How can we get a family of four in Peoria eating dinner together at a table to talk excitedly about our crackers?"

Your overall goal is to come up with a new way of looking at the problem, something unfamiliar that forces a shift in perspective. Some suggestions for such reframing include the following:

- Formulate the issue so that it can be *visualized*—this helps evoke more, and more interesting, responses. It is often useful to start your reframed question with "How could we . . . ?" or "What would it take to . . . ?"

- Keep the key issue as concrete and specific to your organization and its personnel as possible—respecting existing values and constraints that are still valid and important actually helps foster creativity in this context.
- Hone the issue until it is clear to someone who might be addressing it for the first time, ensuring that those you involve will understand the impact and involvement they can have in addressing it.
- Communicate the issue in a way that is connected to something unique about your organization (as opposed to making it an issue that could apply to some other organization in your industry).

Executives from Staples brainstorming on "How can we sell more office supplies?" would likely generate much more exciting results if they started by asking fundamentally, "What does Staples do?" and *then* built upon these results. The goal is to ask the right big initial question. Shawn Coyne, a fellow management consultant, said in an interview that "if you want to be really successful, don't merely steal their idea. Steal the right question that led them to think of the idea."*[8]

As an executive from Ultragames working with your colleagues to come up with new ways to entertain entire families, you could reframe your initial question ("How can we dramatically increase our revenues by making Ultragames the company of choice for families who are looking for a single-source entertainment provider?") and instead ask, "How can we get Ultragames to be the first thing that comes to the mind of a thirty-five-year-old housewife in suburban Milwaukee when she hears the word *entertainment?*" Or, "How can we get a fifty-five-year-old mayor in small-town Kentucky to rave about Ultragames to all of his friends, constituents, and followers?" Or, "How can we get every

---

* Shawn Coyne is co-author of a book called *Brainsteering,* as well as a former McKinsey consultant, and hence could be seen as a competitor of ours in at least two ways. The irony of borrowing this quote about borrowing good ideas is not lost on us.

Baptist preacher in America to give a Sunday sermon about the many character-building benefits of Ultragames?"

Conducting Divergence Exercises

To begin to answer your central question, you'll want exercises that foster divergence, ones that will be stimulating but also appropriate for the specific sort of new boxes you're hoping to create, and any people you might be working with. The exercises that follow are some of our favorites, and are intended to help you see your organization and what it does through a different lens. They are meant to provoke you, to have you consider the very opposite of what you've always thought to be true, and to help you make novel associations between topics and contexts and worlds that generally are thought to be completely distinct and separate from one another. There are a multitude of such divergence exercises, which are generally designed to help you either 1) change your perspective—and thus generate new ideas, models, and approaches; and/or 2) develop new associations, comparisons, and analogies between and among your various boxes.

Some of these exercises will tend to trigger broader "big concept" sorts of ideas likely to be helpful when you're trying to create a broad new core box (such as a new overall vision), whereas others may be particularly helpful when you already have that primary box in place and are trying to "fill it in" with lots of smaller ones (the pen company BIC trying to fill in its new box of "disposable inexpensive plastic objects"). Then, too, you can use many of these exercises to try to see your current boxes more clearly or in a new light, and to reexamine and strengthen those boxes through the creation of future scenarios.

Here are some divergence exercises to experiment with.*

---

* There are more details and examples of divergence exercises at http://www
.thinkinginnewboxes.com.

Describe Your Company Without Using Five Key Words

Imagine if the CEO of Bank of America made a presentation to the firm's board of directors and described the company without uttering the words *money, bank, checking, savings,* or *financial.* Perhaps he'd say, "We help our customers organize and store their most important possession," or . . .

This exercise is particularly useful for developing a broad new box—such as a new overall strategic vision for your firm—because it forces you to abandon some of your most fundamental existing perceptions about your organization. It also pushes you to consider new ways of looking at aspects of what is currently true for your organization. So you can also use this exercise to "fill in" one or more of your boxes with new ideas and concepts.

At a divergence meeting we held with leaders from Champagne de Castellane, a major France-based producer of bubbly, we asked participants to describe their business without using the (French) words for "liquor," "drink," "champagne," "alcohol," or "bottle." After tossing out a lot of interesting and unexpected descriptions, they realized that their company's role was not simply to supply liquor, but rather to contribute to the success of parties and celebrations. Once that simple yet vital insight emerged, a new box was formed in which the executives could think in new ways about the company and its future. This, in turn, led to a range of new product and marketing ideas, a number of which were soon adopted, leading to increased overall sales. For example, in the summer, champagne is often not cold enough, especially if bought as a gift, so the company offered a plastic bag that was sturdy enough to carry the bottle along with a few pounds of ice. Since at many parties, someone is called upon to give a speech, the company offered a free booklet titled "How to Give a Speech" and, as a clever promotional premium, attached it to the bottle. Moreover, as many parties thrive on games and entertainment, the company modified some of the wooden crates that contain its champagne bottles so they could be used as game boards for checkers and backgammon. Of note: About 80 percent of the executives' energy was devoted to the identification of the new broad box, that of contributing to the success of parties. Once that was done, the ideas "filling in" the box came relatively easily.

As an executive at Ultragames, what would it be like to describe the organization without using the words "video games," "entertainment," "adventure/quest games," "gamer/player," or "sports games" (or any synonyms of these words)? What words would you use instead?

Some ways of describing your business—your first real "new boxes" in this exercise—become "we deliver a safe way for the family to enjoy each other's company," "we provide means of escape from reality's drudgery for children of all ages," or even "we help improve hand-eye coordination and visuo-motor skills." One of your colleagues, hearing these descriptions, then latches on to that last point and uses some "yes, and . . ." thinking to build upon it. Worrying that "visuo-motor skills" might sound too boring, that colleague might say something like "Yes, and . . . video games increase resistance to distraction." Someone else, then says, "Yes, and we could also take the 'safe' angle and market our products to preschool and kindergarten teachers and mothers and fathers everywhere, saying we'll give your kids a safe environment *and* help them be better prepared for life and do better in school!" This broad theme of games that help build skills to better prepare for the vagaries of life would respect the company's desire to go beyond purely video games, and hold potential for increasing revenues and inspiring new ideas about how the company could help its customers.

Based on this broad box of "providing safe entertainment that helps prepare kids for school and life" you and your colleagues then think about the following:

- Creating a new franchise of educational games, building on small successes in this product area in the past.
- Researching what it would take to create games specifically targeted at enhancing so-called multiple intelligences, at improving gross and fine motor skills, long- and short-term memory, spatial relations, oral and written language production, and the ability to concentrate and resist distraction.
- Developing a game about building financial and money-management skills that is still entertaining.

- Launching an online sports league in partnership with Little League or other local children's sports associations.
- Investing in development of test preparation software that is much more entertaining than the current options.
- Creating a virtual babysitter, a game that alternately entertains and educates young people; gets school-aged children interested in studying reading, writing, and mathematics; gives them fun study breaks filled with physical exercise; plays confidence-building games with them; and expands their curiosity about the wider world.

During this divergence exercise, you might also think about some of the megatrends or major themes or questions you've been discussing and then try to describe your organization without using any words relating to them. What are some of the primary megatrends affecting your organization and what do you think would be the expected key words it might be useful to avoid? In thinking about this, it may also be helpful to surmise what key words a random person on the street might use to describe your company. Try, for example, to describe Google without using the words *Internet, Web, search, data,* or *information.* Might you describe it as "Home Base for Everyone Everywhere"? Or perhaps "The World's Biggest Meeting Place"? Or "Big Brother"? If one of the megatrends you've been contemplating is "environmentally friendly approaches to business," perhaps you'd describe Google as "The Largest Green Library on Earth."

Break Constraints

What are some of the constraints you identified early on? This exercise involves shattering some of these existing mental models methodically and deliberately, and seeing what possibilities emerge. If you feel your company's different divisions operate in silos, without enough cooperation, what if a new "chief collaboration officer" were put into place? If your goal is to break into the emerging market for navy ships but you only have experience building sailboats, imagine a situation where the top admiral in the navy is talking excitedly about your new product to his senior staff two years hence—how did this happen?

As an example, let's look at the world of solar power. Enough solar energy falls on the earth every hour to power the world for a year. But we are not yet good at harnessing and using that energy. Early residential and commercial adopters of solar power had to invest in the equipment, which could cost $25,000–50,000 to install on the roof. They had to consider different payback times, permit requirements, and various available subsidies. Still, they were able to achieve savings of about 80 percent on the monthly electric bill. What was stopping the typical family from going through this? The uncertain payback time and the large up-front investment. And so a new box was eventually created, after a range of divergent options were explored by different players in the industry, which broke this constraint completely: leasing instead of buying. The solar company installs, maintains, and owns the panels on your roof, and reduces your utility bill by 15 to 20 percent from day one. To quote Lyndon Rive, the head of SolarCity, one of the players in this space, "People don't buy gas stations. People don't buy utilities. Why are we having them buy solar equipment?"[9]

Imagine Your Company Has Disappeared

Do you remember Circuit City or the Sharper Image? What happened to Lehman Brothers or Bear Stearns?

Imagine that your organization no longer exists (in, say, 2025)—and then speculate as to *why* or *how* this happened. Most people normally look at the future by extrapolating from the present; this exercise forces you to imagine the future in a more creative way. Imagine the many fascinating responses you'd get if you asked two hundred top executives at Microsoft to spend thirty minutes trying to explain why their company might not exist in 2025!

How could your organization suddenly evaporate? Perhaps some megatrends you are considering played a role, or your marketing paradigm became irrelevant for some reason. Maybe your products or services were displaced by new technology, or a radical shift in consumer tastes.

We use this exercise to help people stretch the boundaries of what seems possible and, by doing so, expand the way they see their organization. It can be helpful in creating a big new box as well in developing various future-oriented scenarios through which to probe and hopefully fortify your existing strategies and other approaches.

Break Your Company in Two

In 2011, Motorola split its company into two divisions, one for mobile devices and home entertainment equipment, and the other for business-related mobility devices and networking solutions. In October 2012, Kraft split into two separate companies as well, one for its North American grocery business and the other, called Mondelēz, for its global snacks.

In this exercise, you will examine your organization and hypothetically break it up into two mutually exclusive and comprehensively exhaustive parts. How could that be done? How would you suggest breaking your organization in two?

You might imagine your company as split into top and bottom, senior and junior, visible and invisible, aboveground, and belowground, daily operations and innovation, red and black—the possibilities are endless. For instance, when we were in the divergence phase of our work with France's national postal service, La Poste, executives there imagined that the organization could be divided into north and south, male and female, fixed and mobile, yellow and not yellow (yellow is the ubiquitous color of La Poste's mailboxes, delivery vans, and so on). Once you decide upon what the two separate categories are—we would encourage you to make them as surprising as you wish—you can then have fun deciding which groups or individuals within your company would be assigned to or belong in those two respective categories, and thus begin to change the way you look at things.

You can also combine two sets of such distinctions. For instance, if you asked people who work in a diving school for tourists on the Caribbean island of St. John to divide the people in their organization based on whether they are visible or invisible *and* whether they are above the surface or below it, they might conclude:

	Above the surface	Below the surface
Visible	Sales representatives; van drivers; boat operators; instructors who train students at local swimming pools; and billing, publicity, and marketing personnel	Instructors who accompany diving students, interns who work with instructors
Invisible	Bookkeeper and accountant who work from home	

You might then notice the "white space" in the bottom right quadrant, and ask participants to try to come up with more kinds of people who could work for the diving school whose work would place them there. Who could work belowground, and be invisible, yet have a useful impact on the organization and its bottom line? One answer might be photographers who secretly shoot candid photos of divers, to sell to them after the dives. Can you come up with others?

Much like imagining how your organization could suddenly disappear, pondering how it might be split into two stimulates prospective thinking. The ideas you initially come up with often serve you in developing a core new box. And when various ideas come up to start filling in the empty white space (as in the diagram above), you are indeed beginning to fill in that box with "smaller" related boxes.

Imagine Ultragames split into two categories: 1) multiple intelligence and skills development and 2) entertainment. Or 1) new areas and 2) core franchises. Those are relatively obvious—but what about splitting the word *video games* into 1) *video* and 2) *games*? Or considering "day" versus "night," or "what's known outside the company" and "what's known only within the company"? What roles would various employees and executives at the company play within these separate frameworks? What new service and product ideas might you and your colleagues begin to imagine for customers of all ages? One person in your group might envision a "multiple intelligence and skills development" team focused on understanding the latest developments in neuroscience and translating that into aspects of new games, while the "entertainment" team built upon that to make the games fun. Or a new line of "daytime" educational games and "nighttime" entertainment games. Or "civilian" and "combat" ones. Games dubbed "Shakespeare" and others channeling "Dr. Seuss." "High-impact" games and those called "Chillax."

Imagine a Forced Joint Venture

Start this exercise by developing a list of well-known leading players in industries or businesses that have no natural connection to your own. Then pick one randomly, or assign others randomly to one person each, and describe a potential joint venture or opportunity that this business could explore with your company.

What joint ventures could you and your organization create with Facebook, JetBlue Airways, Dunkin' Donuts, the Internal Revenue Service, CBS television, Saks Fifth Avenue, or Outback Steakhouse? What about the Red Cross or United Way?

Let's consider some new products or services that Ultragames could develop in joint ventures with these various entities. Imagine partnering with the IRS to come up with an entertaining "video game" to complete your taxes, or working with the United Way on skills development as an approach to helping the unemployed find new opportunities, or collaborating with the Green Berets to develop games guiding users through sweaty daily fitness regimes. Imagine a partnership with NASA to develop games that teach young school-aged children how to focus in on data, process the information, store it and retrieve it from memory, and bring it to bear in a variety of problem-solving situations and missions. You could envision "sponsored" games to help people pass the time while waiting for a table at California Pizza Kitchen or other restaurants, and games could also be developed in tandem with new CBS or BBC shows, for example, allowing viewers to play along interactively with the newest game show, or even participate remotely in reality shows.

This exercise, based on analogy and combination, can be very helpful in inspiring you to see all sorts of possibilities for new business models, products, services, or approaches.

Adopt a New Perspective

How would your life change if you woke up and discovered that you were the First Lady of the United States of America?

In this exercise we ask you to immerse yourself in a distinct point of view, to adopt an entirely different perspective.

For example, when we conduct divergence workshops, we often ask leaders to come up with a vivid phrase to describe the future of their organization, or some other aspect of its management or operations, from a very specific fresh perspective (for instance, in the voice of a stressed-out freelance musician, a retired widow, the CEO of Red Bull, or a vacationing optometrist).

The goal is to shift one's outlook in a radical and provocative way. It can be especially helpful in stimulating interesting new ideas about your organization's overall vision. You can consider such questions as "How would a detective in Kuala Lumpur describe our business?" or "What would a vineyard owner in Tuscany say she liked most about our products?"

You can also frame questions intended to lead to more specific ideas that fill in a larger box. For example, if you were managing a furniture manufacturing company and had developed a new box focused on the concept of "enchantment and delight," you might ask, "What products could our organization produce to delight a single parent with three children and two jobs?"

Sometimes, too, this exercise is a terrific starting place for developing hypotheses about the future that, in turn, can help you create new scenarios. You can ask such questions as "What social and technological changes would a fifteen-year-old math whiz in Korea tell us are bound to challenge our business over the next five to ten years?" or "What might a nineteen-year-old orphan from war-torn Congo tell us to do differently in the years just ahead?"

Take a second to describe your organization, using one phrase, in the voice of an energetic and enthusiastic seven-year-old child. Now describe it in the voice of a ninety-five-year-old physicist who has been told she only has forty-eight more hours to live. Or you could assume the perspective of people in various professions—an accountant, an investigative journalist, a graphic designer—or imagine placing yourself or your organization in other particular situations or contexts (a street fair, a high school football game, a jazz club).

Sometimes we ask people to take the perspective of their customers, or other specific types of people, to address a certain question or issue. We recently conducted a divergence session with a prominent bank based in Europe that wanted to come up with new ideas about how it could use mobile phones and other communication technologies to enhance the company's product and service offerings. After a megatrend expert had introduced a range of relevant trends pertaining to the banking industry and we had warmed up participants for divergence, we asked one participant to take the perspective of the matriarch of a family with ten people of four generations living under one roof. We asked another to imagine that she was the mother of a family in the Netherlands whose home is in the top 2 percent of average bandwidth usage. The question we put to these participants was "How can we get these various individuals to experience our bank ten times per day in the year 2030?"

As an executive at Ultragames, you build on the central question (that is, "How can we make Ultragames the company of choice for single-source family entertainment?") by taking the perspective of three or four hypothetical families and digging into different ways in which they could be perceiving the company. You ponder how you would answer this question if you were a middle-class "nuclear family" in suburban Detroit with two academically struggling children in their early teens—or a single, poor, uneducated mother in rural Sri Lanka with three young, very studious, and highly driven children. What sorts of products and services would each of those families desire? What kinds of features and promotions would draw them toward Ultragames and its offerings? You might consider the same issues from the outlook of a very well-off family in London with a stay-at-home dad and one five-year-old child.

You also consider how a gregarious, joke-cracking seventy-year-old former NFL quarterback might respond to the same issues. Would he want to sit alone in a comfortable seat and play Ultragames sports games? Or might he be the life of the party, and dream of being entertained along with groups of other fun-loving peers who enjoy following and talking about professional sports? Or might he want his children and grand-children to get the robust education that he never received, a gap that made a life and career in sports his one and only option?

As part of this exercise, you ask what comes to mind when, wearing the hat of these particular customers, you hear the word *entertainment*. For the retired quarterback, key words like *sports* and *bar* emerge, along with a desire for companionship, and profound wishes for the next gen-eration. For the stay-at-home dad, the words *splurge* and *couple time* are powerful associations, while for the single mother, perhaps *me time* would come up, in terms of a short break from it all. *Nuclear family* conjures up images of a family in front of the television set, watching something together, or playing an Ultragames game together, with competition among members of the family. Or it could stir up images of family members experiencing various intense levels of interpersonal conflict and engagement, different levels of being tested in significant ways, moments requiring them to perform their "personal best" and others forcing them to come together in order to survive and triumph.

These conversations lead you to think about two broad themes:

1. *Multiple intelligences and skills development.* To build upon some of the earlier ideas about getting teens better prepared for school and life, there would be family-friendly games based on contem-porary theories of "multiple intelligences" to help users identify their primary intellectual strengths and skill sets, and improve in areas of weakness. For instance, games could help users improve reaction times, build resistance to distraction, memorize informa-tion, and sharpen hand-eye coordination. You could develop on-line competitions in partnership with school districts, with prizes for highest scorers and "most improved" gamers. Imagine fami-lies pushing their kids to compete, because of the advantage it would bring them later on in life. Why not offer points for mile-

stones achieved in these games, linked to Boy Scout badges or Little League participation, to encourage less sedentary activity as well? The marketing for these ideas could be targeted partly at the teens, but also at the parents, exploiting their desire for their children to have every advantage in college and beyond.

2. *A break from it all.* Building on the single mother's desire for some "me time," Ultragames could provide a series of games that are thoroughly entertaining for her kids, while still being safe and educational so that she doesn't feel bad leaving them to play. Perhaps you'd dream up a new box called "Guilt-Free Babysitter." Without even offering games to the mother, you could advertise the children's games to her as a family-friendly way for her to get a break. Going beyond that, Ultragames could offer a game specifically tailored to her needs, where five minutes a day would feel like a substantial break and help her to recharge her batteries. Some of the social-networking ideas could lead to Ultragames-supported playgroups, where groups of parents in similar situations could connect and share stories, while the children are entertained by Ultragames.

These ideas, generated quickly, might end up being useful, though perhaps a bit too straightforward. But you can challenge yourself to take these initial concepts to the next level. On the marketing side of your business, you consider inserting tantalizing, affinity-building Ultragames coupons into the packaging for products that soccer moms use. One coupon might have promotional copy boasting, "Our games can help your kids develop multiple skills and intelligences for life," and be packaged with school supplies or kids' snacks. Another one could be inserted into an upcoming issue of a parenting magazine and promise "The most valuable video game in history. We will not just entertain your kids, we will help identify and build their unique strengths and skills as learners." What would it mean to develop "the most valuable video game in history"? What would it mean to own and control StrengthBuilder, an entertaining educational video game routinely licensed by every elementary, middle, and high school the world over?

Someone then ups the ante by suggesting that Ultragames launch its own "safe" social network aimed at skills development for school-aged children. Another person says, "Yes, and . . . I'm imagining a single mother struggling with a hyperactive teenager, or even one diagnosed with ADHD [attention deficit hyperactivity disorder]—we can build games that are explicitly designed to help improve the teenager's attention span and reduce his or her susceptibility to distraction." "Yes, and use our new social network to enable them to connect and share tips." "Yes, and build games that help engage and enhance every kind of mind, and every type of learner."

To continue trying to walk in the shoes of your customers, you list some of the concerns they would have about these various new proposals and try to come up with ideas that address them. Some of the concerns emerging from your preliminary conversation include the complexity of launching a new social network in the era of Facebook; the ability to reach parents of children affected by ADHD, Asperger's syndrome, or other psychiatric, neurobehavioral, or learning issues; overcoming perceptions that video games are addictive and dangerous; and the need to develop a robust understanding of cognitive science and neurology to really make therapeutically effective games. How might you try to address these issues? You could think about:

- Launching a specific project to investigate the neuroscience and psychology of video games—the multiple wirings of the human brain and what their implications are for game design—and explore how playing certain custom-engineered video games could actually *help* children living with ADHD, autism spectrum disorders, dyslexia, and other such challenges, actually enabling them to build their intellectual strengths and train themselves to become better learners.
- Developing a set of new slogans and partnering with other reputable companies and organizations serving families—PBS Kids, the YMCA, American Girl Dolls, Save the Children—leveraging your long-standing "safe" image to build trust among soccer moms, and indeed parents everywhere.

Write Your Own Newspaper Headlines

Some divergence exercises ask you to reconceive not your organization, but the world: If some unexpected event happened, what new ideas would suddenly appear relevant and helpful? Consider what steps you would take if you were leading your organization, or a central government, and over the next ten years global warming made the entire Southern Hemisphere entirely uninhabitable.

One exercise we often use entails picking a selection of publications—*USA Today* or *The Guardian* or even more targeted ones like *People, Sports Illustrated,* or *Men's Health*—and then asking people to generate headlines about your organization and the wider world at a specific moment in the future (say, 2020). We generally ask them to develop "dream" headlines as well as the "nightmare" ones.

At Ultragames, what might be a dream headline in *People* magazine? Perhaps "How video games saved my family: One mother's story" or "Overcoming ADHD, one (game) level at a time." "Autistic eight-year-old speaks for first time with Ultragames' StrengthBuilder." What about a nightmare headline that might appear in *The New York Times?* Perhaps it would be something like "Video games found to erode short-term memory recall." Or "Video Games Galore launches brilliant new line of EnterTRAIN video games for kids."

Of course, not all of your headlines need be so dramatic—and sometimes they may prove prophetic, or provide sparks for further exploration. For instance, in one of our divergence sessions with La Poste, one participant imagined a headline announcing that French postal workers, who already visited every household in the country to deliver the mail, were successfully selling banking services as well on their daily rounds. We explored other things they could do at the same time, such as helping shut-in seniors or reading the water meter, and as things turned out, La Poste has indeed made strides in this direction, as well as that of offering a wide range of financial services.

Sometimes you may find it helpful to imagine headlines about the organization that might appear in magazines unrelated to the central themes and pursuits of the organization. For example, if yours is a commercial real estate firm, you might ask them to think about headlines regarding the firm that could appear in 2025 in *Sports Illustrated*. Or if you manufacture LED technologies, ask your colleagues what headlines pertaining to their company might appear in *Wine Enthusiast* or *Psychology Today*.

Consider what headlines might appear about you or your organization in 2025 in *Vogue, The Moscow Times,* or *Fortune*. What would be your dream headlines—and your nightmares?

When we ask such questions of people participating in divergence, it generally helps them to think about new "big picture" themes, trends, and visions. But sometimes we use the same exercise to help generate more specific ideas. For instance, instead of asking executives at Google to imagine headlines about the overall company, we might have them write headlines about the company's Gmail service in 2040. In that exercise, they might come up with much more granular suggestions regarding what "email" or person-to-person communication might look like in or around that year. A dream headline in the March 2040 issue of *Wired* magazine might read, "Aggregate Gmail accounts in newly emerging African markets surpass those of all other players combined." Or even "Gmail: Now available for all five senses, with the arrival of smell-o-vision."

Build on Oxymorons and Other Forms of Wordplay

Can you come up with a useless improvement? An old novelty? A form of strict flexibility?

In this exercise, we invite you to use an oxymoron (which is when two logically incompatible words coexist, like "virtual reality") to provoke stark departures from your usual way of thinking about things.

We recently used this approach with a major cosmetics company that wanted to develop products that filled in the box of "routine." At first, we asked the executives to ask themselves: "How can we get people to use our products as routinely as they brush their teeth?" This produced some interesting output, such as products that promoted good health and hygiene, like toothbrushes, or a product with specific daily doses that essentially forced itself into your routine. But then, to go further, we asked them to come up with words that, if juxtaposed with "routine," would create an oxymoron. They proposed such phrases as "unpredictable routine," "unique routine," "sporadic routine," and "once in a lifetime routine." We then talked through how these oxymorons might actually connect to new product ideas. Remarkably, the idea of an "unpredictable routine" actually led the company to develop a line of cosmetic products that varied based on customers' moods and what they wanted to do that particular day.

As an executive at Ultragames, consider what new offerings you could create if you were trying to fill in the box of "safe recklessness." You become even more committed to the idea of using the most cutting-edge graphics and sound technologies to create an extreme and intense experience ("recklessness") for your gamers—dazzling rock-and-roll riffs and 3-D high-definition visuals—while maintaining your historically "safe" principles of avoiding profanity and gratuitous blood and gore. You also might think of what to learn from roller-coaster engineers, tightrope walkers, or bungee jumpers—among other things, studying the meticulous steps they take before putting themselves or others in harm's way would reveal, by analogy, how important it would be for you at Ultragames to develop a deeper understanding of neuroscience before making any public claims about how your products could help children improve their abilities as learners.

Consider going beyond oxymorons as well: For example, imagine a colleague said about your education idea, "We won't just entertain you— we'll entertrain you." Like "bankster" (banker and gangster) or "adulescent" (adult and adolescent), this could apply to your new concepts.

Mini-worlds/Analogies

In this exercise, the idea is to explore a "mini-world"—examples we use frequently include fashion, dance, birds, mathematics, printing, movies, the Vatican, the Olympic Games, spying, decorating, and the navy. You then look for relationships, and possible activities and pursuits that could be arranged between that mini-world and your organization, and to connect these ideas to the issues you are addressing. In the first instance, you're generating broader boxes; in the second, you're focusing in on smaller ones.

Suppose that the key issue your organization has formulated to address is this: How can we create new products and services that people living in big skyscraper-filled cities will want to have in the year 2025?

Now, imagine that you have been asked to focus on the mini-world of . . . professional sports. What can be brought from that arena to yours? What are the key characteristics of that mini-world, and how could they apply to your organization? You can explore how this would change what you do and the way you operate, and new challenges you would face. You can reconsider how to deal with some of the mega-trends you've investigated, and opportunities emerging as a result. How would professional sports evolve by 2025 in such an urban world? What new products and services would you want to be sure to create?

When we used this exercise with La Poste, leaders there imagined the French postal service finding itself in such mini-worlds as the Cannes Film Festival, a New York City exhibit of works from the Louvre, and the Interpol drug-trafficking investigation unit. These conversations led to all sorts of new ideas—from developing payment verification systems for Internet sites to hosting stamp collector expositions, from offering quality "stamp of approval" certification for products, services, and organizations, to creating an online community shopping and exchange site.

Sometimes we alter this exercise by offering up a detailed set of analogous characters or situations, and then asking people to interpret what these things mean for their respective enterprises or situations. Imagine, for instance, a field in which there is a shepherd, a dog, a flock of sheep, and a wolf. Who do these characters represent in the higher education business? In the automobile industry? In your business? You can decide who are the various companies, competitors, customers, and other stakeholders. You can discuss who is protecting whom, who is well fed, who is safe, and who should be deeply worried about surviving the next day!

EDITING AND CRUSHING YOUR IDEAS

Once you have used some of these (or other) divergence exercises to produce a range of new ideas, we then encourage you to edit and "crush" them.

This is another key moment when we especially invite "Yes, and . . ." conversations. For instance, if, during the divergence phase at an ice-cream company's product development workshop, one participant were to say, "We ought to try holiday flavors like Turkey Dinner ice cream," we would encourage another participant to contribute to this process of consolidation by saying something more like "Yes, and we might focus on the cranberries of Thanksgiving to emphasize sweetness" rather than "Yes, but will people want ice cream with meat in it?" The goal of this part of the process is not to weed out "bad" ideas, but rather to reshape your ideas a bit and then to begin "crushing" them.

By "crushing" we mean listing the ideas generated, and then, one by one, changing those ideas in various interesting and often surprising ways. With each round of crushing, another person can suggest another twist on things. Below are some of the verb commands you can pick randomly to use for crushing:

Crushing: sample list of verb commands

1. Make it bigger	24. Make it a collector's item	47. Make it portable
2. Make it smaller	25. Mechanize it	48. Make it collapsible
3. Make it round	26. Electrify it	49. Summarize it
4. Make it square	27. Reverse it	50. Winterize it
5. Make it sparkle	28. Give it texture	51. Personalize it
6. Make it heavier	29. Make it romantic	52. Make it a substitute
7. Make it lighter	30. Add nostalgic appeal	53. Isolate it
8. Make it weightless	31. Make it look old	54. Speed it up
9. Enclose it	32. Make it look new	55. Slow it down
10. Turn it upside down	33. Make it part of something else	56. Make it fly
11. Lay it on its side	34. Make it stronger	57. Pulverize it
12. Stretch it	35. Make it fragile	58. Sharpen it
13. Change its color	36. Be unrealistic	59. Change its contours
14. Make it visual	37. Make it cooler	60. Concentrate it
15. Put it into words	38. Make it hotter	61. Spread it out
16. Put it to music	39. Change the scent	62. Soften it
17. Eliminate words	40. Change one ingredient	63. Harden it
18. Eliminate pictures	41. Add new ingredients	64. Make it satirical
19. Make it glamorous	42. Twist it	65. Purify it
20. Make it in 2-D	43. Make it transparent	66. Contaminate it
21. Change the shape	44. Make it opaque	67. Add comfort to it
22. Change a part	45. Use another material	68. Make it uncomfortable
23. Make it a set	46. Change the package	69. Use a different texture

Crushing is a wonderful way to expand your ideas, opening them up with new features, and suggesting other ways in which they can be stretched or consolidated, refined or intensified.

Take a moment to think about the product, service, or other offering about which you are currently most concerned. What would it mean to pulverize it? To reverse it, or make it more satirical?

Likewise, think about your current job or personal career situation. What would it mean to make it move or electrify it? To fill it up, or make it fly?

What about one of the people you love or care about most on the planet. How could you "crush" your relationship in helpful ways? What would it mean to make that relationship sparkle? To add new ingredients, or solidify it?

What are some of the key ideas you came up with for Ultragames? What would it mean to turn them upside down, collapse them, make them shine, or glamorize them?

One of the ideas suggested earlier for Ultragames was a social network to connect parents of ADHD-afflicted children, who would be helped by a new line of games. You could stretch this idea—why not have live meetings as well? Or flipping the idea upside down, you could use existing social networks to actually find the parents in the first place, and launch your new games there. "Glamorizing" this idea might mean getting some celebrity participation, recruiting some actors or athletes who suffered from ADHD or have children with ADHD to appear in or promote the new games. Yes, and . . . maybe gossip magazines would "leak" some of your latest celebrity users and ideas. Yes, and maybe the game itself would be named "Race to Focus" and be released on Mother's Day next year. "Yes, and maybe we could connect it to fast-paced professional horse racing and call it 'Focus Derby PRO.'"

Suppose the education and "entertrain" idea is being explored: What "Yes, and . . ." concepts could come to mind? Training is tied to the army (basic training), to sports (spring training), to health (retraining a limb, as in physical therapy). How could that apply? You could develop tools to sell to the army or sports franchises, to help develop specific mental or physical skills. You could be reborn as a science-based learning company, running clinical trials to test whether your newly developed games make a difference for children with ADHD or other conditions that can make learning more challenging.

By the end of the divergence process, you'll want to have created a clear list of your edited, crushed, and fully shaped new ideas. This is often a pivotal moment in the creative process, and sometimes an emotional one. You may have generated a long list of wonderful new boxes and now realize that, terrific as they all seem, you'll likely be able to pursue only some of them. You may have a personal favorite that could end up being voted down by others during convergence. Then, too, several or all of you may feel as though you're experiencing a true opening up of new creative possibilities. Maybe you've already begun to coalesce behind an original and novel idea, or a new exciting variation on an existing idea, such that one or more of you are beginning to sense an imminent experience of *Eureka*.

IT IS CRITICAL TO FOLLOW UP

To maintain this well of new creative energy and opportunity—and to maximize the value and significance of the many ideas you created during divergence—we urge you to follow up with anyone who may have joined you for divergence, in a prompt, thorough, and ongoing way. Among other things, such follow-up should include listing and communicating some or all of the ideas you've generated, staying in close touch with those who participated in divergence about their ideas, and then moving into the convergence phase as soon as possible.

We've seen very smart, creative, highly motivated people develop copious ideas during divergence but then fail to take these essential subsequent steps. Rigorous follow-up helps ensure that, at the very least, any participants will feel that their efforts during Step 3 were important and valuable, and will make them more likely to want to participate in additional phases of the creative process going forward. Even before you end the divergence session, you'll want to outline for any participants what they should expect in terms of next steps. And then you'll want to make sure that those steps are in fact implemented in a timely way. Acknowledging the contributions of the participants is also vitally important. Especially if convergence happens soon after divergence and some ideas are put on the path to implementation right away, you'll want to give ample credit to the individuals, and the group as a whole, who came up with those ideas.

Above all, you'll want to keep the lines of communication open with everyone who was involved, as well as with any key people in your organization who were not; share the ideas that were created; indicate what the process will be going forward; and then follow through as promptly and effectively as possible. Soon enough, you'll be selecting, voting upon, and then implementing the boxes that everyone feels are the most sensible and promising to pursue.

HOW TO AVOID CREATIVITY KILLERS

Maintaining a positive and inspiring creative environment is vital to effective divergence—and "Yes, *but*..." is just one of many phrases and attitudes that can stop open-minded, imaginative thinking in its tracks.

To avoid sapping the potency of your divergence sessions, take a look at this list of creativity-killing statements—these are examples of phrases you should do your very best to avoid during this phase of the process:

82 ways to kill a new idea

It will not work	One can fantasize, but . . .	Let's keep our feet firmly on the ground
It is not included in the budget	It would take a lot of time	It's been working like this for twenty years
It is not serious	We're not in China here	The computer is not powerful enough
Stop talking nonsense	You must be realistic	This is a good theory, but practically . . .
It is against the rules	Well, of course	There aren't all that many solutions
It is too expensive	We'll not change the world	Our competitor doesn't do it, either
We already tried	Let's stick to the point	You might as well say that we are closing down
It has already been done	People will not understand	You shouldn't bite off more than you can chew
What will our clients think?	People like us think that . . .	Why do you want to change at any price?
Let's talk about it another time	We're not a lab	Did you measure the risks, consequences?
Let's do a market survey first	We're losing our way	We can see what you're leading up to
We've always done so	Nothing will come of it	I already heard this idea somewhere
Let's get back to basics	Have a bit of common sense!	We don't have the staff, the equipment
It is politically unacceptable	While we're at it, why not . . .	They will be shocked
You don't mean it	Let's form a committee	Maybe that isn't stupid, but . . .
I've got a better idea	It's not our business	I am not a specialist, but . . .
It is not as simple as you think	They'll think we're nuts	Too academic

It only solves part of the problem	Wait and see	The only problem is that . . .
Even if we wanted to do it . . .	Let's put it in writing	There are only twenty-four hours in a day
It is technically impossible	People don't want to change	This is not a priority
This is unworkable	Calm down	This is not concrete enough
This is not legal	I don't see the relationship	You don't understand our problem
The boss will never accept it	It's not in line with our strategy	Don't exaggerate
Beautiful idea, but not for us	It is not our business	Don't make me laugh
Let's get back on track	It will give us more work	Let's ask the opinion of an expert
I'll have warned you	It's too early	This is not in our culture
Is there any precedent?	It's too late	Let's get to the point
You'll never change . . .		

Of course, we are not saying that you should *never* use any of these statements. But during the divergence phase, you'll want to do everything you can to stay in "Yes, *and* . . ." mode rather than using the "kill the idea" phrases indicated above (or by conveying a stance that communicates the same sort of skeptical "Let's get back to reality" negativity).

Take a moment right now to think about all the many ways that you, or people you know, tend to squash new ideas. Perhaps you could list some of those ways so that you'll be more aware of them, and freer to "call them out" when they occur. Here are some that we have observed:

- *Blaming yourself.* We often hear people say things like "I have no new ideas about that," "I'm not really creative," "We're too small for that," "We're not a lab," or "I can't dance the tango."
- *Blaming or second-guessing other people.* "You're dreaming," "You're being ridiculous," "You need to be realistic," "You don't understand our problem," "You haven't measured the risks."
- *Worrying about others' judgments or attitudes.* "The boss will never go for it," "What will the clients think?" "People don't want to change," "The competitors don't do it this way."
- *Worrying about resources.* "That will take a long time," "We don't have the equipment," "The computer isn't powerful enough," "We don't have the data," "It's too expensive."
- *Generally negative attitudes.* "That's impractical," "That's not the question," "That's fine in theory but in practice . . . ," "You're on the business side of this company, not the creative side."
- *Apparently neutral statements hiding negative underlying attitudes.* "Write that up in a memo and send it to me," "Let's set up another meeting to

discuss that down the road," "I have a different idea," "Keep me posted!" "Let's check with legal."

The antidote to all these sabotaging statements and the "not going to happen" mindset they represent is to use "Yes, and . . ." statements and to adopt a much more "can do" approach. During convergence, you will have plenty of chances to decide which ideas are worthwhile and which ones should be relegated to the back burner. During divergence, strive to use much more reassuring and rewarding statements, such as:

"Why not? In fact, we could also . . ."

"That is a bit like . . ."

"There are a lot of ways we could try that . . ."

"What if we test that idea *and* . . ."

"How interesting! Let's dig deeper on that one . . ."

GENERALI INSURANCE: DIVERGENCE IN ACTION

Try to visualize what the insurance business was like in 1831. Much of the Western world had already moved past the simplicity of "mutual aid societies," where neighbors committed to help each other rebuild, and to an industry centered on ships. Ship owners, merchants, and ships' captains would meet in maritime cities with people willing to underwrite maritime travel and transport. This is the context in which Generali was founded in 1831 in Trieste, Italy, the then-booming seaport city.

Fast-forward almost two centuries: Generali is still headquartered in Trieste, but not much else has stayed the same. The world around it has shifted in almost every way you can imagine, as have the kinds of accidents and disasters people are keen to insure against. Today's concept of insurance against fire and maritime disasters might be recognizable to someone from 1831 Trieste, but the policies' legal details, the actuarial models used to set the premiums, the intricacies of the deductible and the "copay," and the concepts of automobile insurance, "reinsurance," and ties to pension funds and other complex asset-management models would be way beyond them. And that is not even to mention the Internet, and the computers where every policy is essentially bought and sold: This online world is the one in which Generali operates today. Currently in more than 60 countries, the insurance giant in 2010 boasted 85,000 employees and 70 million clients worldwide, while the French division alone wrote 15 billion euros in premiums to 5.5 million clients. Back in 2007, this division was coming off an excellent year, and opted to strive for *Eureka* by pursuing a broad strategy review while the going was good. One of the key projects we pursued together entailed overhauling the company's Internet strategy.

At our first meetings, the executives had relatively conventional objectives. They wanted to determine which Web-based products and services held the most promise over the next several years, the likely costs of producing them, the revenues they had the potential to generate, and how this analysis should inform the company's overall business model and strategy. They were also eager to assess the feasibility and attractiveness of several existing initiatives pertaining to the Internet and to entertain new ones if they arose in our work together.

At the time, Generali had developed effective partnerships with banks to market life insurance products online. But many of the company's Web offerings were lagging behind those of its competitors and the Generali brand was not as prominent in the digital space as it could be.

A significant component of our initial role, then, was to introduce a prerequisite level of doubt—as required in Step 1 of our approach. We worked with these executives to understand not just what was (or wasn't) working in their then-current Internet strategy but also just how broad and powerful the Web-based opportunities ahead of them truly could be. Even before launching into divergence sessions with Generali, we sat down with our clients and together realized that they could go beyond simply redesigning the company's website and then declaring that they had executed a new Internet strategy. We helped them shift perceptions, exchanging the old box of "we're a well-established insurance company" with a new box of "we're a brilliant new e-company that is active in the insurance business." Specifically, we all eventually acknowledged that, rather than implementing a standard online portal reflecting what the company was already doing, they could completely reinvent the company in fundamental ways, creating the sort of e-company that would make its own mark in the industry, would be quick to react and adapt, and would soon lead, rather than follow, what similar companies were doing.

As we all grew to understand just how momentous a shift they could make, they realized that they wanted to invent all sorts of new capabilities, features, and approaches to doing business on the Web, creating a new overall paradigm that would really resonate with the public, generate buzz, and increase the company's market share. In other words, they wanted to reinvent several fundamental aspects of the company in ways that would not only make sense from a business model perspective but also really differentiate Generali from its competition. The broad emerging question: How can Generali transform itself into a leader online for all aspects of marketing and commercializing insurance?

During Step 2, we helped Generali conduct intense research regarding its customers while also boosting its competitive intelligence, looking closely at best practices across industries in the Internet space (with a focus on what competing insurers like Geico and Progressive were doing to interact with the public on the Web), studying some of the most innovative approaches to customizing end users' experiences on the Internet, and probing other key trends, such as Web 2.0.

Over a period of several weeks, we also explored how various teams within Generali were then approaching the Internet. This involved assessing their general attitudes and beliefs about the value of the channel, and analyzing the more than thirty existing Internet-related projects that were then under way across the company. For example, one project sought to develop a customized "extranet" for large institutional clients. For each of these initiatives, we noted Generali's main goals, the key stakeholders they involved, and the proposed approach and timing for implementation. The company was eager to try to embrace all these various approaches and outlooks (many of which were conceived and being championed by specific subgroups within the organization) while also helping people across the company adopt a common overall vision and strategy.

We then embarked on a series of divergence sessions, several of which were hosted in a beautiful chateau where executives could step outside their usual workspaces, breathe in country air, and free their minds to see new perspectives. We first met in a plenary session of about forty participants. Most of them were top managers, including some of the company's most senior executives. Everyone seemed eager to participate, because of excitement about the future, but also practically because the company's top leaders were present and conveyed a lot of excitement about entering into a creative process, setting a tone that was unusually positive, upbeat, and enthusiastic.

After introducing all of the participants, we set the stage with some illusions, brainteasers, and other warm-up exercises together to help introduce the concept of doubt and remind everyone of the importance of identifying and challenging your current boxes. We asked the group to try to describe what the company does without using obvious key words, as in the first of the divergence exercises outlined on page 131. We asked them to imagine themselves in a very concrete, easy-to-visualize setting, such as giving a speech explaining what the company does, but underscored that they should not use such words as "uncertainty" and "insurance." During this warm-up, executives described Generali by saying such things as "We contribute to the comfort of people throughout their lives." "We offer each person the best possible protection." "We permit our clients to face the future with serenity." "We provide a simple and immediate solution for people who want to be more secure." "We protect the world and its belongings from the hazards of the future."

These phrases may seem tame, but we were still warming up, and it was helpful to understand how they viewed the company and customers to date. Following further discussion, we helped the same executives begin to concentrate on six recurring themes: protection, daily life, serenity, hazards, solutions, and the future. These themes would not bind the participants during divergence, but they were helpful in stimulating their creative juices and giving them confidence that they could not only generate a range of ideas on any given topic but also come to agreement regarding those that seemed the most valuable, helpful, and urgent.

Next, we moved into our main exercise, dividing the participants into four groups of about ten to begin to come up with lots of ideas. We asked the executives in each group to meet in separate rooms, where, to get things started, they were asked to develop imaginary headlines for a gamut of popular publications (ranging from *Astrology* magazine and *Elle* to technology-related publications like *Wired* and *PC Expert*), as in the exercise mentioned on page 143. We asked each group to focus on one of four distinct key issues, namely how the company could use the Internet to 1) enhance and improve the products and services it could sell, 2) tie its clients to these online offerings, 3) reinforce and improve its relationships with sales agents and brokers, and 4) enhance the quality of its internal communications and dealings with employees.

As each group thought about these issues and what sorts of stories and headlines they'd lead to in these various magazines, they began to generate all sorts of fanciful ideas. For instance, the group focusing on what products could be sold online imagined a story in *Sailing Monthly*. It featured "pay as you sail" insurance, in which the premium rate would be determined in real time based on the weather risks and the distance you were traveling using an application tied to your mobile phone and GPS technology. In a magazine about Internet technology, they envisioned a story about Generali insuring avatars in virtual reality, and one about insurance policies protecting people and institutions against occurrences of copyright infringement or libel online. The group focusing on how to link clients to such new product offerings thought that an article could appear in *AutoMoto*, a French car and motorcycle magazine, announcing car insurance policies that you could purchase at the time you bought a new automobile, where the cost of the premium would be included in the overall cost of your car. In something of a more whimsical suggestion, another participant in this group imagined a feature story in *Elle* announcing that Generali would be insuring all clients against the risk of not being sufficiently fashionable. Customers would be able to upload their own pictures onto Generali's website and subsequently receive sartorial advice, coaching on their style choices, and claim payouts if they suffered certain fashion mishaps.*

As the four groups of executives began to open their minds to various new possibilities, we worked with them to "reformulate the question" carefully. Rather than suggesting they brainstorm around "What should our Internet business model be?" or "How can we be a leader online in the insurance space?" we nudged them to ponder much more evocative questions inviting increased induction and prospective thinking. For instance, we asked them to consider the following:

- How could we get the personal computers of everyone in Europe to include Generali.fr in their favorites list?
- How could we offer a new insurance experience to people just now entering the workforce?
- How could we use the Internet to get customers to do the work we have been doing for them?

We also had a magician come in the evening and perform for the participants, as an unusual way to foster doubt while entertaining. Toward the end of this show, there was one trick that the magician repeated multiple times to show people exactly how he was doing it. As part of this trick, a sweeping motion made by his right hand drew people's attention away from what his left hand was doing. His masterful sleight of hand offered a poignant and persuasive reminder of how our eyes—and brains—are constantly misleading us and causing us to distort reality. His various tricks and moves helped underscore our lessons

---

* Once again, remember to silence your voice of judgment as you read this! One key goal of the divergence phase is to get a lot of ideas on the table, and as we've already stated, no idea is born good. Or as in a quote sometimes attributed to Albert Einstein, "[I]f at first the idea is not absurd, there is no hope for it!" This phase provides the fodder that will be sifted through and iterated upon in good time.

about doubt and impress upon everyone that if they could shake themselves free of their old boxes and open up to changing their perceptions, they would then be able to look at things in dramatically new ways.

A few days later, we met again to build upon the output from the first session and to begin imagining the new online insurance site and its features. Participants started answering some of the above reframed questions and expanding on some of the headlines they had previously created in a "yes, and . . ." way to try to get to some very specific new possibilities. As it turned out, we ended up with more than 140 distinct ideas in total—the room was literally wallpapered with flip charts. We then grouped these ideas into fifteen themes, among them:

- Creating a community among our customers.
- Exploiting additional information for better pricing (for example, share information about your driving habits, so that if you are a safe driver you'll get a discount).
- Building on the contributions/desires of our customers (for example, many of our seniors do art in their spare time—maybe we should sponsor art classes or exhibits).
- Creating product extensions and Web services that build on existing products.
- Offering mini-products and partnerships (for example, free movie tickets for the unemployed).
- Hosting an e-library (for example, an "internal Google").

Participants then compared the fifteen themes to the more than thirty existing Internet-related projects at the company. Though there was some overlap, and a range of new ideas that weren't part of the thirty existing efforts, there were some elements to add as well, including developing B2C channels online, developing specific sites for major clients, offering virtualization, and redesigning the company's internal processes (for example, its intranet).

In all, there were now twenty-one themes, each of which had somewhere between one and nineteen semi-developed ideas relating to it. Participants then grouped these twenty-one into four major categories:

1. The client/end user's role in the value chain.
2. The broker's role in the value chain.
3. New product concepts.
4. Optimizing the internal value chain for employees of Generali.

Soon after these workshops, Generali entered into the convergence phase, as we will explain in the next chapter. To begin with, four separate "e-teams" were launched to investigate one of each of the four respective categories, with the mandate of researching relevant benchmarks (insurance or other industries), outlining revenues and costs, and assessing the attractiveness of each based on a variety of qualitative and quantitative criteria and metrics, such as feasibility, cost, and potential impact. Each of these teams was then on the hook to make presentations to the executive committee eight weeks later, much as if they were entrepreneurs making a pitch to venture capitalists. These pitches, in turn, were summarized and submitted to a special "board" that decided how to prioritize them and then, over a one-month period, developed an overall business plan pertaining to their implementation. This part of the process, together with Step 2's focus on investigation, was critical. At one point, a leading executive said, "I can taste the special sauce, but where's the beef?" He and other senior managers who at times had felt relatively skeptical during the more divergent phases of our work with the company were especially appreciative of the balance everyone ultimately struck between induction and deduction, bold experimentation and hard-nosed analysis.

Once the entire Generali team agreed on how to proceed, the company invested significant resources into implementing its new Internet strategy, essentially creating a whole new sixty-person business unit from scratch. Because many of the company's leaders in this area had gone through our five-step process together, they reported feeling as though they were all now speaking a common language. "Our genetic makeup has changed as a result of this process—now we're in sync and making lots of things happen together," explains one top manager at the company. "We've learned how to reinvent ourselves, to think about everything we do in a new shared light." Given all the excitement and enthusiasm that had been generated across the company, people were eager to get involved in this new digital division: More than one hundred internal candidates applied as soon as the unit was announced. Generali also decided that it should support these efforts by investing more than 50 million euros in back-office improvements and website updates. These additional expenditures represented at least 20 percent of the company's overall annual IT budget.

Generali also "filled in" its new box with all sorts of new features and offerings. After only a few months of preparation, the website was completely relaunched, boasting a gamut of new products and services, reorganized user-friendly screens, real-time optimization, and searching. In light of all the new ideas generated during divergence, the company's new Web strategy included numerous "first ever in the company's history" components: a platform for small- and medium-sized brokers to access new services (such as a help page featuring best practices and another one sharing sample sales contracts), a Web marketplace for wholesale virtual brokerage (which enabled extensions of the product line), a platform for groups to update their own risk profiles (for example, an employer that covered five hundred employees' lives), and a platform to consolidate coverage for individuals and groups (for example, people who use Generali to insure against multiple risks). In some cases, these added features and new ways of reaching and serving customers online were seen as game changers within the insurance industry. And the company's community of agents was appreciative that, as much as these new features helped customers interact with the company, they didn't remove the important role, and human touch, of the agents themselves. Generali soon won awards for its new website. Its insurance-agent-based and direct-to-consumer businesses both grew. And the company evolved from laggard to undeniable leader in the digital domain.

SIX

Converge

□□□□□□□□□□□□□□□□□□□□□□□□□□□□□□□□□□□□□□

Select the Right New Box(es) to Focus Your Vision

Whenever you see a successful business, someone once made a courageous decision.[1]

—PETER DRUCKER

RY THE FOLLOWING MANEUVER: Turn your right foot in counterclockwise circles and, without stopping, begin turning your right hand in clockwise circles.

Can you do it? Without looking, we are confident that the answer is no. Your body isn't wired that way. And although divergence and convergence represent a symbiotic pair of functions, they are fundamentally separate processes, distinct ways of thinking: Your mind isn't wired to do both at the same time. They should not be pursued simultaneously, but rather iteratively.

In convergence, you change from a purely creative, brainstorming-type mode, in which you try to withhold judgment, into a mode of analyzing what really has the best chance to succeed. This is a completely different type of thinking from divergence—convergence requires you to evaluate your ideas, choose the most promising among them, and then zero in on which should be implemented, or in what order you think they should be pursued. You're called upon to apply logic and practicality, discipline and shrewd strategy to take all of these many boxes and select the ones you're actually going to put into action. Convergence is about applying your best skills of reasoning and good judgment, focusing in, winnowing down, and, in the end, making decisions you can then go on to execute.

Unfortunately, it is all too possible to come up with brilliantly creative and promising ideas that end up "going nowhere"—in the corporate world we've all seen exciting possibilities get buried in committees or simply forgotten. One famous example is the now-ubiquitous computer mouse—the first marketed version of a mouse for PC users came with a personal computer marketed by Xerox in 1981 called "Alto." The Alto mouse was clunky, expensive, and broke easily. The mouse remained relatively obscure until Steve Jobs visited Xerox in 1979, tried the Alto mouse, and decided that he and Apple could do better.[2] Several years later the Apple Macintosh appeared—with a nimble, more durable, and affordable mouse—and was one of the most revolutionary and popular personal computers ever. Xerox had been unable to make the decisions that would have transformed the idea of the computer mouse into a market success either early or effectively enough. Jobs later said: "If Xerox had known what it had and had taken advantage of its real opportunities . . . it could have been as big as IBM plus Microsoft plus Xerox combined—and the largest high-technology company in the world."[3]

Convergence is about beginning to translate ideas into reality rather than simply trying to give birth to more and more new ideas; it is about prioritizing decisions so that you can act on your best ideas. It's worth noting, however, that even with a fresh focus on judgment and deduction, you need to continue to foster an open-minded attitude of "doubt"; otherwise you risk eliminating any ideas that depart too much from the status quo. Keeping these in the mix can enable you to arrive at fundamental broad new boxes. To use the example above, the mouse is not simply an improved keyboard; its introduction changed the broad box of "the best way to enter data" for almost everyone.

Often, in the midst of a convergence discussion, new ideas may still pop up here and there, and you may decide to change or refine some of the ideas you developed during divergence in interesting ways. You shouldn't permanently shut off creativity as you converge. It can continue to play a helpful role so long as your critical and analytical faculties dominate your thinking. Just make sure you are not trying to do both at the exact same time, especially with other people—the least productive situation possible is when half the room is in divergence and the other half in convergence, as everyone will be frustrated (and the two teams' results could just cancel each other out). Trying to converge when you're still diverging is a little bit like trying to repair a bicycle tire while the wheel is still turning. You need to stop the spinning wheel, at least temporarily, before you're going to be effective.

Decades of fascinating "split brain" scientific research (and centuries, at least, of philosophical thought ranging from yin and yang to id and ego) suggest that divergence relies on one set of cognitive functions (many of which occur predominantly in the right side of the brain) whereas convergence depends on a discrete set of such cognitive functions (which occur mostly in the left side of the brain).* Divergence calls upon your imagination, your ability to brainstorm in a free and uninhibited way, to make numerous creative leaps, to generate all sorts of ideas without worrying about how smart or sensible or valuable they may end up actually being. Convergence, by contrast, relies upon judgment and analysis, your ability to put ideas into practice, to render them operational, to make specific practical deductions, to decide which ideas will, in the end, be more meaningful and valuable than others.

In most organizations, indeed in most human contexts, there are some people who are better at one process rather than the other, some who tend to be more "divergent" thinkers naturally talented at coming up with numerous "wild" ideas, as compared with others who are wired to be stronger "convergent" thinkers and thus more gifted at selecting the best of someone else's far-fetched ideas—and actually making them happen. Many of the most successful collaborations involve

---

* One of the earliest and most important such researchers was Roger Wolcott Sperry, who won the Nobel Prize in Medicine in 1981 for his work in this area.

the combined strengths of divergent and convergent thinkers. Hewlett-Packard. Rolls-Royce. Yves Saint Laurent and Pierre Bergé. Even Bill Gates and Paul Allen represent such a fortunate pairing of divergent/convergent thinkers.*

While some people may tend to see divergence as where the "magic" happens, our experience suggests that the convergence phase is really where perceptions begin to change and become more concrete.† This is where a wide set of ideas suddenly shift in people's minds, like the flipping on of a high-voltage switch, into the realm of fully illuminated plausibility. Indeed, we have often seen participants' eyes widen and brighten when they realized, "Hey . . . this could *be* something. We could really run with this idea and change our business . . ." Or "If we combine these two ideas, we'd really have something that would transform the market . . ."

To understand how divergence and convergence function together in sequential back-and-forth "rounds," consider Thomas Edison's development of the lightbulb. Prior to Edison's work, to produce light you had to start and then maintain a fire; that is, you had to keep wood burning in a fireplace, wax in a candlestick, oil in a lantern. Hypothetically, an effective process of divergence and convergence might have led Edison or others to try to develop better sources of light, to come up with a more efficient type of oil, a better wax, more useful wicks, safer protective lantern glass, or other such improvements.

But instead, Edison and his peers and assistants came up with a wholly new box: incandescence. The fundamental premise of the incandescent lightbulb is to preclude the filament from burning, that is, to

---

* We do not know these people personally, but Paul Allen claimed in *Idea Man* (New York: Portfolio, 2011) that "I was the idea man, the one who'd conceive of things out of a whole cloth. Bill listened and challenged me, and then homed in on my best ideas to help make them a reality." Analogous stories suggest Rolls, Hewlett, and Saint Laurent were the more divergent members of each pair. Not to mention de Brabandere compared with Iny.

† This is of course an oversimplification: perceptions do not really "begin" to change, since perceptions are very personal and shift in a very binary way, like a lightbulb going off. Still, within a group or a company, there will be early adopters, whom we are basically referring to when we say "begin to change."

produce light by *preventing* something from burning. History attributes this new idea to Edison, though he also relied on the contributions of others. Remarkable as it was, this new box did not immediately lead to the invention of a usable lightbulb, and Edison had to do significant additional tinkering, testing, and analyzing before he could claim victory.

Engaging in multiple rounds of divergence (to come up with new ways of looking at things) and convergence (to select the next approach to try), Edison tested platinum and numerous other possible metal filaments before he finally came up with a carbon version that could last up to forty hours. When asked if he felt like a failure and should perhaps give up, Edison famously said: "Why should I give up? I now know over nine thousand ways that an electric lightbulb will not work, and so success is almost in my grasp." Shortly after making this statement, his optimism indeed bore fruit. He continued to improve the technology and eventually patented a carbonized bamboo filament that lasted over twelve hundred hours.

Of course, once this fundamental shift occurred—an incandescent lightbulb lasting not just for a few days but for weeks—there was plenty of room for additional rounds of divergence and convergence, allowing future generations of innovators to develop different shades and intensities of light, various colors and styles of glass, different types of filament, lightbulbs with various specific purposes and durations of use. Indeed, though you can use divergence and convergence to develop a new box, you can also rely upon these two essential processes to refine, enhance, and improve upon that box.

DECIDING WHOM TO INCLUDE IN THE CONVERGENCE PROCESS

As we saw with divergence, you may choose to involve others in the convergence process. In most cases, you'll probably flow relatively swiftly from divergence to convergence, and thus end up using the same group for both steps, whether that means yourself with bits of advice from friends or colleagues, or a broad set of experts. This approach is often both sensible and efficient because anyone involved in divergence will be very familiar with the full range of ideas you came up with together (and sometimes quite invested in them) and thus likely to be sensitive, wise, and appropriate about determining which ones may make the most sense to pursue.

But in other cases, one group will be effective at divergence but quite another will be helpful and important during convergence. Convergence is generally best achieved by people who are deeply knowledgeable about the issues at hand and thus qualified to make informed judgments about them.

A few examples: If you're trying to come up with a creative new press release, you might diverge and converge solo, or possibly do a few quick exercises over lunch with some friends. On the other hand, if you are trying to come up with a broader new box, such as a new strategic vision for your organization, you'll probably want to attract those of your colleagues who have a solid understanding of your organization's current business model as well as those of your most important competitors. And if your focus will be on "filling in" an existing box for a company— for instance, coming up with new product or service ideas—you'll most likely want to involve those individuals who understand the target market for new products; the costs of developing, manufacturing, and distributing them; the existing landscape of competitive products; and other similar factors.

Granted, your organization may be so small that the people involved in convergence should and must be the same ones who handled divergence. But in larger organizations, you may find that certain people will have more helpful expertise than others, and the convergence phase should be handled primarily, or exclusively, by these expert individuals.

Deciding who can be most effective during convergence will vary based on the unique dynamics and needs of each organization. For instance, when we were working with an apparel and accessories company in the Midwest—let's call the company Vamp—we helped the company's leading executives organize several rounds of divergence and convergence over numerous weeks. These sessions were attended by distinct sets of individuals. First, senior executives at Vamp came together for a round of divergence and convergence during which they generated several broad themes pertaining to new product development such as "Green Market" (wherein consumers are especially keen to purchase products and services that are environmentally friendly) and "Olympian Triumph" (where they are inspired to acquire items linked, figuratively if not literally, to the feeling of winning the Olympic Games). Following this initial visionary "big new box" process, fifteen up-and-coming leaders at the company came together for another round of divergence and convergence during which they brainstormed in a lively way on each theme in order to "fill in" the larger boxes their supervisors had initiated. This second contingent emerged with a carefully selected group of highly creative product ideas for Vamp to consider pursuing going forward, such as women's skirts that looked as though they were made out of bamboo, women's blouses that were adorned with layers and layers of something resembling banana leaves, and men's and women's running pants that included a small chip that would emit triumphant music if and when the person wearing them achieved a certain velocity in running. Over the next several months, product development and market research experts within the company then conducted significant further convergence exercises to probe, test, and strengthen each of these ideas and thereby determine which ones should actually be produced and distributed by Vamp both in its own chain of domestic boutiques and in big-box stores like Target worldwide.

Moving into Convergence

Once you've selected the most appropriate participants and you're ready to begin the convergence process in earnest, you'll need to determine three important things:

1. Any key "make it or break it" practical *constraints* related to the decisions you're about to make such as budget limitations, technological standards that must be respected, and/or laws or regulations requiring or forbidding certain practices or actions.

2. The more subjective *criteria* you believe should be used to decide which of your ideas to pursue, such as cost, the effort and time that will be required to execute each idea, your and your colleagues' relevant background and experience, or whether the idea comports well with your organization's culture and current product or service offerings.

3. Your *selection and voting procedures:* how you intend to prioritize the range of ideas; how you will weight the different criteria, whether anyone you may have invited to participate will get to vote just once (or, for instance, whether there will be several rounds of voting) and whether each person's vote will be weighed the same (or whether certain individuals—such as your CEO or some third-party expert—will have a more heavily weighted vote, or the final one). How much of this will be done today versus over the coming days or weeks using additional data, and how will the different criteria be weighted?

Identifying any "do or die" constraints should always be your starting place. A *constraint* is an absolute restriction: It either can be satisfied or it cannot be. If, for example, you're a creative executive at Vamp and you're selecting from among a group of new clothing ideas, you could potentially have constraints regarding the textiles you could decide to use. If, for instance, the worldwide supply of silk is so diminished that you already know that you won't be able to use silk cost-effectively in any of Vamp's products, you won't want to waste time during the convergence process entertaining proposals for new products using silk.

Although, as we've seen, some assumptions and rule-sets within any organization can sometimes be bent (or broken) to spark new creative ideas and possibilities, during convergence organizations may face constraints that, as a matter of objective reality, simply cannot be violated without causing harm to the company, its employees, or customers, or constraints that, if ignored, will make it impossible for you to execute on one or more of the ideas you're considering. Some other constraints could include the following:

- Caps on internal or external resources;
- Practices or activities that are restricted, or forbidden, by existing contracts or other agreements or policies to which the organization needs to conform; and/or
- Industry standards—such as territory-specific voltage requirements for electronic products—that must be respected.

As this sample list suggests, some such constraints may be external ones (FDA approval for a certain compound will take at least another three years), and others may be internal to your organization (you and the top management of your green TV food network are committed to airing shows on organic vegetarian cooking—so proposals for new programs for meat lovers called things like "Carnivore's Heaven" or "Pigs in Mud" are not worth considering during convergence—unless they're actually about replicating the taste of meat dishes using all vegetable-based ingredients). During your most expansive, divergent, highly creative moments, you'll want to take risks and leaps of the imagination that include shattering some of these assumed constraints (for instance, by imagining what would happen if the government ended all regulation of drugs and medications or if all food needed to be made artificially because of dire shortages of most vegetables and animals). But during convergence, these constraints need to be respected, since this will help ensure that neither you nor your organization loses time or resources "going down rabbit holes" by pursuing decisions that, when implemented, would end up being inappropriate, damaging, or simply not feasible.

Another important discussion to have prior to the convergence process is one in which you set out the *criteria* you plan to use to evaluate your decisions about which ideas to take forward and which ones to eliminate. By discussing and agreeing upon these benchmarks *before* you actually try to vote and make decisions, neither you nor anyone else will be tempted, either arbitrarily or inadvertently, to steer your decision-making toward any specific possibility. If for any reason during the convergence process you realize that one of your criteria is not helpful or relevant, or that you need to use additional criteria, you can always make these adjustments (or you might need a neutral facilitator to help you do so). But by and large, the process will go more smoothly if you've thought through and identified these key decision-making nodes in advance.

There is a seemingly infinite number of criteria that you might use in making any decision. And you could probably conduct numerous divergence and convergence sessions just in order to determine which ones you think would be the most helpful to apply.

Some of the criteria you might decide are relevant—especially when trying to develop a big new core box—include the following:*

Alignment

- *Strategic outlook.* Is this new idea consistent with your organization's overall strategy, objectives, and goals?
- *Competence.* Does the new box leverage your organization's capabilities and competencies, its knowledge base, its experience in the relevant area?
- *Values.* Does this new box more or less comport with your organization's culture, values, and philosophy?

Feasibility

- *Resources.* Can this new idea succeed relying on your organization's current resources, assets, and people?
- *Time horizon.* How long will it take to implement? Does that timing fit well with your organization's current planning?
- *Financial returns.* Is pursuing this new box affordable? Is it likely to produce sufficient revenues soon enough? Or could funding it seriously threaten the health of your existing business?

* For helpful lists of such criteria, see Nilofer Merchant, "Strategy Matters: How to Develop Criteria for Achieving Business Goals," *Entrepreneur*, December 11, 2008, www.entrepreneur.com/article/199154; and Alan Chapman, "SWOT Analysis Template," found on numerous business-related websites including www.businessballs .com.

- *Marketing requirements.* In terms of the marketing, sales, and distribution infrastructure of your organization, how poised are you to make it a success?
- *Geographical requirements.* To what extent do the locations and geographies pertinent to the new box fit well with those of your organization?
- *Regulatory and legal feasibility.* To what degree will pursuing this new idea trigger problems with accreditation, qualifications, certifications, or other legal requirements?
- *Technological development.* Will this idea require new technological development? Will it fit well with your current technologies?
- *Research and information resources.* Will implementing the new box require any new research or data resources?

Impact

- *Reputation/brand.* To what extent will implementing this idea support your reputation and goodwill? Does it relate appropriately to your brand or trademark? Does it add value or detract from that brand or trademark?
- *Competitive advantage and differentiation.* Will it enhance or detract from your ability to compete against others and exploit others' weaknesses? Will it differentiate you from your competitors in the eyes of customers?
- *Externalities.* How will pursuing this new box change or influence your immediate community, the industry in which you participate, your state, the global community? Will it have a positive impact? A negative one?
- *Operational efficiency.* Will implementing the new box enable your organization to save money or resources, or operate more efficiently? What economies of scale could the new box rely upon or would it be likely to achieve?
- *Risk/consequences of failure.* What would it mean to the organization if the new box failed? Are there "no regrets" type moves that can be taken right away, or opportunities to pilot or test on a small scale before making dramatic or irreversible shifts?

Often the specific nature of the ideas you're considering will dictate the criteria you decide to contemplate.

We have also seen people decide to measure the potential of their big new ideas based on such measures as:

- *Change.* Will this new box truly help us change the way we see and do things?
- *Leap in value.* Does this new box represent a valuable departure from the past?
- *Credibility.* Will this new box be credible to others (our colleagues, customers, clients) and easy for them to visualize and thus understand, embrace, and act upon?

To determine the immediacy, strength, and imaginativeness of a new box in this more high-level way, you can also ask people to describe that box as if they were speaking to a seven-year-old child (who probably possesses less business or technology savvy than you and your colleagues), presenting it in a forum attended by everyone in your organization or industry, or pitching it to the public as an exciting new sports event, movie, or city building. Along similar lines, you can ask others to try to articulate the new idea to "a stranger on the sidewalk." Often the ideas that you find most compelling, appealing, and worthy of implementation will also be those that you can quickly and succinctly make vivid to a clueless outsider.

To test your new boxes for this sort of creative and forward-looking robustness, ask such questions as:

- Did we have to fight for it?
- Will it make us take a risk?
- Will it lead to a paradigm shift?
- Is it simple?
- Is it special?
- Can it be drawn?
- Will there be a "before" and an "after," with a clear distinction in people's minds?
- Will we remember when and where it was created?

To be clear, we are not claiming that for every new box, the answer to all of the above should be "yes." But it can be helpful to consider these questions to gain further confidence that you're really moving toward something new. No matter what sorts of boxes you're hoping to create, the criteria you select—and the questions you ask—will help you test them in an implicit way, to run something of a "reality check" so that you and your organization move ahead only with those that you believe have a decent chance of succeeding.

As you become more sophisticated about the convergence process, and especially when the stakes seem significant to you and your organization—for example, "Are we going to launch into this very costly new area of business?"—you'll want to work together to identify several of the most relevant criteria based on the particulars of your organization and the issues it is currently facing.

So long as you remain aware of these risks, and do your best with your colleagues to agree ahead of time on the most sensible criteria, you'll handle convergence in a successful way.

PRIORITIZING, VOTING, AND MAKING YOUR RECOMMENDATIONS

To dive into the ultimate decision-making process, you and whoever may be joining you in this process should remember the key objective or issue at stake, go over all the ideas being proposed, indicate the relevant constraints and decision-making criteria, and then outline what approach will be used to prioritize, evaluate, and vote upon the various ideas (and to communicate them to your colleagues in the organization).

But how are you to know which new box—or boxes—to pursue? Even if you are brilliant in your analysis—and fair and systematic in how you vote on the various proposals—how will you know you're taking the best possible road to success?

In most cases, you won't. There is usually no single real right answer—there are always many possible boxes, and even the best strategy remains a working hypothesis. And so the process of selecting one or more to pursue is inductive, not deductive. In other words, faced with all the facts and figures in front of you, the constraints, criteria, and their application to your ideas, you're going to have to induce or "generalize" as to what makes the most sense for you and your organization. You are going to have to make a decision, make a choice.

Today we can celebrate the wisdom of the leaders at Philips who, after analyzing megatrends relating to the rise in healthcare spending and consumer market preferences, decided to pursue the development of easy-to-use home healthcare systems that now represent a product unit of substantial size within the company. At the time they made this decision, as we saw earlier, it surely was not the only rational one that they could have pursued. It was not a purely objective, logical, obvious move—instead, there was a significant subjective element to it, a leap of faith made based on the executives' best individual and collective judgment.

We often encourage our clients to create grids or matrices that help them measure each idea against their preselected criteria. The criteria can be weighted, or you might determine that your criteria should all be deemed to have the same relevance and importance (in which case weighting them will be unnecessary). You might create two-by-two matrices to compare specific advantages and disadvantages, such as costs and benefits, or feasibility versus impact.

You might then move on to apply more elaborate criteria, testing your ideas against each respective criterion thoughtfully and thoroughly.

You might enforce a rule whereby each person in the room gets one vote. Or you might give key decision makers more votes (or simply weight these key persons' votes so that they count more). You might forbid people to vote for ideas they proposed, or give everyone, or select leaders, the right to veto any idea. You can agree that there will be just one round of voting. But we often suggest holding several rounds of voting in which ideas that score the lowest are eliminated early on. In this way, you can get rid of the "noise" and focus in on those ideas that, as a group, you are the most excited about. Above all, given that the people in the room should be—and therefore probably will be—among the key individuals involved in implementing and executing the new ideas, it is important that everyone feel that they have been appropriately involved in assessing them.

As a general guideline, when people are discussing and voting upon any new box, we discourage them from simply "caving in" to the apparent consensus or "letting go" of any lingering worries. Whereas divergence is a time to try to transcend constraints, suspend judgment, and generate lots of ideas, convergence is the time to apply your most clear, analytic, and practical thinking—and to be courageous and persistent in voicing your questions and assessments, your thoughts, anxieties, and concerns. If you're in a group that is leaning toward making a specific decision and you don't feel quite right about it, now is the time to pipe up and say something! Not everyone will be happy with every decision—and you may be the one who ends up "taking one for the team." But if you're feeling uncomfortable, and don't say anything, your colleagues won't have the benefit of your concerns. If there is a facilitator or moderator, that person should check in with all participants from time to time, asking questions such as "Is everyone comfortable with the emerging consensus?" "Does anyone want to offer any additional suggestions, objections, questions, or concerns?" "Are we all satisfied with this?"

Convergence should not be an impulsive rush to judgment (though that is often our natural instinct). Instead, it is about being thoughtful, methodical—and patient. So if the decision-making process seems to be going too quickly, or in an overly perfunctory or systematic way, speak up! It is not unusual to have to go through several cycles of divergence and convergence. If you end one round, and are not at peace with what you've decided, go back, reevaluate, and try again.

Whatever specific approach you opt to use to prioritize your various ideas, you should compare the outcome of your convergence process with your original goal, largely because this will help bring you "back to reality" or "back to your day job." Conducting divergence and convergence sessions is intense work, and it often helps to reground yourself and any participants with a reminder about what you were hoping to achieve and specifically what the target outcome is. Are you hoping to create new products or services, or a new overall concept for the business? A new marketing plan, or new approaches to growth? Operational strategies, or scenarios for the future? Sometimes, toward the end of convergence, you might find yourself entertaining a concept or idea that, brilliant as it may be, is quite tangential to your overall mission. By contrast, you might discover that an idea that you had long ago rejected, or considered a low priority, suddenly makes sense to you and seems like one worthy of considering. In either such case (or in other similar ones), neither you nor anyone else in the room should ever have to fear speaking your mind. You are in the midst of making decisions of consequence. It you've gotten off track, there's always the opportunity to regroup and find your focus again. If you've come to see an old idea in exciting new relief, now is the time to step up, speak out, and help make things happen.

CONDUCTING MULTIPLE ROUNDS OF DIVERGENCE AND CONVERGENCE

We can't stress enough how helpful it can be to take your best ideas and then submit them to additional rounds of divergence and convergence. Especially when you have begun by creating a rather broad box, set aside additional time, either on your own or with others (who could be the same group as before or a different one), in order to use your best thinking and creativity to "fill it in" with more specific ideas to execute. This is not about repeating the same exercises or questions as before and seeing if something different comes out—that can be an interesting academic exercise but it is generally not the best use of people's time. Rather, it's about taking some of the output that has been generated and building upon it, either through looking with a fresh perspective, trying some "yes, and . . . ," building off the spark an idea generated, or combining specific ideas to form something bigger.

During your divergence sessions at Ultragames, you and your colleagues ended up producing dozens of ideas for the company, from new games for working mothers to leveraging the "safe" image. And imagine that through several days of iterative convergence discussions, and several rounds of voting, you then arrived at four broad boxes filled with possibility, namely:

- Develop a range of games for new market segments such as teenage girls, seniors, mothers, and more, building on existing game development expertise.
- Explore the "entertrain" concept, with a range of options from test preparation to tailored courses for companies.
- Learn more about the neuroscience of specific learning disorders, particularly ADHD, and the benefits that video games can offer, with a view toward developing therapeutic games.
- Engage in a proactive marketing blitz focused on the "safe" image you have maintained over time and leverage it to communicate that Ultragames offers games that are not only "safe" (your old box) but also "good" (your new box), games that *should* be used for long sessions over many years, games that build children's intellectual strengths over time, games that are "guilt-free" for concerned parents and educators everywhere.

Sorting your list of ideas into categories such as these may take a couple of hours, or a couple of weeks, depending on the complexity of your particular situation. And depending on the ambitiousness of these ideas, you might require not just a few hours, but a few additional days or weeks to decide together with your colleagues whether you should pursue all of these ideas, or just one or two of them. Further, if you decided that your company should select just one of them, you might need still additional time to analyze which of these would be the most worthwhile to pursue.

As leaders trying to select ideas falling within each of your four buckets, prior to convergence you and your colleagues at Ultragames have already moved on from your original constraint of "We need to target teenage boys and men in their twenties" and, in the spirit of growth, decided to challenge the "We are not big enough to maintain our existing franchises and launch more than one to two new games per year" constraint, which came from the historical perceptions of the two founders.

You and your colleagues also decide to open that $5 million line of credit with your local bank. Though you won't be required to use the line to borrow money, you can now be open to thoughtful risk-taking and expansion.

By way of criteria, you and your group at first decide that you are looking for ideas that will have short- to medium-term financial payback because of your (and your CFO's) underlying nerves relating to the line of credit, and that are low-risk to the extent possible. Then the founders add another one to the mix: They would like Ultragames to make a difference in people's lives, to change society to some degree. They have recently been inspired by seeing what Bill Gates and Warren Buffett have done with their money, and they are keenly interested in a "new box" kind of shift that will change the world in some way, rather than simply staying the course as a purely profit-driven organization. You then all agree in advance that the most measurably important priorities are the payback and risk levels, with the criteria about "making a difference" being important in an entirely different way, as a vital guidepost and inspiration.

Given the $5 million constraint and your limited personnel, it has become clear to you that even with the willingness to explore dramatic growth plans, Ultragames does not have the bandwidth to execute on all the ideas that have been raised (even if they all made sense). And so you invite your colleagues to explore the different possibilities under each of the four buckets, to begin to consider the combinations that might have the most potential without requiring significant risk, and to try to flag those that might change the world.

After some discussion, you realize that some of your peers (perhaps led by your risk-averse CFO) are not excited about anything that would involve spending much money or tapping into the line of credit. Their mantra is "If it ain't broke, why try to change it now? Why try to grow when things are fine?"* Assuming that Ultragames has a strong cultural preference to proceed by consensus rather than majority vote, you might decide that this is a good time to pause. You promise to do some additional investigation before reconvening the group.

---

* Some people say there's no need to reinvent the wheel, but we should be glad that many individuals did just that. The wheel has come a long way in recent centuries.

After some exploration, you find out that one of your strongest game developers and two of your star salespeople have been getting bored with the status quo, churning out and pushing updated editions of the same basic games year after year, and are thinking of leaving the company. You are keen to retain them, and think that giving them responsibility for some new projects would persuade them to stay. In addition, you spend some time with the founders, who have become particularly excited about neuroscience and the potential therapeutic value of video games of late, and start putting together a specific proposal for what this idea could entail. After a small number of interviews with experts in the field of neuroscience focused on multiple intelligences, as well as specialists in ADHD and other learning challenges, ranging from pediatric neurologists, occupational therapists, and psychiatrists to teachers, guidance counselors, and parents, your proposal includes a specific timeline and plan for what it would take in terms of personnel, time, and cost to get this idea off the ground. You also learn that ADHD is the most commonly diagnosed neurobehavioral disorder in children, with estimates that it affects about 5 percent of children worldwide—a substantial global market. ADHD also often continues into adulthood, which bodes well in terms of your ability to make a difference, and is diagnosed several times more frequently in boys than in girls, meaning that your target segment may not actually shift so dramatically, even if your product does.[4]

Once you circulate this new plan to your team, and the group reconvenes, several people ask for more particulars about how this would fit with the existing organization, and about some line items in your draft budget. You then refine and improve your plan as a result, adding more specific details on the people who could take this forward, their expected relationships with the existing business, and the specific cost details requested. The CFO tries to insist on a more "risk-free" approach but is eventually convinced that sticking to the status quo would pose an even greater risk than making a shift, given the likelihood of losing key employees, not to mention the threats identified earlier regarding mobile phones and the world changing around you.

After further group discussion, you all eventually agree to:

- Invest in researching and developing the neuroscience/ADHD opportunity, assigning a now-excited star salesperson and game developer to understand the market and flesh out the specifics of how a product designed to help people living with ADHD would work. You agree to use part of the $5 million line of credit to fund these R&D expenses.
- Explore the "entertrain" concept further, in a relatively low-risk way. Specifically, the other star salesperson who was looking to leave seems energized to focus on new business development, looking at ways to train corporate executives, offer continuing education to military personnel, sell test-prep software, and more. He is even going to embark on additional divergence to explore this idea further, with the idea that he will have relatively minimal funding to actually develop new products until he confirms any deals, in a "pay-as-you-go" approach that seems to work in other industries.
- Use another part of the line of credit to hire high-performing new people to replace these employees in their existing jobs, to ensure the existing game franchises continue to grow and bring in revenues while Ultragames is moving into these new areas.
- Shelve the idea of a "safe" marketing campaign, and of developing new games and franchises for seniors and other segments, at least for now. Instead, you decide that StrengthBuilder is a much more exciting new box.

Over the coming months, as the ADHD idea takes shape, it also becomes clearer in the eyes of you and your colleagues. You see it as a way not only to change the world but to fundamentally change your company from one that is primarily about the entertainment of teenage boys to one that is about recognizing and helping support the multiple intelligences of all people and thereby improving the educational and life experiences of children and teenagers everywhere. As the prospects for the new product look better and better, you realize that people's common perceptions of video games as "bad for you" will eventually be turned around 180 degrees, thanks to this shift into healthy "good for you" video games, games specifically designed to help kids with ADHD and other learning disorders become better lifelong learners in spite of the challenges they face, games that may actually help children work around—maybe even cure—the symptoms of their neurobehavioral conditions. In some ways, you are going to transform Ultragames into a sort of multiple intelligences learning and StrengthBuilder company— or what could even be seen as a healthcare company, with ongoing plans for conducting clinical studies using brain imaging and for exploring different ways to rewire challenged circuits. Over time, this broad new box, this new vision or way of looking at the company, could open the door to further research into ways to use video games to combat all sorts of learning issues, as well as psychiatric disorders such as anxiety and depression. And, of course, for Ultragames, these new pursuits could contribute mightily to continued growth and massive competitive advantage.

None of this would have been possible if you hadn't first strived to foster doubt, to challenge your initial sense that extending your existing games into the mobile arena with your existing segments was the safest and best way to go. Your new strategy and products make sense only in the context of your new "good for you" box. *Eureka!*

THINKING IN NEW (MAIL)BOXES: DIVERGENCE AND CONVERGENCE IN ACTION

When we worked with France's national postal service, La Poste, to develop an overarching theme it could use to inspire and guide its future activities, little did the executives there initially realize that we wouldn't ask them to conduct just one but rather a dozen divergence/convergence workshops! With the proliferation of e-technologies (especially email and social networks) and the deregulation of many aspects of delivering packages in France (leading to competition from FedEx and others), La Poste was eager to find new sources of inspiration to help make itself as relevant and profitable as possible at the dawn of the twenty-first century. In other words, La Poste needed to create a big, overarching new box. By way of analogy, imagine trying to help the U.S. Postal Service make itself as vibrant and relevant today as it was in 1950.

We used numerous divergence exercises to generate a tremendous number of new themes and ideas. Participants talked about La Poste from a variety of provocative and wildly disparate perspectives: those of a drug addict, a colicky infant, the president of Microsoft. They came up with dozens of key phrases attempting to capture La Poste's future, from "Reinvent Proximity" to "Make Life Possible," from "Always by Your Side" to "Don't Move; La Poste Will Bring You the World." They brainstormed countless fun new ideas. Some pertained to improving customer service at post offices: showing relaxation videos or having live musical performances in all local post offices; hiring professional writers to help local post office customers craft letters; installing playgrounds or meeting rooms at every post office. Others involved whole new potential areas of business: an online PayPal-type offering, an encryption service for people sending one another emails, a mass-market Web-based tool to help people determine local real estate values.

It took us several sessions, over many weeks, to focus in on six key themes that La Poste's top leaders believed the organization could unite behind. And it took yet further sessions, and a lot of additional thought and consideration on their part, to converge upon three possible major boxes based on the original six: 1) becoming an exchange platform, 2) serving as a trusted third party, and 3) providing support in life.

We then looked for overlap among these three concepts by helping La Poste assess many of its current key products and services and seeing which ones related most logically to each. La Poste decided to boil them down to just two overall concepts: a vision focused on trust, and another based on exchanges. The first idea entailed cultivating the trust La Poste could achieve with its customers. From years of studying customer survey results—and simply based on conventional wisdom—it was clear to everyone involved in our workshops that La Poste is one of the most trusted institutions in France. The second idea involved seeing La Poste as a central hub for all sorts of exchanges, not just traditional ones (like getting letters and packages from senders to recipients), but also less obvious ones, like helping people send money to one another electronically or enabling them to make donations to not-for-profit organizations online yet without worry about Internet security issues.

After still further divergence on these two themes, including using bold analogies to imagine and talk together about other worlds in which "trust" and "exchanges" could be seen as relevant and valuable (such as the Russian-American space program prior to the fall of the Berlin Wall or organizations overseeing human organ donation), the top leaders of La Poste subsequently converged once again. They explored what it would mean to compete against FedEx and DHL regarding exchanges, or against the electric utility and large banks regarding trust—what assets did they hold, and where would they be advantaged? They eventually decided that the simple yet powerful notion of "trust" was the most essential, inspiring, transcendent theme of all, and a theme that La Poste could leverage successfully for many years to come.

Specifically, several of the leading executives at La Poste realized that the organization had accumulated years of public recognition as a trustworthy operation, given the omnipresence of post offices across the country, the visits of delivery personnel to homes every day, and the tremendous investments La Poste had made to preserve its reputation for discretion, honesty, and reliability. La Poste avoided aberrant delays. It kept its promises. It was careful not to make mistakes in billing people. It avoided labor problems at all costs so that people across France would receive their mail and enjoy all other key services provided by La Poste without any disruption or delay.

During one set of divergence exercises, workshop participants had looked at Google and eBay as models for what La Poste could accomplish. Google offered people confidence about the searches they were conducting, while eBay was a safe, trustworthy venue for selling things. Both companies built their essential value through numerous key technological innovations, but both, too, emerged as significant platforms grounded in trust. Arguably, La Poste could boast an even greater trust quotient among its customers who routinely see La Poste as an ever-present, ever-impartial, and honest partner.

In deciding upon trust as its primary theme, executives at La Poste considered numerous criteria. They asked themselves:

- What new sources of revenues will a model based on trust offer?
- How will it help La Poste compete against other organizations (such as banks and courier services) that offer similar services?

- What percentage of the relevant markets will La Poste be able to dominate? What new investments will be required?
- What sorts of early results seem likely?
- Will it help La Poste grow?
- Will it help La Poste soar in the Modern Age?

And as Georges Lefebvre, La Poste's director of human resources and labor relations (and an active participant in the divergence/convergence sessions we conducted with La Poste), recently said to us, the organization asked itself above all, "What will we have to do differently tomorrow? Why is it legitimate for us to claim this, and what will this mean for our key stakeholders?"

Following all of the divergence/convergence sessions La Poste's senior management aligned behind the notion of trust. Trust satisfied every criterion they could imagine. As Lefebvre explained, "We always knew we scored high on trust from customer satisfaction surveys. But we never understood until now that trust could be a lever to bring us all forward together. We started thinking about what we might *stop* doing, and what we needed to *start* doing. We realized that we have always earned people's trust, and now we could own it as a legitimate claim. We just had to change our perspective. Customers were on board because it fit with their long-held perceptions of La Poste. It really resonated with them." In fact, trust, in and of itself, seemed to offer an unassailable benchmark for most everything La Poste had accomplished historically and everything it wanted to achieve going forward. Many of the other key themes that had seemed reasonable and important during divergence now merely seemed to be valuable *subsets* of trust. For instance, during divergence, many managers had mentioned "proximity" (that is, the fact that there are so many post offices across France and postal workers have access to every community, neighborhood, and home) as a paramount aspect of La Poste's operations. But once the convergence process began to enter its final phases, the same executives had come to share a changed perspective. They could now see that it was more fundamentally because of trust that people in France would allow postal workers from La Poste to deliver their personal mail—and sometimes even enter their homes with letters and packages. Proximity was important, but it was made possible by, and therefore fell within the larger rubric of, trust. "Trust," Lefebvre told us, "has become the real root of our shared vision."

Once Lefebvre and his colleagues had converged on "trust," it almost instantly seemed to make sense not just as a theme for internal and public communications but also as an intrinsic part of the organization's ongoing strategic plans. With respect to La Poste's new forays into consumer credit, trust would mean not investing in any unreliable mortgage deals. As for its interest in facilitating customers' connections to charities, it would mean protecting customers' privacy and developing a whole new range of online tools to allow individuals to rely safely upon La Poste when making donations to their most cherished not-for-profit organizations. During additional divergence and convergence sessions to "fill in" the trust box with ideas for new products and services, participants proposed (among many other ideas):

- Operating a moving company that would leverage La Poste's famous brand and its presence in communities across France.
- Launching a consumer rating service that would certify the quality of specific products, services, and/or commercial establishments—at one point participants even reconsidered the possibility of acquiring Michelin's travel and restaurant guidebook business to help jump-start La Poste in this new area of potential growth.
- Offering a broader array of e-services (not only those then offered, for instance, by Yahoo! or Gmail, but also such services as custom-made stamps, where you can go online and create your own personalized stamps using images and themes of your own choosing).
- Delving even more deeply into the online space, where trust is essential, to offer secure virtual document retention, delivery, and management, and an online voting tool that enables businesses to conduct secure elections, for example, when nominating and voting for union representatives.

Of note: This last concept, that of a "digital safe," was not new to the world, or even new to La Poste—it had actually been considered and rejected several years earlier. Now, however, in the concept of a broad "trust" box, it made perfect sense. This is another example of looking at old ideas differently, and the importance of changing perspective.

All of these innovations comport in an organic way with the firm's new box of trust. Jean-Paul Bailly, president of La Poste since 2002, recently explained to us that the emergence of trust as such an important shared vision at the organization marked "a decisive moment in the history of La Poste," one that affected the firm's management decisions, how it trained and evaluated employees, and the decisions it made about which new products and services to pursue (and which ones not to). According to Bailly, before the workshops, La Poste lacked a clear central strategy regarding where the organization was headed. The notion of trust, he said, offered a new all-encompassing value, a shared starting point and baseline against which La Poste could examine nearly all of its most important potential choices, initiatives, and opportunities. "Trust," he explained, "has become our faith."

SEVEN

Reevaluate Relentlessly

□□□□□□□□□□□□□□□□□□□□□□□□□□□□□□□□□□□□□

To rest upon a formula is a slumber that, prolonged, means death.[1]

—Oliver Wendell Holmes, Jr.

O IDEA IS GOOD FOREVER. No matter how brilliant, how resilient, how imaginative, how timely and effective, every box you conceive will benefit from being modified, improved, and ultimately replaced. The creative process is constant, and our five steps remain in continuous play. You will need to use each of them again and again, though not always in the same sequence.

Coming up with new ideas, even ones that turn out to be exceptionally valuable and perhaps celebrated the world over, does not put an end to your process. The ADHD-mitigating game experience you've created at Ultragames could be trumped tomorrow by a competitor's even-more-effective game, or by a helmet that produces brain waves that neutralize the symptoms of the disorder, or a magic pill that cures all ills. You can never stop doubting.

There is no idea that will remain valid in perpetuity, and to achieve sustainable creativity, you must continue creating, modifying, selecting, implementing, rejecting, and, at some point, replacing your boxes.

To be successful, it is imperative to create one new box after another, embracing change, and knowing when it's time to discard one box and replace it with another. Rather than waiting for *Caramba*—and rather than believing that success today guarantees success tomorrow—some companies consistently anticipate the impact of change and thus do a good job of replacing their boxes.

As an exemplar, we would point to the news organization Reuters, which has consistently evolved in brilliant winning ways. The company's overarching box of message and news delivery dates back to its founding in 1850, and it has remained consistent ever since. How did Reuters keep its broad box the same in the face of so many changes in the world since then? It initially implemented this box using homing pigeons, followed by the telegraph (in 1851), and then the telex machine (in 1882). These technologies were then discarded and replaced with radio (in 1923) and satellite communication (in 1962)—and today the company boasts whole new approaches featuring sophisticated Internet-based news delivery applications.

Paul Julius Reuter founded the company in 1850, in Aachen, Germany (then Prussia). The telegraph, at that time, was a new invention, but there was a gap in the line between Aachen and Brussels, so he used homing pigeons to bridge that gap, enabling news to move more quickly between Berlin and Brussels, among other routes.

Knowing that carrier pigeons were not a technology of the future, Reuter looked for new approaches to news and message delivery (or put another way, he looked for new successful boxes that would "fill in" the broad original box he and his colleagues had originally created at the company's inception). Reuter appears to have been incredibly gifted at coming up with lots of new ideas, exploiting them for as long as possible, and then replacing them with new ones if and when necessary.

After moving to London in 1851, Reuter took advantage of the newly laid telegraph line under the English Channel, between Dover and Calais, and began providing stock prices from the London Stock Exchange to brokers in Paris, as well as prices from continental Europe to brokers at the LSE. Reuter opened more and more offices, and in 1865 his private firm became a corporation called Reuters Telegram Company. In 1865, he was also the first in Europe to break the news of Abraham Lincoln's assassination, after the news took twelve days to cross the Atlantic.

Around 1882, Reuters implemented another new paradigm when it began using the "telex," a sort of column printer that is an ancestor of today's terminals used by some hearing-impaired people, to communicate news and stock prices across its network of offices, which enabled longer missives than the simple telegraph. This continued the overall mission of getting news and stock prices communicated broadly and quickly, while also continuing to take advantage of shifting trends and technologies in the world.

In 1923, Reuters helped develop new uses for radio, including methods for transmitting news internationally and a service of stock quotes and exchange rates sent in Morse code by long-wave radio. This ultimately turned into Reuters's primary service in Europe, and eventually the world as the radio transmitters grew stronger.

Reuters continued to be agile and flexible. In the 1960s, the company implemented a fifth new box when it embraced the potential of satellites, and a sixth when it developed a new box relating to the Internet in the mid-1990s. Remarkably, though the company's overall broad box—of news and stock price transmittal—has stayed the same as the world changed, Reuters has repeatedly developed new exciting boxes to "fill it in" and thus remain both relevant and successful.

As the world changes around you, conditions will change, leading to the constant need for new boxes. Events—from political upheavals to technological revolutions, from deep unexpected economic crises to whole new realms of society, culture, and opportunity—may contradict scenarios that were developed earlier, in a different environment. Unforeseen, high-impact events may disrupt the validity of the previously "new" box. And, of course, sometimes even well-known threats (such as competitors with whom you're very familiar) can have unexpected impact. In fact, after Reuters was merged into the Thomson Corporation to create Thomson Reuters in 2008, it was probably widely assumed that one of the newly reorganized company's key competitors in the area of financial news and analysis would be Bloomberg. But following the 2008 recession, Thomson Reuters's Markets division suffered when, among other things, its new Eikon desktop financial data program performed below expectations and failed to compete effectively with Bloomberg's established terminals.[2] Reuters was a successful company for more than one hundred years because it constantly evolved—and today it must evolve again and find another game-changing box.

Step 5 is about making sure that, like radar constantly scanning the skies to collect information, you subject your boxes to rigorous, ongoing critical examination. It's about striving to ensure that the information you gather is not constrained by your wish that those boxes remain valid forever. And it is also largely about avoiding denial, or at least knowing when you are in fact resistant to seeing or accepting the truth before your eyes.

In many ways, Step 5 necessarily returns you to Step 1, since both steps entail being profoundly vigilant—and constantly questioning your current boxes. In chapter 1, we used the analogy of breaking free from a prison: You can't get out of a prison if you haven't acknowledged that it exists, mastered how it operates, and learned about its vulnerabilities. Step 5, then, is all about making sure that you do not become imprisoned once again (or that, if you do, you promptly forge new keys or escape routes).

You must always do your best to notice how your current boxes are serving you well, and how they are holding you back. "Progress," playwright George Bernard Shaw once opined, "is impossible without change, and those who cannot change their minds cannot change anything." In other words, you can't move forward if you're not continuously reexamining and recalibrating your perceptions.

Step 5 asks you to reevaluate your boxes consistently and carefully enough to prepare, as best you can, for the uncertainties of the future and the inexorable flow of change. It helps ensure that you neither hold on to your new boxes for too long nor abandon them too quickly. Put simply, we would implore you to *keep on doubting*, and recall one of Nike's classic corporate taglines: "There is no finish line!"

REPLACING YOUR BOXES WHEN IT'S TIME

In the summer of 2011, Netflix's CEO, Reed Hastings, having carefully studied reams of data showing that more and more consumers were moving away from DVD rentals in favor of streaming videos, decided that he should split Netflix into two.[3] One part, subsequently named Qwikster, would be launched as a new company that would mail DVDs to customers in vivid red envelopes, with convenient prepaid postage for the return of the DVD to the company following viewing, as Netflix had traditionally done. The new Netflix, by contrast, would cease to provide that mailed DVD service, instead focusing exclusively on the relatively new, rapidly growing video-streaming business.

Soon after making this decision, Hastings sent a mass email to Netflix's subscribers, stating the following:[4]

> We are separating unlimited DVDs by mail and unlimited streaming into two separate plans to better reflect the costs of each. Now our members have a choice: a streaming only plan, a DVD only plan, or both.
>
> Your current $9.99 a month membership for unlimited streaming and unlimited DVDs will be split into 2 distinct plans:
>
> Plan 1: Unlimited Streaming (no DVDs) for $7.99 a month
> Plan 2: Unlimited DVDs, 1 out at-a-time (no streaming) for $7.99 a month
>
> Your price for getting both of these plans will be $15.98 a month ($7.99 + $7.99). You don't need to do anything to continue your memberships for both unlimited streaming and unlimited DVDs.

Not long after Qwikster was announced and Netflix's subscribers received this email, some 800,000 of them dropped Netflix, many of them sorely disappointed that it would no longer offer its mailed DVD service except via Qwikster (and that the price had gone up from $9.99 to $15.98 for the combined streaming/mailed DVD service).

When financial results were announced at the end of the third quarter of 2011, Netflix's stock price had decreased by more than 25 percent. According to *The New York Times,* Netflix had "underestimated the unquantifiable emotions of its subscribers who still want those little red envelopes, even if they forget to ever watch the DVD inside."[5] Hastings told the newspaper that he realized that he had made the decision to split up Netflix (even as he approved the fee increases) based on hubris and a surplus of confidence (about consumers' growing preference for video streaming). He had erred, he said, in "moving too quickly," and the company opted not to make the change.

We would tend to agree that Hastings acted prematurely in separating out the "mailed DVD" concept in favor of the "streamed video" one. He failed to recognize that many of the company's customers were not yet ready to replace one box with another (indeed, many still wanted to be able to enjoy both options, or the variety that the streaming service was not yet providing, without a dramatically increased price point). They were still enamored of the "mailed DVD" concept and unwilling to put it aside for a new world in which they would instead have to obtain all of their audiovisual entertainment exclusively by downloading digital files.

Of course, if Netflix failed to recognize that many consumers were not yet fully ready to replace one box with another, many organizations are at least as prone to making the opposite kind of error, that is, clinging to an old box for too long (rather than not long enough). When it comes to thinking in new boxes, you want to avoid jumping the gun, but you don't want to rest on your laurels, either. No matter how many consecutive *Eureka* experiences you've had, or how brilliant your most current boxes seem to be, you're also forever at risk of encountering *Caramba.**

Granted, in order to get things done, you'll always have to hold on to

---

* Following this episode, Netflix did have an excellent 2012, with a deliberate focus on the fast-growing market for streaming video, which the company had made a focus of its attention even at the risk of cannibalizing its DVD-by-mail business. From our perspective, this is a solid acknowledgment that the world is always changing.

your current boxes for a while, "freezing" everything so that you can take action. For instance, if you are selling products in distinct market segments, the segmentation and resulting sales strategy you create on the first Monday of the month will probably still hold value on the second and third Mondays of that month. For efficiency's sake, you'll want to rely on that initial approach for a while, "freezing" it for a time so that you can focus on selling your products. But the world is constantly changing, and those consumer segments will eventually be out of date.

Organizations nowadays are often awed by how quickly things can change. For instance, in 1960, a U.S. company among the top 10 (based on revenues) in its industry could, on average, expect to remain among the top 10 for forty years. Statistics show that by 1990 this average period had decreased to only fourteen years, and today it could be for only ten or even fewer years depending on the industry![6] The same statistics show that the percentage of U.S. companies dropping out of the top-3 rankings (by revenues) in their industry grew from 2 percent in 1960 to 14 percent in 2008. The data underscore the importance of resilience and adaptability, of reviewing and revising your boxes regularly.*

People often have a hard time noticing gradual changes, as with the "boiling frog." For instance, parents don't tend to notice day-to-day changes in a child's growth but then, all of a sudden—poof!—their child seems to be much bigger and more mature. Checking in periodically can help, as aunts, uncles, and grandparents know—and the same is true for your boxes.

The good news is that you can sharpen your capacity to scan for

---

* In this context, we stand on the shoulders of several of our colleagues, notably Martin Reeves, who have recently explored the importance of achieving an "adaptive advantage." Given today's constantly evolving market positions, overwhelming flows of information, fuzzy company and industry boundaries, and huge "meta" changes in the overall social, cultural, and ecological environments we face worldwide, achieving adaptive advantage calls upon organizations and their leaders to be shrewd, experimental, and highly resilient in how they select, implement, and manage their future strategies. We see the successful reevaluation and replacement of boxes—the ability to know which new boxes to pursue and when to do so—as fundamental to inducing and exploiting such adaptive advantage. For more details see https://www.bcgperspectives.com/content/articles/future_strategy_business_unit_strategy_adaptive_advantage/.

change and sensitize yourself so that you're more aware of such gradual, under-the-radar shifts, and so that when there is ambiguity about
what particular signs or signals may mean, you ask even more questions, and dig even deeper.

The history of numerous organizations reveals the importance of
such heightened perception, and of agility—of not releasing effective
boxes too soon yet properly scrapping boxes when they become threat-
ened or obsolete, then quickly moving on to others. One classic example of a company that at least initially demonstrated this sort of resilience
is the Ford Motor Company, especially its founder Henry Ford's development of the Model T and the remarkably efficient assembly-line manufacturing process used to produce the storied car. Gottlieb Daimler
had already invented the four-wheeled gas-powered car in 1886,[7]
whereas Ford came onto the scene only in 1903.[8] Ford's first box, which
his company refined over about five years, was the inexpensive four-
wheel car, beginning with the "quadricycle," which had a very simple
frame, a gas-powered engine, and four bicycle-like wheels.* But Ford's
genius, among other things, was his realization that this small box
would soon be both insufficient and irrelevant. Consumers wanted
more. They wanted the power and efficacy of self-starting gas-powered
cars, but they also wanted them to be easy to repair, maintain, and modify, and they wanted to pay less for the privilege of owning and driving
them. Then, too, they and their counterparts in foreign countries
wanted cars that could withstand bumpy countryside roads.[9]

Ford's development of the Model T in 1908 transformed the car from
a relatively expensive, fragile, difficult-to-keep-up luxury item into an
affordable, sturdy, fast, efficient, and easier-to-maintain commodity for
the masses. Not only did he develop numerous innovative features
(such as lighter materials, stronger suspension, and a one-piece under-
side shell), he drastically reduced manufacturing costs (and therefore
the car's cost to consumers) by adding a movable conveyor belt to the
assembly line, thus shortening the car's manufacture time from what

---

* Indeed, the reason it was called Model T? They had started with Models A, B, C, K, N,
R, and S first.

had been 12 hours to a mere 93 minutes.[10] This broad new box—mass production of a sturdy, lower-cost car—led to explosive growth in the company and transformed the entire industry.* Production of the Model T ended in May 1927, but by then the company had produced 15,458,781 units of the car worldwide.[11]

Still, it is difficult to adapt and maintain continuous agility—to perfectly time the replacement of one brilliant new box with the next again and again.

Henry Ford remained steadfastly stuck with the Model T for years, but with urbanization, the popularity of increasingly glitzy Hollywood films, and Americans' ever-more-sophisticated cultural tastes, interests, and aspirations, automobiles soon became a means of communicating social standing and financial success as much as a mode of transportation.[12] Or as we see things, the box changed from that of "efficient cars" to "efficient cars that reflect who you are and how much money you're able to spend"—or from "vehicle" to "status symbol."

General Motors anticipated this dramatic cultural shift—and reflected it in the products it developed—but Ford Motor Company changed little about how it was designing, manufacturing, and marketing its product. General Motors introduced customer financing, numerous lines of cars (Chevrolet, Pontiac, Oldsmobile, Buick, and Cadillac, in increasing order of snazziness), offering more and more dazzling features and talismans of luxury, and created year-to-year models making customers with last year's car look like sorry outmoded also-rans. Meanwhile, Henry Ford remained perilously enamored of his reliable but lackluster monochrome (all-black) Model Ts.

As captured by Harvard Business School historian Richard S. Tedlow in *Denial*, a book illuminating the failure of many business leaders

---

* Notably, Henry Ford helped not only to innovate "more of the same" (that is, new features that made his company's cars faster, lighter, and stronger) but also to effect fundamental change by radically altering the efficiency with which cars could be manufactured. It is this latter form of creativity—in other words, not just coming up with new features or iterations of an existing product or approach but shifting things in a much more broad, essential, and powerful way—that is at the heart of the "new paradigm" sustainable approach we advocate.

to respond effectively to change, for the rest of his life Henry Ford was unable to recognize the momentous socioeconomic revolution that took place all around him.[13] Even when close family members pointed out what they felt he was missing, he remained rigidly committed to his once-winning car. For decades, GM and others enjoyed ever-increasing market share as Ford lost out on it. By the end of World War II, Ford Motor Company nearly reached bankruptcy.

How to "Know" When It's Time to Move to the Next Box

Learning how to know when it's time to replace an existing box with a new one requires you to fine-tune your prospective mindset. It requires you to become much better attuned to many of the various things that may change in the future over the midterm and the long haul, and be better able not only to detect the early signs of such change ahead of time but also to act upon these signals promptly and effectively. And it requires you to realize that even when everything is going well, you still need to be on the lookout. There are always forces at play that could wield tremendous influence over your organization at any moment, lifting it up or tossing it into a scalding fire of "if only we had realized the importance of this soon enough."

The signs of change—and your ability to see and prepare for them— occur along a spectrum. At one end of the spectrum, you're encountering vivid paradoxes and instances of *Caramba* that are relatively easy to detect and, hopefully, respond to. At the other end of the spectrum, you're scarcely able to see, or may be entirely blind to, the inevitability of change and the constant prospect of failure. You're so intoxicated by your success that unless you do what it takes to anticipate and respond to change, you may end up like Henry Ford, delivering an old model to a marketplace that has moved on. Sometimes when everything superficially appears to be moving along just perfectly, the truth is that you are a "sitting duck."

All along this spectrum are various sorts of "weak signals" that are difficult to detect because of your own current biases and perceptions (even though they may seem obvious to other people within or outside of your organization). Some typical signals: the entry of new competitors into your industry, growing anxieties among your organization's top people about the impact of new technologies, or changes, including apparently minor ones, in your organization's core performance metrics. Sometimes you notice the weak signals yet say to yourself, "no big deal."

WATCH FOR *CARAMBA*

One very strong indication that you need to reevaluate your current box is a *Caramba* moment or the occurrence of a *paradox*, where some of the key things you are currently observing seem markedly inconsistent with your existing approaches, beliefs, paradigms, or other boxes.

With *Caramba*, you are hit over the head with change. You're a cellphone manufacturer and the iPhone comes along. You're a traditional perfume shop and Sephora, with its enchanting new box of "try it for yourself," is now decimating your sales. Or perhaps nobody is buying your overpriced, watered-down coffee because a new, laptop-friendly, loungelike competitor with an array of delicious coffee blends just moved in next door. If a competitor brings massive change to your industry—*Caramba*—pay close attention and consider how you can promptly rethink your current boxes. It may seem like it's too late, and it *will* be tough to recover, but rethinking your boxes is the way to continue to thrive in spite of that *Caramba*.

You may also perceive the need to reconsider your existing boxes when you encounter a paradox: when multiple observed phenomena seem inconsistent with one or more of your current mental models.

In physics, for many years there was vigorous debate regarding the nature of light and matter. One theory initiated by seventeenth-century Dutch scientist and inventor Christian Huygens was that light behaved like a wave. The alternative, put forth later by British physicist and astronomer Sir Isaac Newton, was that it behaved like a set of particles. Subsequent research by leading physicists including Niels Bohr and

Albert Einstein found new data that contradicted each of these theories, and eventually the current theory, essentially that light and all matter have a "wave-particle duality," has emerged as a fundamental principle of quantum mechanics. Like these great scientists, we all tend to stick with a theory until it is no longer tenable, until contradictory information arises, until we reach a paradox.

Another interesting example entails the commonplace theory that, largely because of the economies of scale they can achieve, bigger enterprises can offer consumers lower, more competitive prices. The assumption is that when consumers compare a massive Home Depot "superstore" with a small local hardware store, they will inevitably, in the end, expect cheaper prices for similar products at Home Depot. The same could hold true for a giant grocery store as compared with a small local corner outlet. If you were conducting your own business analysis, you might develop a logical theory, a working hypothesis in your mind, that bigger size implies lower prices. But would this assumption prove true, as well, for commercial banks? Here's the paradox: In many cases, the small local bank is actually able to offer better service, features, flexibility, and even sometimes interest rates to local customers because of the personal connections that can be made with customers, the access to local knowledge about them, and thus the reduced risk of default. In this context, your original theory that "bigger size implies lower prices" was too broad—and thus it led to a paradox. This paradox, in turn, is an invitation to replace your first theory with a new and more useful one, that is, with a new, more helpful box.

Some simple and easy new boxes, in this example, would be "bigger size implies lower prices, except sometimes for banks," or "bigger size implies lower prices for grocery stores and hardware stores." But perhaps a more thoughtful new box would be "bigger size implies lower prices for tangible products where there are economies of scale in the supply chain." Of course, you might be able to imagine several other such boxes as well. When you detect a paradox, it will beckon you to refine your theory—or, what is much more likely, to develop a completely new one.

In business, and in life itself, when your observations about what is occurring "in front of" you no longer correspond with "the way we do things at Smith & Company" or "the way we've always thought about things here in Memphis," it may very well be time to seek a new box. A *Caramba* moment and a paradox are among the most obvious signals declaring that it's time to think in new boxes: You *know* that change is required.

Look around: You'll realize that there are numerous companies or organizations you know that have recently been confronted with such roiling paradoxes. For instance, consider those faced by someone like Peter Gelb, general manager of the world-famous Metropolitan Opera. Gelb told us that when he assumed leadership of the New York City–based organization in August 2006,[14] he "was painfully aware that radical steps needed to be taken" to address the company's growing financial difficulties, to make the Met more relevant to a broader group of people, and to address the reality that opera audiences were getting older and older. He remembered an era when the glitzy hall at Lincoln Center was absolutely packed with people of all ages—Gelb was an usher at the Met when he was a teenager. And he was struck by how one of the world's most celebrated and highly innovative cultural institutions could be suffering from such profound uncertainties. They were doing everything they were supposed to be doing, in terms of delivering quality opera, often to packed houses, and yet the finances were a struggle. These challenges inspired Gelb to conceive of all sorts of new measures to try to revitalize the company's audience, that is, to come up with a useful new box for the Met.

He worked to reimagine the Met's repertory with fresh productions of both classic and contemporary operas, sometimes bringing in widely known theater, film, and dance directors to oversee them and thus hopefully attract new (and more diverse) groups of operagoers. He helped launch Metropolitan Opera Radio, a twenty-four-hour satellite radio channel featuring both live performances from the Met as well as historical recordings—and initiated the live streaming of performances through the Met's website every week, reaching people across the globe for free. Gelb also began offering free dress rehearsals for the public and arranged for the company's opening-night performance to be projected onto giant screens at Times Square and Lincoln Center Plaza, where people living in or visiting New York City could come to enjoy the opera in the open air, free of charge.

But what about developing a whole new way of looking at the problems the Met was facing? Gelb knew that opera and other arts organizations worldwide were watching their costs rise more rapidly than the ticket revenues that could be raised—especially if they wanted to keep ticket prices affordable to the general public. This fundamental truth led to obvious budget difficulties, which most organizations were dealing with by trying to trim administrative and other costs in various ways and increase revenues from other channels (for example, from foundations and individual donors).

Gelb subsequently considered whether the Met might increase ticket revenues in some other interesting way—he and his colleagues moved into divergence. Assuming that total ticket revenues were defined roughly as the cost per ticket multiplied by the number of seats in the hall, how about increasing the size of the auditorium? And how about doing so not by decreasing seat pitch and legroom and cramming in additional rows of seats like the airlines have been known to do, but instead by creating an even more radical, more ambitious new approach?

Fashioning what can most certainly be deemed a brilliant new "box," Gelb helped launch *The Met: Live in HD*, a Peabody and Emmy Award–winning series of performance transmissions that are aired live simultaneously in movie theaters around the world. The series allows hundreds of thousands of people to watch the Met's performances simultaneously at a price point that is much more modest than that of most tickets sold at Lincoln Center. The broadcasts are in high-definition video and give audience members the feeling of having front-row seats (or even better seats, since the video cameras capturing the performances can zoom in on the stars and soloists of each opera, but also pan out to capture the biggest dramatic ensemble sequences). *The Met: Live in HD* is now broadcast on more than 1,500 screens in more than 50 countries to an average of 250,000 viewers—in six continents—worldwide. So much for declining audiences, and so much for plummeting revenues! These dazzling new live high-definition performances are delivering the Metropolitan Opera Association Inc. upwards of $11 million in additional revenues each year.

Most every paradox is an invitation to creativity, an opportunity to develop a new box that responds to it.

WATCH FOR WEAK SIGNALS, TOO

No two people can (or will) ever see or interpret—within them—any stimulus in front of them in exactly the same way. No matter how objectively "bright" or "dim" various signs may be, people and organizations, based on their unique subjective mental frameworks, will tend to see some of them more clearly and quickly than others. That is why you must create your own customized list of these more elusive signals, especially those that are likely to be the most relevant to you, your organization, and/or your overall industry. Armed with this list (which we hope you'll continue to monitor and revise), you can then scan for them carefully and respond proactively if you notice them beginning to occur.

Some common signals to watch out for:

- *A changing value proposition.* For instance, it's getting harder to charge a price premium for the product you're marketing—you're in charge of a luxury bus company and notice that there are a range of new companies that have far less luxurious bus interiors but pick people up at specific spots on the street and offer online $19 fares between Manhattan and Washington, D.C., whereas yours are all $75 or higher. Or perhaps there are substitute versions of the same product that cost significantly less, for example, you're a book publisher who notices that ebooks are retailing for $3.99, displacing the hardcover books you're currently selling for $24.95.
- *New unmet consumer or customer needs.* For example, you're running a company that manufactures laser printers and you're still making only black-and-white ones, whereas most consumers have come to ex-

pect color as a standard option; or you own an office products store and see that following the introduction of the iPad, there are no inexpensive, attractive protective cases for them yet available in the marketplace.

- *The entry of new competitors, new suppliers, or menacing changes in what your direct business partners are doing or offering.* For example, you're T.J. Maxx, and then H&M arrives on the scene; you're a high-end builder of luxury apartments and you're still sourcing granite from New Hampshire while your competitors are getting better-quality stone, at lower prices, from suppliers in Italy and India; you're Sony Music Entertainment and see that many of the musicians whose songs you used to distribute are now selling songs online independently; or you're managing Ultragames' traditional video game business and realize that your competitors are all close to launching mobile versions of their key franchises while you haven't been taking that channel seriously.
- *The advent of new breakthrough technologies and/or product or service offerings.* For example, the airline you're operating offers only coach-class passenger seats, organized in tightly squeezed-in rows, whereas several of your competitors are offering premium coach-class seats that provide extra legroom and recline into beds; or you're still manufacturing and distributing conventional wristwatches whereas newbie innovative companies are offering Wi-Fi-connected "Wrist-Pods" that not only tell you the current time but offer voice-recognition GPS and glow in different colors to indicate the weather wherever you happen to be.
- *Changes in your organization's core performance metrics.* For example, quarterly sales of one of your most important products suddenly increase or decrease, your inventory across all product categories is stagnant for long periods of time, or your annual revenues are much lower this year than last. We often like to compare the challenges of monitoring such metrics with the act of flying a helicopter. A helicopter pilot has to pay attention to many different dials that show critical aspects of the flight and need to remain within expected parameters. Of course, some dials are more critical than others. But in general, if

one key dial exceeds its parameters, the pilot needs to pay attention to that particular issue; if two dials show unusual results, a broader problem may be affecting the helicopter; if three or more dials are abnormal, there may be an emergency. Of course, managers can operate in this way only if they have a clear view of which "dials" need to be monitored and optimized. You need to know the metrics that matter before you can notice—and act upon—the fact that they're not quite right. Depending on your organization, these "dials" could be inventory levels, monthly revenues, share price, weekly expenses, hits on your website, sales in a particular segment, utilization rates of your service staff, market share, requests for brochures about your products, or any number of other metrics. For instance, at Ultragames, if you notice that sales of a newly launched update of one of your normally top-selling franchises are 30 percent below expectations, the time may have come to reexamine several of your existing assumptions.

- *Unfulfilled business and other potential opportunities.* Sometimes you may be astonished to notice something that has *not* yet occurred or been fulfilled, and therefore it signals to you an opportunity—and the need to replace your current boxes with new ones. For instance, if you were an executive at a traditional television news network in the 1970s who couldn't sleep, turned on the television, and wondered, "Why isn't there any twenty-four-hour network dedicated to covering the news around the clock?" you might have decided that it was time to replace the "We summarize the news at six o'clock" box with the "We cover all the news, all the time" one. If you worked in business strategy for a bus company and noticed large numbers of farm and factory workers milling outside of a newly constructed casino ninety miles from Manhattan—that is, large groups with apparently no way of getting home after a night of gambling—you might decide it's high time you tried to come up with some new routes for the company, including special buses going to and from the casino and similar venues.
- *Broad disruptive events.* You may also feel motivated to reexamine your current boxes in light of relatively broad disruptive events signaling that change is afoot. Among other things, these could include a new

regulatory scheme, a shift of all production in your industry to over-
seas facilities, a prolonged drought or change in environmental patterns, macroeconomic changes such as ongoing inflated commodity
prices, or sociological changes such as increased movements for democracy in the Arab world.

- *Premonitions, anxieties, and/or intuitions.* Sometimes the signals may
be even more subtle or insidious. Perhaps your assistant mentions to
you that your phone has been ringing much less than it did in prior
years. Or maybe several of the workers in your production department
mention that they're worried about water leaks in the factory windows,
and you develop renewed anxieties about vulnerabilities in your organization's overall physical plant. At Ultragames, perhaps you get word
that some of your star salespeople and game developers are getting
bored, as we saw earlier. Such worries, inklings, and realizations can
often be valuable warnings of significant impending change, of new
risks and new opportunities.

Again, these are just some examples of weak signals. As you think
about all the different factors influencing you and your organization
going forward, you will be able to identify many others.

In the late 1990s, Philips encountered such a situation when it realized that its coffeemakers were primarily traditional multi-cup drip coffee brewers, whereas more and more consumers want to make their
own personalized cups of coffee, select their own favorite specialized
flavors, and feel as though the coffee they're drinking is a premium
"luxe" product. In other words, *Caramba* had not yet occurred, and
there was no stark paradox—but it started to become clear that they
were overseeing the development and production of relatively standard
drip-filter coffeemakers, whereas consumers were eager for ones that
offered exciting new features and possibilities. The broad box of "same
coffee for everyone, at the same time" was showing hints of becoming
stale, and with time, these executives could have become the Henry
Fords of home coffee brewing, continuing to design and sell simple
models while the rest of the industry moved on.

Instead, and fortunately for Philips, the company quickly developed and began marketing its remarkably convenient and innovative single-serve Senseo coffeemaker, in partnership with Douwe Egberts, a Sara Lee subsidiary with a history dating back to 1753 as a traditional coffee roaster. Both companies—the appliance maker and the roaster—had started noticing the weak signals and they decided to address them together. In 2001, when Senseo was launched in the Netherlands, the market for coffeemakers was crowded and highly competitive, and the demand for coffee in general was relatively stagnant, increasingly crowded out by cold beverages and those without caffeine.[15] Even for a company as forward looking as Philips, there probably was a significant temptation to keep pace with the competition simply by innovating "more of the same," for instance by adding a few new features to an existing model of coffeemaker, or developing a coffeemaker that prepares the beverage more efficiently or inexpensively. In the extreme, it might even have been tempting to simply give up on the entire "coffeemaker" category.

Philips recognized the following relatively strong signal: It was still clinging to the well-established product paradigm focused on relatively expensive do-it-yourself coffeemakers whereas many consumers were gravitating toward the new box of relatively inexpensive yet highly personalized and sophisticated individual coffee-making.

Philips went into action. By building upon its ample experience creating, marketing, and distributing coffeemakers and other such small appliances—along with Douwe Egberts's expertise in quality coffee roasting—Philips generated a whole new coffee-making experience, and a wonderfully successful new box.

The engineers behind the Senseo coffeemaker recognized several key consumer trends that existing coffeemaker producers were not addressing as well as they could. These trends included a growing penchant among consumers to prepare their own separate cups of coffee whenever they wanted it (rather than brewing an entire pot, much of which eventually ended up in the sink), and a similar desire to personalize the taste of their individual respective cups of coffee. These designers understood, too, that people wanted increased speed and efficiency when preparing their daily coffees as well as a sense of the "luxury" of drinking a foamy Italian-style espresso. The Senseo addressed all of these things, allowing users to select separate pods of coffee (available in all different flavors) and brew their own separate cups of foamy espresso-like coffee within just half a minute. The Senseo also boasted a unique forward-leaning design and initially a clever blue color (although it's now available in numerous fun colors), distinguishing itself from other coffeemakers and giving it a sleek elegance that some say only adds to its aura of luxury. Of consequence, too: The Senseo coffeemaker cost much less than most espresso machines, which were a key alternative for single-serve coffee, retailing for about $70–$130, depending on the model.[16] In the first four years of its introduction alone, Philips sold 15 million Senseo units worldwide, and as of 2012, it remains the leader in Western Europe in its category, despite a much more crowded competitive landscape.

The story is not yet over: As always, the world continues to change, and some of the newest observed trends relate to consumers always wanting the ultimate in freshness for their coffee. And even if single-serve remains useful most of the time (for the sake of convenience and variety), there are times when customers want to be able to make a whole pot, for example when they have guests. And so in late 2012, Philips, still in partnership with Douwe Egberts, launched the Senseo Sarista in the Netherlands, with additional country launches planned for 2013. With a simple twist, Sarista grinds the beans before making the coffee, something no other single-serve coffee machine can do, meeting the freshness criteria—and it also allows you to prepare one cup, two cups, or a full pot of coffee at the touch of a button. The world continues to change, and Philips's coffee offerings with it.

Hindustan Lever Limited: Overcoming *Caramba* and Learning to Heed Weak Signals

In August 1999, John Ripley, a senior vice president at Unilever, looked out at the audience gathered before him and concluded his remarks by saying "it's that learning process that has caused our company, world-wide, to once again re-invent ourselves. We are no longer a company that satisfies the needs of a select group of people, we are a company that provides for all people. We at Unilever have looked at the new market and the new business paradigm before us and have not asked the question of *should* we compete, but rather *how* will we compete." He reflected on everything that had taken place in recent years as he left the podium.[17]

The story of Hindustan Lever Limited (or "HLL"), the local subsidiary of Unilever in India, during those years, reflects what can happen when corporate executives are not fully cognizant of weak signals, along with a best-practice example of recovering from that. Leading with a hugely popular brand called "Surf," HLL, by 1965, had grown to dominate India's market for various consumer products, claiming a 70 percent share of the Indian laundry detergent powder market. Initially, HLL's competition was not another brand of detergent: It was the traditional Indian practice of washing clothes with hard bars of laundry soap. To encourage people to switch, HLL developed a network of sales-people who traveled around the country, showing people how to use detergent and explaining how easy it was in comparison with soap bars. HLL backed this up with a strong national advertising campaign. For years, it was king of India's so-called organized sector of premium laundry detergent manufacturers, and by all accounts, HLL scarcely noticed or worried about other players in the broad, down-market "unorganized sector" that lacked HLL's big-company resources and whose products were inferior.

Competition emerged in the 1970s from an unexpected source: a brand named Nirma, a less efficient but much cheaper form of detergent. Developed in his own home by an entrepreneur named Karsanbhai Patel, Nirma cost one-third of the price of Surf, and it became popular even though it did not contain any perfume and neither bright-ened nor softened the clothes that were washed with it. Nirma had no field force or sales organization (the earliest orders were fulfilled by Patel himself, riding on a bicycle from shop to shop); it grew based on word of mouth along with simple advertising and promotion. The com-pany avoided paying sales tax by appointing distributors as commission agents, eventually developing a system using vans and then trucks that was dramatically simpler than HLL's countrywide sales agent distribu-tion.

Nirma became phenomenally successful—by 1977, it was the second-strongest detergent brand in India, selling just under a third the volume of Surf, boasting a market share of 12 percent, versus Surf's 30.6 percent.

As Nirma grew, several aspects of its strategy remained distinct from that of HLL. Whereas Surf was sold in classier (though more expensive to manufacture) paper containers, Nirma's yellow powder was mixed and inserted in polythene bags by low-cost manual laborers. Nirma also benefited from an innovative logo—Patel designed an image fea-turing his daughter (rather than the Indian housewife typically used by many of the other cottage manufacturers of laundry detergent)—and Patel's advertising using this trademark, together with an unforgettable "Nirma washes clothes white as milk" jingle, became ubiquitous across India.

Many of the customers who became loyal to Nirma were less afflu-ent; they had never used Surf, instead switching directly from inconve-nient soap bars to Nirma's increasingly famous coarse yet relatively cheap and effective yellow powder.

HLL did not notice this new threat for some time. As often can hap-pen to companies doing business in emerging markets, HLL identified its potential customers as India's wealthier consumers and thus did not immediately notice this lower-cost competitor. Nirma was right in front of HLL. But, absent *Caramba*, HLL for years did nothing to address Nirma's growing presence in the marketplace. Indeed, in 1977, when HLL's then marketing director, S. Sen, finally started to notice Nirma's increasing market presence and wrote to HLL's branch manager in

Ahmedabad requesting information on the company, the branch manager reportedly fired back, "You don't expect me to know about every junk product coming out of Ahmedabad."

At that point at least, HLL leaders were too confident about HLL's position in the marketplace to grasp Nirma's formidable, ever-growing position among consumers in the laundry detergent marketplace. Between 1977 and 1985, Nirma's sales grew at a compound rate of 49 percent. By 1985, Nirma was selling 200,000 tons a year—and its market share was 58 percent compared with Surf's 8.4 percent. But critically, HLL was still not significantly attuned to Nirma's market position, if only because its own market was still in fine shape. HLL still perceived its core market as "affluent Indian consumers" and Surf's sales and revenues were still growing and helping drive profits for the company. Arguably, HLL was not quite yet able to acknowledge what in retrospect might seem to have been a clear set of weak signals: the rapidly growing market for consumer products among lower-income people in India and Nirma's increasingly dominant grip on sales of laundry detergent in that very market. For a while longer, HLL stuck to its established strategies and outlook.

But then, in 1986, challenging HLL's once-controlling position even further, Nirma announced that it was testing a new detergent bar that would compete directly with HLL's leading Rin detergent bar product. After Nirma began marketing this new detergent bar, Mr. Sen of HLL, referring to Mr. Patel, reportedly conceded: "[W]e lost consumers and profits to him." After years of eluding HLL, the threat from Nirma became much more difficult for HLL to deny. It was time for HLL to toss out its old boxes—boxes that concentrated on affluent consumers only, on producing quality products rather than reasonably priced ones, on using a large and costly national sales team—and replace them with new ones that would head off Nirma.

Once this *Caramba* moment happened, HLL moved into high gear. It cut costs by changing packaging (from cartons to poly bags) and by simplifying the approach to distribution. It ran a national advertising campaign to show that Surf, with double the amount of detergent of Nirma, was closer to Nirma in price than first appeared. It developed an innovative approach for deciding exactly *where* to establish new plants based on information about the availability of raw materials and the sales potential of its products in specific regions throughout India. And to benefit from the same low-cost-labor approach that Patel had always relied upon for Nirma, HLL set up small third-party manufacturing units in each of these optimal locations. Each of these production units was an independent contractor that could hire local workers and thus reduce costly labor conflicts.

Then, too, refocusing its R&D to explore the needs of the rising but less affluent Indian consumer, HLL introduced a new low-cost detergent brand in India called Wheel. HLL created advertising distinguishing Wheel from Nirma, asserting that Wheel offered extra power, better lather, and was "safe on hands and clothes." HLL also relaunched its Rin product, using advertising that claimed that Rin offered a less expensive wash with more lather than the competing Nirma product. Soon HLL was successfully competing with Nirma in the popular, lower-cost segment of the market. Perhaps because of HLL's improved vigilance and awareness of competition, when Procter & Gamble entered India in 1990 with a high-end laundry detergent called Ariel, HLL responded promptly and proactively, stepping up advertising for Rin and Surf, and using an aggressive expedited product development approach to come up with Surf Ultra, a new, higher-quality, more expensive premium laundry product. Surf Ultra would be a more concentrated product: A little bit of Surf Ultra would go a long way in cleaning your clothes. Remarkably, the product development approach that previously would have taken HLL two years to accomplish instead took the company only four months. Laboratory testing of the product, creation of its packaging and promotional materials, work on its scent, its test marketing, and the development of its production and distribution models all happened simultaneously during that highly coordinated four-month period.

The outcome was a big win for HLL. Its new-product development, marketing, manufacturing, and distribution approaches—its expertly conceived new boxes—were just what the company needed to stave off Ariel's growth. In 1992, when 11 percent of India's overall laundry detergent market was generally attributed to concentrated premium detergents, HLL dominated the sector: Of the 11 percent HLL scored 7 percent (3 percent with Rin concentrate and 4 percent with Surf Ultra); in comparison, P&G held only the remaining 4 percent. And HLL's total value share of the overall laundry detergent market went up from 39 percent to 42 percent. Perhaps more than anything, HLL seemed to have learned a valuable lesson about the importance of maintaining a nimble strategic outlook that anticipates, notices, and acts upon "weak signals" rather than just waiting around for the most obvious and dramatic instances of *Caramba*. As an organization, HLL decided that a key theme going forward would be "edge," staying on top of the competition by maintaining "marketing edge, distribution edge, and technology edge." S. Datta, then the chairman of HLL, stated, "[I]f we come up with a new vision, we must review our structures and procedures to match that new vision. If our current ways of working impede our ambition, we must change these ways of working." And as John Ripley mentioned, HLL was now a company that provided for all people, not just a select group. It was no longer about whether HLL should compete, but how.

EYES WIDE OPEN: KEEP ON DOUBTING AND EVOLVING, EVEN IN SUCCESS

There's a counterintuitive exercise we often ask our clients to ponder: If you are the CEO of the perfect company where operations are superb, everyone and everything functions with perfect efficiency, and the company is bringing in excellent revenues and profits each year, what would be your role as CEO? Many people respond by saying, "Keep doing what you're doing!" Or simply, "Sit back and relax." That might work in a world that wasn't changing. But our answer, from the perspective of seeking robust yet also sustainable creativity, is that your role is to reevaluate things relentlessly, to work constantly to help your company determine *which* new box(es) to implement next, and *when* exactly to begin doing so. Even when your creativity is empowering you to generate all sorts of valuable, game-changing new boxes, even when you have just experienced *Eureka* and released a highly profitable new product, the struggles continue. Surviving success can be just as challenging as succeeding in the first place.

In other words, even when you are not being dogged by obvious paradoxes or *Caramba* moments, and even when you see few if any weak signals, you must do your very best to keep your eyes wide open. Even when things seem to be moving along well, you can be vulnerable.

Consider, for a moment, the legendary creativity of chef, entrepreneur, and serial innovator Ferran Adrià, who presided over elBulli, an award-winning eatery near Barcelona, Spain, that was, until its recent closure, one of the most revered restaurants (and coveted dinner reservations) in the world.[18] Adrià won numerous accolades for his inventive combinations of ingredients (imagine: "seaweed waffles" or "pumpkin seed and peanut risotto with saffron jelly and curry air") served in a beautifully designed space in a spectacular coastal setting. elBulli was open only for dinner (serving just fifty people each night) and closed down for six months every year. This was originally driven by seasonality, but even after Adrià could easily have filled the restaurant every day, he insisted on this schedule to allow him to refresh his boxes regularly. In its final years, as many as two million people clamored for the opportunity to eat there each year, but only eight thousand got the chance to do so.[19] In 2007 *Restaurant* magazine named elBulli the "best restaurant in the world."

In addition to the quality of elBulli's food, much of Adrià's and his colleagues' renown could be attributed to their seemingly constant generation of ideas and endless reevaluation of what they could do to expand, improve, and build upon the enterprise. Or, as we like to say, Adrià mastered Step 5 by persistently reexamining the mental models, or boxes, that he and his colleagues were using to operate the business and forge its future. Adrià made sure that, in addition to carefully studying and mastering the science of cooking (and the range of approaches that chefs can use to prepare, combine, and present various ingredients), he and his staff met for ongoing group creative meetings. Together they regularly produced all sorts of new ideas for recipes, new approaches to presenting dishes, new menus, even new concepts for the pottery and cutlery the restaurant used.

But Adrià's generation of ideas did not begin and end with the "filling in" of the "We are a restaurant" box, or even the "We are the best restaurant in the world" box. Presumably knowing that the ideas behind this restaurant (and the meals it would serve) would remain relevant (and interesting to the public) for only so long, Adrià also worked diligently to broaden—and constantly revisit—the organization's overall vision and business paradigm. "First it was a search for survival," he said about his and elBulli's fundamental strategy, "and later, for creative freedom."[20] Adrià sustained the business by creating a catering company, a consulting firm that helped develop new restaurant and culinary concepts for hotels and other companies, and a publishing company that released lavishly illustrated books on the philosophy of cuisine (books that other publishers had rejected).

In 2010, Adrià decided to close the restaurant.[21] "Part of my job is to see into the future, and I could see that our old model is finished. . . . It's time to figure out what comes next," he told *Time* magazine.[22] At a special event to fête the closing of the restaurant in 2011, Adrià told members of the press and numerous famous chefs who had come to mark the occasion, "My brother Albert said we had to kill the monster. . . . But I said, 'No, we have to tame it!'"[23]

In the spirit of transformation and reevaluation rather than death, Adrià announced plans to use it as an international creativity center and to launch a not-for-profit foundation to keep the enterprise going. To identify a sustainable model, Adrià sponsored an MBA case study competition to seek submissions from students from a range of business schools, including ESADE, Harvard, Berkeley, Columbia, and London.[24] In what is by all accounts his quintessential fashion, Adrià solicited a broad range of ideas for how the foundation should be set up such that it would build on best practices but also promote creativity and innovation. As Carles Abellán, a former member of the elBulli creative team, once said of Adrià's fierce inquisitiveness and relentless collection, examination, and reexamination of ideas: "[He always] made me question everything, rethink everything. . . . There was one requirement: the interest to comprehend the 'why' of everything."[25] In yet another creative postscript to elBulli, in mid-2011, PepsiCo announced a new "innovation partnership" with Adrià, whereby he would work with PepsiCo to create new methods and concepts for creative food innovation, particularly focused on healthier foods, breakfast options, and more.[26]

As we see it, inherent in Step 5 of our approach to creativity is just this: constantly asking "why?" Step 5 calls upon you to doubt the status quo, to wonder why you are currently finding success (rather than assuming it will continue forever), to take new risks, and, perhaps above all, stretch yourself to learn, much as Adrià demonstrated in his ruthless quest for new possibilities and approaches, both how to accept and how to transcend your inevitable experiences of *failure*.

Consider, on this score, the amusing anecdote shared with us by a friend who recently stumbled upon a group of employees at a major office products company celebrating together boisterously, sipping on champagne and munching on delicious hors d'oeuvres. When our friend asked them what the occasion for the party was, one of their senior executives explained, "We're celebrating the failure of a project," and when asked to elaborate, he explained that that meant they were still a company that was open to taking creative risks.

Along similar lines, consider the "Heroic Failure" awards reportedly offered to certain executives in the New York offices of Grey advertising. According to *The Wall Street Journal,* the Gotham division of Grey grants these awards in recognition of highly risky acts of creativity that, though they led to failure, reflected keen inspiration and a willingness to break with convention. Amanda Zolten, a senior vice president at the firm, apparently qualified for this accolade when she tried to impress potential clients from a kitty litter company by meeting them in a conference room and, at the end of the meeting, letting the prospective clients know that none of them had detected the odorless box of the company's kitty litter product that had been sitting under the conference table the entire time (together with the feces of Zolten's cat, Lucy Belle). Two of the potential clients walked out, and at the time her boss gave her the award, for taking an extraordinary risk, it was unclear whether they would win the business.[27]

Taking risks, failing in order to succeed, and learning to recognize when your current box needs to be exchanged for a new one are all fundamental to creating an organization that not only keeps pace but stays ahead of the proverbial curve.* Not every new idea will succeed, and that's fine. In fact, as wonderful as it can be to come up with a new idea, recognizing when it's the right time for an existing box to be adjusted, or an old box to be revived, can be equally valuable.

As an effective leader at Ultragames, you will be constantly reevaluating the new ideas that were recently selected and launched to make sure they are still valid and viable. You'll be checking in on the "business development" progress of the salesperson focusing on entertrainment. You will check the status of the research and game development for the therapeutic product designed to fight ADHD or other learning disorders, and simultaneously keep an eye out for new data about diagnoses and treatment approaches. You'll be scanning the activities of your competitors—both video game companies and education and healthcare companies targeting learning and other disorders—to see whether they're copying your new boxes or perhaps coming up with some of their own. You'll be analyzing key relevant trends in the world around you to try to determine whether your new areas of focus are well placed and whether you shouldn't also begin considering other market segments and other new innovative directions. You might even return to the lists of ideas you previously generated during divergence and convergence, combing through for concepts that, though rejected at the time, might still be worth considering for the future.

Above all, Step 5 entails ensuring that your ongoing creative process is an inductive one that allows for—and engages—complexity and critical uncertainties. Remain vigilant. Look for ways in which you may be failing or falling behind and acknowledge them when they occur. Listen to your intuitions about impending revolutions in your industry. But these precautions will not be sufficient. To survive success, you

---

* Keeping pace with change is critical not only to achieving dazzling innovations but also to simply making sure that the good things you have going for you don't slip away. As the character Tancredi Falconeri says in Giuseppe Tomasi de Lampedusa's posthumously published novel *The Leopard:* "In order for everything to stay as it was before, everything has to change."

must also frequently revisit the process of divergence and convergence—indeed all five steps that we outline in this book—rather than, for example, merely reinstituting last year's plans and "deciding" (or often just hoping) you'll grow sales again by 10 percent.

More than anything, we believe it is critical to reward people for asking interesting questions and challenging the status quo and, for your part, to do your very best to remain open to the constant and inexorable flow of change, to new visions, new concepts, new trends, to the infinite range of new possible boxes.

From Inspiration to Innovation: Building Bold New Boxes—and Then Filling Them In

□□□□□□□□□□□□□□□□□□□□□□□□□□□□□□□□□□□□□

If you can dream it, you can do it.

—WALT DISNEY

MAGINE IF YOU WERE ABLE to wear a special suit equipped with wings and then, much like the mythical Icarus, fly on your own, soaring from great heights to land safely at your desired destination. Could this ever be possible? What would have to change in your perception so that what had always seemed fundamentally impossible to you was now suddenly *possible*?

In March 2012, Swiss daredevil Remo Läng leapt out of an airplane flying over the Verbier ski resort in Switzerland, jumping in a free fall from more than twenty thousand feet above sea level.[1] Wearing a fabric wing suit, he flew sixteen miles across the Swiss Alps, landing seven minutes later in the Aosta Valley, in neighboring Italy.

Source: Marcel Kuhn and Remo Läng, used by permission

Läng encountered temperatures plummeting below minus 50 degrees (whether you prefer Celsius or Fahrenheit), reached speeds exceeding 300 miles per hour, and transcended the summit of Grand Combin, which is more than 14,000 feet high. By all accounts, this was the first time in world history that a person wearing only a wing suit had flown over a mountain range.

How did Remo Läng come to think that flying hundreds of miles per hour over a dangerous rocky mountain range in a mere wing suit would ever be possible? How did he shift from fear to confidence? Exactly what had to happen inside his mind before he would agree to take his very first solo flight?

In our theory, he first had to replace the box that said, "Humans cannot fly on their own—that's impossible" to one that said, "Of course humans can fly, why not?"* Once he made this dramatic shift in his thinking—from the very broad box of "impossible" to the equally broad one of "possible"—he was then able to create paradigms that were slightly more narrow, but still quite grand in scope (and still equally optimistic), such as: "Humans can fly on their own . . . like birds" or "Humans can fly on their own . . . like airplanes."

Of course, none of these shifts in perception, at least at first, presented a perfect hypothesis. An airplane does not take flight in the same way a bird does—and a human being in a wing suit cannot do so exactly like either an airplane or a bird. Indeed, when engineers were developing the wings and other technologies that enable airplanes to fly, they were not well served by modeling them slavishly after the bodies and aerodynamics of birds. It took time for them to realize, for instance, that it wouldn't work well to build airplanes equipped with flapping wings! As a practical matter, then, an airplane is not, and cannot be, a replica of a bird. In the same way, a cannon is not an improved version of the catapult, and a lightbulb is not an improved candle.

---

* Remember: Any box that you create will always be a *simplification* or reduction of reality. It is your mind's way of creating a new category or concept or outlook to try to understand the world in front of you. The idea that anything is "impossible" is such a simplification but so, too, is the idea that it is "possible"! When you shift between the two, you're exchanging one snapshot of reality for another.

Remember that creating new boxes, especially paradigm-shifting ones like these, is a saga of working toward freedom. And then more freedom. When the engineers who first created the box leading to the development of the airplane said, "Flying in airplanes *is* possible," they then became free to consider the idea "Airplanes can fly like birds." Yet they also had to abandon their initial hypothesis to develop a vehicle that many people would agree to fly in.

Likewise, once Läng and other daredevils saw some appeal and practical possibilities in "Humans can fly on their own like birds" or "Humans can fly on their own like airplanes," they could then use these big new inspiring ideas, in turn, to imagine and experiment with all sorts of new approaches to fulfilling them. Sure, Läng and others in his field were restrained by certain core principles of engineering and physics (which govern both birds and airplanes). But they also had to challenge some of the existing protocols before they could ultimately decide that creating a wing suit would be the most appealing and feasible approach.

And then, once Läng and others developed this new core box of "Humans can fly using a wing suit"—and then perfected the technology to make it as safe and effective as possible—they were free to envisage all sorts of courageous wing suit journeys they could make. Each of these subsequent ideas for the stunts Läng and others could execute—"I could leap off public monuments," "I could jump out of the window of one of the world's tallest skyscrapers," "I could free-fall from an airplane over rocky snow-covered mountains in Switzerland"—is yet another box that fits within the big one of "Humans can fly using a wing suit."

Boxes come in all shapes and sizes, and you can come up with a seemingly endless number of further boxes that fit within one, almost like so-called Russian dolls.

As you begin to use our five-step process, you'll quickly discover these boxes within boxes within boxes. And as you create more and more specific "boxes within boxes," they'll lead you to more focused objectives and more useful ideas.*

---

* Eventually, you'll find yourself engaged in the separate though related process of innovation, where you and your colleagues will take one particular box—such as a spe-

As you move between these various "levels" of boxes, you will need to use our five-step process to constantly reexamine and modify your thinking. Each time you create another core box—or box within a box—you make at least one if not several shifts in perception. These shifts are the fuel of creativity.

In this chapter and the next one, on scenarios, we will outline some of the most useful applications of "thinking in new boxes" that we have seen in the business world. The first of those is the new "core box" that is described above. Organizations often ask us, "What is going to be our next big thing? How can we leverage the value of our brand more broadly? Where should we focus our attention in the future? How can we create a bold new vision?"

Building a new box after addressing such questions can bring about a dramatic shift in strategy, or one that may seem relatively subtle. Sometimes a new box is formed that, though it is closely related to the original one, nudges the organization toward new businesses or toward a new orientation within its primary field. Michelin and IBM moved into new boxes when they changed from a product or technology orientation to a services or solutions one—without abandoning core products or technologies. Michelin, the tire manufacturer, shifted its broad box to become a road safety specialist, which led to its becoming a travel guide publisher, while IBM has entered the consulting business. Their examples show that building new boxes can complement core businesses—and, if necessary, replace them.

Sometimes, however, thinking in new boxes is about revising a box (and the nature of a company) more fundamentally. Take, for instance, Danone, the food giant. It made a significant shift in its self-definition as a company, from a vision based on "good taste" to one focused on "good health." Once it overhauled its basic strategic outlook, Danone sold off businesses relating to beer, biscuits, and sauces and began focusing on baby food, yogurt, and other healthy-product lines.

---

cific idea or process improvement or application—and then iterate on it in new and exciting ways as you "implement" and bring it into reality, where it will continue to be enhanced and improved upon over time.

Apple was originally a manufacturer of popular personal computers, and leveraged its expertise to expand into the multimedia business. Initially there was no obvious reason for it to contemplate taking on Sony and its ubiquitous Walkman. But once Apple had created a new box and viewed itself through a different lens—as a multimedia company that knows circuits and bytes—the notion of a digital music player was perfectly logical. This kind of paradigm shift demonstrates the limits of customer research (without negating the value of it). Steve Jobs said, "it's hard for [customers] to tell you what they want when they've never seen anything remotely like it."[2] This was in reference to desktop video editing, but it could just as easily be applied to the iPad or iPhone.*

Once a broad new core box has been created, our system can also be used to "fill it in"—as when BIC filled in its new "disposable objects" box with lighters and razors. This entails following the five steps to come up with lots of new ideas that help implement a broader mission, or strategic vision.

"There hasn't been an exciting innovation in our industry for some time," people often say to us. "How can we be the ones to come up with it?" Or: "Our competitors are developing all sorts of new business models and products—what can *we* do?" Or: "We've invented an amazing new technology. What specific applications of it can we develop that will be relatively quick and easy to bring to market?"

In each of these instances, we take a "larger" box and help the organization envision "smaller" ones that fit within it.

Imagine, for instance, that a group of executives at the hypothetical Happy Coffee Company said, "We're one of the greatest coffee shop chains in the world. How can we sell more coffee in our stores?" They might immediately toss around ideas for all sorts of new coffee-related products: coffee from all over the world (Bali, Guatemala, Timbuktu, etc. . . .), coffee of different roasts and strengths (Mega Dark, Super

---

* Henry Ford is often quoted as saying something similar, such as "If I had asked people what they wanted, they would have said faster horses," but it seems he didn't actually say that, according to Patrick Vlaskovitz's research. See http://blogs.hbr.org /cs/2011/08/henry_ford_never_said_the_fast.html.

Lite, etc. . . .), coffee with added flavors (Nutmeg, Bourbon Cream, Hot Pepper, etc. . . .). This so-called brainstorming might churn up an idea that would help them sell more coffee.

But that type of brainstorming is yet another illustration of the challenges inherent in trying to think outside an existing box. For Happy Coffee Company, that box would be "we are sellers of coffee."

Now consider what might happen if those executives first asked themselves, "What is the Happy Coffee Company?" What sorts of new product and service offerings would those same executives have imagined if, through the five-step creative process, they had come up with numerous unexpected answers to that question? What if they had had fun considering many of them, rejecting some, and embracing and refining others, before settling on a few broad core boxes they could use to spark ideas for new products and services, such as "Happy Coffee serves as the largest office in the world" or "We rent a huge amount of real estate" or even "Happy Coffee is Yuppie Headquarters, the home away from home for the young and affluent"?

After coming up with these broad boxes, the executives could develop all sorts of ingenious new offerings that transcend "more of the same." So perhaps, by thinking in the new broad box of "Largest Office in the World," they consider offering Skype-style teleconferencing, document scanners, printing-on-demand, iPad and laptop quick chargers, and even soundproof conference rooms. A similar range of potential new products and services could be imagined for each of the other such "broad" boxes the executives might have come up with. And indeed, we recently read about a coffee shop in Moscow called Tsiferblat, or Clockface Café, where drinks, snacks, printing, and wifi are all free—all customers pay for is the time they spend there.

How did Nintendo, which started out as a playing card company, change into a global leader in high-tech video consoles (which the Ultragames founders would likely have played as boys), and the games and applications that run on them? How did Tiffany & Company go from a stationery company to selling high-end jewelry? LG launched as an industrial chemical manufacturer. What had to change inside the minds of its leaders in order for them to decide that LG should become the innovative high-tech appliance company it is today? They thought of new boxes. None of these companies could have undergone such radical transformations until their leaders significantly modified one or more of their basic assumptions.

Only once they did that were they free to create a new box that either immediately made sense or, as is more often the case, inspired several new ones within it, and then maybe even still more boxes within one of those.*

Granted, the old paradigm for creativity can produce some good ideas. If executives at Nintendo had simply sat down and said, "We're a playing card company, but we should be doing something new, so what should that be?" perhaps they would have succeeded, but more likely, they would have ended up running around in circles within their existing box of "We're a playing card company." They would have been trapped in the prison of their old biases and assumptions, their tried-and-true ways of thinking about Nintendo.

The five-step process—which begins with the all-important process of *doubting* your most important boxes ("What is Nintendo?" "What is a game?" "What kind of children want our products?")—is a much better way to shift your thinking, which, in turn, will free you up to generate such winning ideas as the Nintendo Wii or its bestselling Super Mario Bros. games.†

As Step 5 of our process suggests, continuously examining your old boxes—and allowing your perceptions to evolve—is the best way to sustain your creativity.

---

* *Eureka* can happen early in the creative process (for instance, through the development of a wonderfully imaginative new corporate vision that promptly spawns brilliant new product ideas, as in BIC's case) or much later on, as in La Poste's case, or even perhaps after you've gone through the five steps not once or twice, but numerous times.
† And as we like to remind people, it is critical to do everything you can to "survive your own success" by continuing to pursue the five steps over time, constantly reevaluating your boxes and replacing them with new ones. Even with its tremendous initial success with the Wii console, Nintendo has recently seen increasing competition, especially from designers and distributors of games and other apps that run on tablets, mobile phones, and other PDAs. See http://www.gamesdiviner.com/nintendo-struggles -against-mobile-games.html.

CHICAGO PUBLIC SCHOOLS: SHIFTING FROM
VIGILANCE TO PREVENTION

In some cases, a shift of perception can be the difference between life and death.

With more than 400,000 students, the Chicago Public Schools system (CPS) faces profound challenges, but arguably none is more pressing than the horrifying number of students each year who are shot. In the 2007–2008 school year, 211 CPS students were shot and 23 of them died; in the following year those numbers rose to 290, with 32 deaths. More than 500 school-aged children shot and more than 50 killed in just two years! These shootings did not occur on school property, and 35 percent of them occurred during the summer holiday, with 33 percent on weekends and school holidays. Still, a number of the shootings occurred when students were on their way to or from school, creating an oppressive climate of fear in many of the city's schools.

Chicago's established strategy for coping with this violence was *vigilance*. Based on the assumption that many of these shootings could be attributed to gangs, the conventional wisdom for a number of years had been that CPS, the Chicago Police Department, and the entire community needed to be increasingly watchful and build an enhanced security infrastructure. Significant effort and expense were being put into things like more surveillance cameras in high-crime areas, and additional security guards.

These measures were helpful—in fact, vitally important—but as the death toll climbed, CPS leaders began to doubt whether these measures were sufficient. They wondered, "Shouldn't we come up with creative ways to keep our students from being shot?"

CPS partnered with some of our colleagues in Chicago to accomplish this critical mission. We all understood that before they would be able to come up with creative new measures, these leaders, and their counterparts in various city agencies, needed to shift their perceptions. Their mental model had long focused on using stepped-up surveillance to apprehend perpetrators. As we began our work with them we began to focus more on *prevention*, that is, how to keep students out of harm's way.

After studying reams of data about each of the more than five hundred shooting incidents, we worked with these civic leaders to come up with ways to identify at-risk children *before they got shot*. For each shooting, we asked: Where did it happen? At what time? In what sort of area did it occur? We looked at the profile of each victim: age, gender, race, and family situation. We looked at each victim's attendance record and academic record, and whether he or she had faced any disciplinary proceedings. We noted, too, the type of school for each victim (that is, whether it was a general school, a charter school, a remedial one). We ended up looking at more than fifty factors, from a wide variety of sources, and then we looked at the same factors for the general population (more than 110,000 high school students).

We began to create a new paradigm of violence prevention based on the idea that if you could actually predict which students were most likely to be shot, you could protect them in a much more proactive and effective way.

Working with CPS, we found a range of factors highly correlated to a student getting shot, and then tried to focus on those factors that were within the control of CPS. We identified four key risk factors: attendance (those who got shot missed an average of 40 percent of school days, compared with 15 percent for the general population), academic performance (victims were five times more likely to be not on track to graduate), in-school behavior (victims were eight times more likely to have committed a violent act at school), and the type of school (victims were vastly more likely to attend an "alternative school," where CPS administrators placed students when the traditional neighborhood schools couldn't handle them).

With this focused profile, one can imagine solutions that would address the issues at the alternative schools and improve attendance, academic achievement, and classroom behavior. But instead, as the leaders at CPS began to shift their outlook to a very proactive one aimed at early prevention, we all agreed to use the model to project the probability of each student being shot. Accordingly, we developed a model that used the data to assign a specific probability of being shot to each student and thereby identified a small set of students who were most at risk.

The entire population was grouped into four primary categories: First, about 200 students were deemed "ultra-high risk," with a risk of getting shot of more than 20 percent, more than 50 times higher than average; about 1,000 students were deemed "very high risk," with a risk between 7.5 and 20 percent; about 8,500 were deemed "high risk," with a risk between 1 and 7.5 percent. The remaining 100,000 students had a risk of getting shot under 1 percent.

The model suggested that 10 percent of the "shot" population would fall into the "ultra-high risk" category, with 20 percent in the "very high risk." All of that meant that we expected 30 percent of the shootings to come from a group of 1,200 students, about 1 percent of the CPS population.

Once CPS had this new box of "prevention," it could then "fill it" with strategies to protect *those* students, rather than trying to protect everyone equally. Those programs continued, for example through awareness-enhancement programs implemented directly in the school curricula, and other experiments including one-on-one mentoring. Our analysis showed that most of these young people didn't have any meaningful relationships with adults. Not surprisingly, they were often truant, and got into trouble even when they *were* able to show up at school. And so in parallel to the risk assessment, CPS developed more aggressive interventions, beefed-up security in particularly risky neighborhoods, and a "safe passage" program to help students make it across gang boundaries—in addition to directly impacting gun violence, studies have shown that students worried about personal security do not perform well academically, continuing the downward spiral. In some instances, CPS helped relocate students to schools where they would be safer.

In the 2009–2010 school year, there was a 16 percent drop in shootings, and a new ethic of cooperation began to take hold in Chicago's 120 high schools. Still filling in the box of "prevention," CPS used the data on students to create a "safety metric" for each school based on its specific location. This normalizing across all neighborhoods makes it possible to compare best practices across schools, and also increases accountability, since "we operate in a bad neighborhood" was now taken into account. CPS has discovered that those schools with poor safety-metric ratings generally rely on security guards and surveillance cameras, as opposed to, say, social workers and personal mentoring. Top-performing schools are the ones that help their students cope with the social-emotional problems underlying the violence swirling around them.

Although the problem of gun violence unfortunately remains in the headlines nationwide, CPS's violence-prevention program is a new box it can be proud of. Cities across the nation are now looking to it as an innovative and vital new model.*

MANY SHIFTS, MANY BOXES

Just as boxes come in many sizes, so, too, do the kinds of changes that can and must occur in your mind to empower them. Some of these cognitive shifts may be more provocative than others. Some may suddenly help you recognize new opportunities (during almost any moment of our five-step process) and others may "tweak" your perspective in a way that fosters your creativity but still requires you to continue using the process before you "land on" what you and your team decide should be your next important new box.

Some of these shifts alter the "big picture." For instance, you might change your threshold perception from seeing something as impracticable ("Leukemia can *rarely* be cured") to very much within reach ("Leukemia can *often* be cured"); from an unbendable rule ("All music must follow the basic rules of tonality") to something open to challenge ("Music may break those rules and be atonal"); or from preposterous ("Let's manufacture and market a pet rock") to wildly profitable (in the early 1970s, advertising executive Gary Dahl sold more than 1.5 million

---

* According to Michael Casserly, executive director of the Council of Great City Schools, the new program is "strikingly well planned," and he says he knows of nothing "that has the promise this initiative does." "Case Study: BCG, Chicago Public Schools Team to Reduce Gun Violence," *Consulting*, March 24, 2011.

of these novelty items). In each case, you're shattering a bias or assumption, breaking a seemingly "unbreakable" rule, or daring to perceive a situation in some radical new way.

Some changes in perception may be more particular or subtle, or at least seem so. You might change from thinking about an idea in a relatively simple and singular way ("We make hamburgers with 100 percent beef") to a slightly broader or more complex or variable way ("We make patties" or "Horsemeat is scrumptious"). Just this slight modification in your outlook, however, might lead your restaurant to triple its revenues when health-conscious people line up to purchase your patties made of portabello mushrooms, turkey, chicken, or lentils. Likewise, you might change your perception from seeing two things as being *unrelated* and *incompatible* to being *related* and *complementary*—and thereby create a tremendously exciting and lucrative new box.

"Mmmm, *chocolate!*" raves a handsome blond-haired man as he takes a big bite into his chocolate bar, swaggering down a city street.

"Mmmm, *peanut butter!*" coos an attractive brunette as she eats the unctuous treat out of a jar, strolling on a street that's perpendicular to the one he's on.

The two come to the same street corner and collide.

"You got chocolate in my peanut butter!" says the young woman with an accusatory tone.

"You got peanut butter in my chocolate!" replies the bemused young man.

In this vintage ad campaign, Hershey's, which had acquired the Reese's business, made vivid the idea that two previously unrelated foods could be enjoyed together, and promoted its new box of "peanut butter cups" in a memorable way.*

This is similar to the way the Rosetta Stone was deciphered. In 1822,

* For nostalgia's sake, consider watching this video: http://www.youtube.com/watch?v =DJLDF6qZUXo.

Jean-François Champollion published the first translation of the Rosetta Stone hieroglyphs, showing that the writing system was a combination of phonetic and ideographic signs, building on contributions of Thomas Young. If you had imagined it as purely phonetic, or purely symbol based, you'd never solve it—you needed to change your box from "or" to "and," to combine those two theories to decipher what was in front of you.[3]

Another simple example: We know of a relatively athletic business consultant who loves biking and the beauty of the natural world. But when he and his wife had a little girl, he was so eager to spend every free moment he had with his daughter that he stopped spending much time exercising on his bicycle. His core belief of "I should spend as much of my nonworking time doing things with my daughter" seemed to conflict with his belief that "I really need to be spending more time training on my bike." Months later, he saw a man zip by him on a bicycle with a baby boy on the back in a child seat. Suddenly our friend saw the possibility of bringing his two separate boxes together. Within days, he was spending several hours each week training on his bicycle and enjoying lovely, bucolic scenes with his daughter in tow.

Some other examples:

- Most computer companies traditionally built computers and then sold them—Dell's just-in-time production approach changed this to "we sell computers and then build them."
- The "apéricube" cubed cheese helped shift the box from the traditional European box of "cheese always comes after a meal" to "cheese can also be eaten before the meal," thanks to a deliberate marketing campaign positioning it as an appetizer.
- Fishermen in Greenland dismayed about global warming and depleting fish stocks realized they could go into mining since the ground wasn't as frozen as it had been for generations.
- Most people would say that the box for a television network is to entertain viewers, or to develop interesting programs. The CEO of a major French network, Patrick Le Lay, once said, "Our job is to help [advertisers] sell their product."

There are innumerable perception shifts that can lead you to create valuable new boxes. In almost any context, you can create a new box by shifting your perspective, as in the real-life examples below:

Before . . .	After . . .
Is irrelevant or low-priority ("No one will want to read a book on a screen.")	**Is relevant or high-priority** ("Half the sales of our top-selling novel were purchased in ebook format . . . who is masterminding our digital strategy?")
Makes no sense ("How audacious for Mr. Stravinsky to have written that dreadful music. Let's throw eggs at the musicians performing it.")	**Makes perfect sense** ("Let's hire our musicians to perform *The Rite of Spring*!")
Is uncomfortable or unacceptable ("Women in the U.S. military may not go into combat.")	**Is comfortable or acceptable** ("Some of our best assets on the ground in Afghanistan are women.")
Works over there, for them ("Semiconductor chips work well in the hardware business, for use in computers and mobile phones.")	**Works over here, for us** ("Semiconductor chips can work well here at our biotechnology company, to help us sequence the human genome.")
Can only be this way ("We create binoculars for use during the *day* when there's *light*.")	**Could also be the opposite way** ("We could also create a special type for spying at *night*, when it's totally *dark*.")
Too risky or foolish to accomplish ("We cannot intervene to free the hostages. If we try and fail, we'll look like fools.")	**Too risky or critical *not* to accomplish** ("If the hostages remain in enemy hands, they'll be used for years to blackmail us. Let's send in the Navy SEALs to rescue them. We'll be heroes!")
Is not part of what we do or too early ("We're not a video website, and not enough people have the technology they need to upload personal videos, anyway.")	**Is just what we should be doing and now is the perfect time** ("Let's create a service called YouTube. People will come to it sometime soon and the opportunity will only grow.")

We hope that you will be inspired to think about all sorts of cognitive shifts that can help you free up your creativity. Depending on the context in which you are trying to create a new box, you might ponder one or several of the ones suggested above, or you might also come up with your own list. Something that has long seemed worthless might now appear priceless. What was humorous could be seen as serious and urgent. Whereas you once said, "never," perhaps today you'll say "always," or "sometimes," or "on every second Thursday." The important thing is that you are opening the doors to creativity.

NATURA: SHIFTING FROM A PERSONAL VISION TO A COLLECTIVE ONE

If you ever have the chance to visit Natura's beautiful headquarters in the countryside near Cajamar, a small town outside São Paulo, Brazil, one of the first things you'll see upon entering the contemporary glass-paneled main office building is the company's slogan etched into a stone wall: "Bem Estar Bem," which literally means "well being well" but also can be translated as "being well by doing good."

The campus has several buildings with large panels of glass that enable employees to enjoy the verdant surroundings—rolling grassy lawns, palm trees, eucalyptus forests—even when indoors.

Brazil is one of the rapidly developing economies of the world, with a population of about 200 million people, including a disproportionate number of young people. However, there are serious problems with the educational system: Some 3.7 million school-aged students are not currently attending school, and fewer than 50 percent of those students who go to high school graduate on time. The quality of teaching in the country, especially in the upper grades, is poor. Students in Brazil perform the worst among sixty-five countries in terms of the proportion of them who meet basic requirements in reading and mathematics.

Natura Cosméticos is the largest seller of cosmetics in Brazil, and while the link between cosmetics and education may not be obvious, Natura is working tirelessly to change perceptions and make a real difference in educational outcomes and standards in its home country.

Natura manufactures, markets, and distributes cosmetic products based mostly on natural and organic ingredients, and has calculated its ecological impact upon the environment (an "environmental chart" is on the packaging of every product). It has worked to reduce its carbon footprint by doing such things as limiting the amount of packaging for its products and making many items available in refillable containers.

Natura employs a "direct sales" model rather than relying on a traditional retail model with brick-and-mortar stores. It has only 7,000 employees, but it also works with more than one million "consultants" or direct salespeople across Brazil (and upwards of 200,000 such freelance salespeople in other territories). Since the company was founded, in 1969, it has grown significantly, and by 2010, it boasted more than $3 billion in annual revenues.

Natura seems genuinely committed to serving all of its key stakeholders—its employees, consultants, consumers, suppliers, and supplier communities—with extraordinary care and thoughtfulness. Executives at the company say "bem estar bem" is Natura's bedrock reason for existing. The phrase captures how your "well-being" depends in large part on "being well," that is, on doing good things not just for yourself but also for society and for the planet. Natura has committed itself to using eco-friendly natural products, to using ordinary women rather than supermodels in its advertisements (a strategy later adopted by Dove in its "True Beauty" campaign), and to working closely with suppliers and local communities to minimize environmental impact and promote sustainability. The company also encourages and supports its employees' volunteer efforts in their own communities, especially in Cajamar. Nurturing all your most important relationships, says the company, is what matters the most in this life—and this value is at the center of everything it does.

Given this commitment to "do well" by its people and their communities so that they can, in turn, "be well" and "do well" for others, Natura set up a sister organization known as the Natura Institute.

Established in 2010, the Natura Institute is a not-for-profit foundation that oversees social initiatives such as community building and the enhancement of the company's local sustainability efforts, as well as improving education in towns and villages across Brazil. Even before the institute was founded, Natura had several significant education-related projects, financed by sales of a special line of products called

Crer Para Ver (Believing Is Seeing). Since its founding, the institute has managed all the profits from the Crer Para Ver line, which represent a significant investment in public education in Brazil.

In 2011, leaders at Natura asked us to help clarify the institute's strategic vision. We were told that there were a variety of opinions regarding how the institute could be most effective and that a big part of our job would be to help its top managers and other key stakeholders (including governmental entities involved with the institute's activities) come to agreement about the organization's fundamental identity, purpose, and vision.

Put another way, we were asked to help them make a major shift in perception among these various powerful people—to move them from "my way" to "our way." The participants included two of the company's three founders, along with the president of the institute and a former education secretary for the state of São Paulo. We knew these players would provide an exciting array of divergent ideas because of their very different backgrounds and perspectives. That also meant they would each have distinct boxes pertaining to education. Some were most interested in the fundamentals of primary and secondary education in Brazil: how to improve teaching methods, testing procedures, and classroom resources. But others perceived education in a more philosophical way, as the sum of all the ways people develop their knowledge about the world—and develop themselves as individuals—across their entire lives.

We conducted an ambitious beliefs audit (and in-depth interviews with the founders and CEO), which helped us identify many of the current mental models the participants were using to think about "education in Brazil." We asked them to think about the following profound institutional questions: What is the institute's mission and initial focus? What are the principles that will guide the institute? How will you ensure its continuing impact and relevance? What are some of the potential avenues that excite you most?

Several said they very much wanted the institute to serve as an extension of Natura, to reflect the company's values and build on its mission and vision. The institute, they argued, should launch initiatives that would encourage all the groups involved in teaching to do work together to elevate the quality of education in Brazil. It should especially address such issues as community, renewal, and sustainability.

By contrast, those participants looking at the issues from a governmental angle saw education in a more traditional way and thus were seeking clarity about how best to make educational resources available to as many people as possible. They were especially passionate about ensuring that young Brazilians achieved a baseline level of proficiency in reading, writing, and mathematics and that schools, books, teaching staff, and other such essential components be allocated equitably throughout Brazil.

How could we help these two groups move from "my way" to "our way"?

We first reviewed troves of primary and secondary data about education in Brazil: the quality and performance of its schools, how students were faring, especially in their earliest years. We invited several thought leaders in education to make presentations. This was where we quantified and learned more about the many intense challenges faced by Brazil's educational system. The experts also told us about some of the various kinds of educational programs that had proven effective in other countries. They discussed best practices for supporting vulnerable schools and communities, using technology to foster learning and teaming, motivating and training teachers, and involving parents in an effective, ongoing way.

We held a day-long workshop at the founders' office in São Paulo, and as a starting place, building on the "doubt" and "explore" phases just described, everyone agreed that we should focus on enhancing primary education in Brazil, and on developing programs that would be multi-local, that is, programs targeting all the local areas where Natura operates. As we began to get more specific about the participants' most basic ideas regarding the institute, they found that they shared significant common ground. They all thought it important to look at education holistically, involving many interdependent actors, including teachers, students, parents and other family members, administrators, policy makers, and community leaders. They all wanted to make Natura a presence "in the field," where education actually happens in cities and towns across Brazil, instead of simply working with the Ministry of Education in state capitals and Brasília. They agreed that cultivating efficiency in how education is managed is critical, but also that fostering an entrepreneurial approach, too, made good sense. Enlisting principals and other school administrators to embrace a more progressive and unified outlook to education in Brazil would be important, as would creating broad, society-wide awareness and engagement.

These early conversations helped sensitize Natura's top leaders to some of the "boxes" they were relying upon to think about the institute and about what it could and should accomplish. Our goal was not so much to debunk these notions, but rather to make them fully apparent to everyone involved. We hoped that by making them absolutely clear, some of the key differences in their various perspectives might be overcome—and we might create a new vision statement that would unite the Natura Institute's leadership.

We then opened an interesting discussion about some of the current boxes they were using to think about education in Brazil. To spur this conversation, we asked an open-ended question—"What, in today's world, does it actually mean to *teach*?"—and showed a short video about the research of Sugata Mitra, now a professor at England's Newcastle University, who embedded an Internet-equipped computer in a wall in a slum and watched poor, uneducated children essentially teach themselves to use a computer and surf the Net.[4]

That sparked a vigorous debate about the nature of modern-day education, and about who the central players are. Some felt the premise of the video was ridiculous, that teachers were and would always be a critical part of the equation. Others were intrigued by the possibility of helping poor children to teach themselves. Some spoke about what it means to "teach" today, about the variety of materials and tools typically used in classrooms (from standard books and three-ring binders to iPads and smart boards), and about traditional curricula as compared with "radical" ones. They then discussed what it would take to change the people of Brazil's mindset about education so that it would be less about what the government and schools could do for kids and more about how people could develop a deep consciousness about just how rich and stimulating lifelong education can be. Although the conversation took many thematic directions, it eventually focused on a shared understanding: A long time ago, education was primarily a relationship between a student and a teacher, but students today also learn by "exchanging" information and ideas with *screens*. Education has changed, then, from a two-way (student/teacher) relationship into a three-way one among students, teachers, and screens. This realization, this "box," gave us a new way of looking at the situation. The workshop participants wondered whether in the future, students might rely primarily if not exclusively on screens, with teachers merely facilitating the process. They agreed, in any case, that the old box of "student/ teacher" would need to be replaced with new boxes that reflected the growing relevance of computer-guided teaching on screens. They agreed, too, that the concepts of "education," "teacher," and "student" would all need to be redefined.

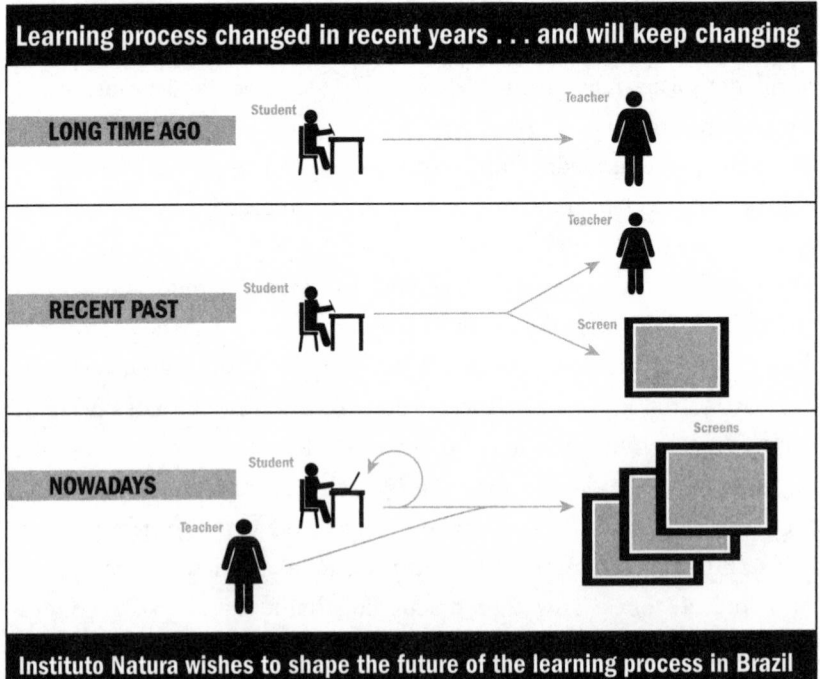

And so, in this first part of the divergence phase, we started to generate all sorts of ideas about what "teaching" and "learning" might mean in the future. There were some heated arguments; in fact, when we eventually broke for lunch, it was not immediately clear how we would pull it all together in "convergence." Still, the participants stuck to the plan, and we moved into more divergence pertaining to the institute's strategic vision and to the particular words that might be included in it.

Specifically, we wanted to come up with the raw materials we would need during convergence to help the participants give birth to a sentence that aptly and persuasively expressed the Natura Institute's vision. This part of divergence was divided into three phases:

1. The "to do" phase—finding a *verb* to describe the education process.
2. The "doer" phase—defining the subject of the verb, that is, for whom the "to do" would be intended.
3. The "impact" phase—defining what outcomes should ideally result from the actions of the doer, that is, the object of the verb.

During the first phase, participants came up with words such as "change," "connect," "promote," "improve," "create," "enable," and "enchant."

During the second phase, they thought about those words from different perspectives—that of the teacher, the student, the administrator, the government, the institute, the entire Brazilian people.

Then, during the third phase, they identified desired potential outcomes and criteria for measuring success, with the goal of doing so in a surprising way (rather than just saying "better test results" or "better graduation rates"). These included the hope that 1) more and more Brazilians would want to help teach other people, 2) more pupils would want to learn, 3) more of the country's top students would become teachers, 4) Brazilians would respect teachers more, and teachers would have an enhanced sense of their worth, and 5) someday, there would be no such thing as an unsuccessful student in Brazil.

Once the workshop participants placed this range of ideas on the table, we encouraged them to begin to converge, to decide what specific direction the institute's new vision should take.

To start our Step 4 convergence process, we picked out some broad elements that resonated with the group. Two key objectives the group promptly agreed upon were 1) the importance of *showing* Brazil what was possible when it comes to educating the nation's people and 2) *using volunteers* to help connect the nation's demand for people with a diverse spectrum of educational skills with its ample supply of such wide-ranging talent.

We then started talking about the central question: "What do you think the institute should *do?*" Participants volunteered single words as well as phrases. One person said "catharsis" and "catalyze." Another said it should "create conditions for quality education." Other participants insisted that "teachers and parents should become educators," and that when it comes to learning, "we should change the perspectives of age, time, and geography . . . it is a continuous process."

But it was when one of Natura's founders mentioned the phrase "learning community" that there was finally a real click of recognition in the room. It was a magical moment, and there was a palpable sense of relief as we began to explore what this could mean, and how it could help not only to pull everyone's views together but also to differentiate the Natura Institute from other foundations.

By the end of this conversation, the group concluded that it really wanted the Natura Institute to shape the learning process and education in Brazil, with the words "learning" and "education" to be interpreted very broadly. Everyone concurred that the institute should articulate a modern view of education that recognizes how quickly everything is changing socially, culturally, and technologically. Dogmatic "one size fits all" teaching, they stressed, should be replaced with more nimble systems that recognize individual differences in how students learn. They also underscored that the institute should help shape "protagonist citizens" who are conscientious about the impact of their actions not just on their immediate communities but across the entire planet. Much as Natura Cosméticos itself was founded on a philosophical conception of the individual linked with nature in a system, the

Natura Institute should respect and encourage study of the relationship between the individual and the creation of knowledge.

When next we focused in even more, to try to decide upon the words to articulate this vision, we held six rounds of voting. The first round was difficult because it entailed agreeing upon the verb. Each participant had two votes but was not permitted to vote for something he or she had suggested. After conducting these two rounds, the group settled on the verb "create." This verb held significant meaning for the participants; it was more apt than words such as "enable" and "connect," and better than "improve" (which they felt suggested something more incremental). They agreed that they wanted the institute to bring about a fundamental shift, to create something new.

They then worked together to converge around the object, that is, *who* would benefit from the institute's efforts. After some debate, they settled not on primary school students or teachers, but instead, the full set of citizens of the country, "the Brazilian people." Someday, they decided together, there would be no unsuccessful students in Brazil.

After additional rounds of voting, the workshop participants concluded they should strive to turn Brazil into a lifelong "learning community." Accordingly, by the end of our workshop, the institute's leadership decided that the foundation's specific vision statement should be *"To create the conditions for the Brazilian people to become a learning community."* Although they had started off the workshop with relatively rigid personal outlooks, they had created a collective vision.

Within a few months, the institute had developed a strategic plan. It would cultivate programs aimed not only at improving but at *changing* education. It would help people "learn how to learn," and how to recognize and develop their unique talents. And it would encourage everyone to embrace the idea that not all learning stems from an act of teaching—much of it is experienced outside the classroom through the full range of human experience.

The new vision and strategic plan of the Natura Institute were designed to serve as guiding principles for the leaders of the organization for years to come. Even the work already under way could be viewed through this new lens: Shortly after this project, Brazil's Ministry of

Education agreed to expand an already-existing nationwide reading and writing program for elementary school children. The institute had launched this program in 310 schools, collaborating with them to develop stronger classroom materials and boost the quality of teachers' training. This was so well received that the project has now become part of the entire nation's public educational policy and is being implemented in upwards of two thousand cities. Soon it will reach approximately 72,000 schools, 140,000 teachers, and more than three million children across Brazil—the potential for the future of Brazil and the concept of the learning community seems huge.

CREATING A NEW STRATEGIC VISION

As we have shown with the Natura Institute's workshop, one of the most common applications of our five-step process is developing a new strategic vision—a beautiful example of a shift in perspective.

A rich body of literature debates the best way to define a strategic vision (and how it should be distinguished from an organization's mission or purpose or identity) and this book will not attempt to resolve that discussion. But we, and many of our colleagues in the field, generally define a strategic vision as *an ambitious image or box relating to the future that is radically preferable (or a necessary alternative) to the current box.* Our experiences advising companies suggest that an organization's vision should apply to every aspect of its business, and therefore to every employee. A good strategic vision is simple yet broad enough for everyone to understand, but rich and deep enough that its implications for action in every area of your organization are clear.

We have seen many organizations with ghastly "visions" that are variations of this:

> *Our vision is to maximize shareholder wealth by exceeding customer expectations for* (insert product or service here) *and providing opportunities for our employees to lead fulfilling lives while respecting the environment and the communities in which we operate.*

That is not helpful! It might temporarily satisfy some stakeholders, but it is not a clear or distinctive image of the future. Your vision should not be something your competitor could appropriate simply by inserting its name (let alone a random company in a random industry, as in the vision on page 240).

Two examples that fit these criteria: AT&T Labs' vision, as of late 2012, was "to design and create in this decade the new global network, processes and service platforms that maximize automation, allowing for a reallocation of human resources to more complex and productive work."[5] Boeing's evocative vision in the 1950s, as the world was just moving into the realm of commercial air travel, was "to become the dominant player in commercial aircraft and bring the world into the jet age."

The Key Components of a Strategic Vision

The most important elements of a well-framed vision statement are 1) the *vision* itself—the firm's fundamental aspirations for the future, 2) the *values* upon which the firm and the vision are built, and 3) the *promises* the firm would like to make to its employees, customers, and other stakeholders.

#1: The Vision
A strategic vision is a rallying cry designed to appeal to a wide and diverse group of people (especially the organization's employees and customers). It is easy to confuse with an organization's "mission" (or "purpose") and indeed both are core mental models—or boxes—with some overlapping qualities. But we generally see a vision (that is, "what we aspire to become, to achieve, and to create") as *building upon* an organization's mission (that is, "what we stand for and why we exist").[6] In our framework, a mission or purpose tends to be more static, probably shifting quite slowly and imperceptibly over time, as if it's somehow intrinsically connected to an organization's very essence, its "DNA." A vision, by contrast, contemplates the direction an organization's leadership would like to take over a relatively short or midterm time frame (that is, a five-year strategic vision, or a ten-year or twenty-year one). A

vision helps answer such questions as "Where are my organization and I excited to go from here?" A vision is the big inspiring new box we can create today that my team and I will be able to fill in with lots of exciting new ideas tomorrow.

#2: Values

A vision must capture the basic values—or ideas we have of the way things should be—upon which your firm is built. Some commonly cited values: integrity, client satisfaction, team spirit, and authenticity. Avis Budget Group's vision statement, building on commitment, integrity, and responsibility as values, is "We will be a leader in the vehicle rental industry by focusing on customers, our people, growth, innovation and efficiency. All of these elements will drive bottom line success and show that Avis and Budget are stronger together than they could be alone."[7]

Land O'Lakes says its vision is "to be one of the best food and agricultural companies in the world by being: our customers' first choice; our employees' first choice; responsible to our owners; and a leader in our communities." And according to its website, Land O'Lakes' core values are "people," "performance," "customer commitment," "quality," and "integrity."[8]

To help you start thinking about your firm or organization, we have assembled a list of such values. When pondering your vision and the values that should inform it, begin by considering the list on page 243 and then picking out, say, the three, five, or ten values you think *currently* apply best (later you can also explore ones you think your organization should stand for in the future).

In addition to using this list, you might spend some time with your team—indeed, you might organize a dedicated divergence/convergence session for such purposes—to create your own list of values and contemplate which ones best reflect your organization.

Another way to think about your firm's basic "values" is to ask yourself questions like these: What would my organization and I be willing to *fight* for? What essential aspects of my organization do I want to see transmitted to my children? What do I hope my company and I will be remembered for? What basic elements of my company, if they were to vanish, would end my reasons for wanting to work there?

Of course, even when you do this deep thinking, and come up with a list of values that seem paramount, you will not necessarily be able to develop consensus about what they signify and what their implications should be for your vision statement. Any of these values can mean different things to different groups of stakeholders. But by doing your best to identify a shared set of values, you will begin to understand not only where your organization is today but also what you believe its "radically preferable future state" or "radically preferable view of the future" should be.

55 values

INNOVATION	SPEED	PERFORMANCE	DIFFERENTIATION	SERVICE
INTEGRITY	LOYALTY	HUMANISM	GLOBAL ATTITUDE	ENTHUSIASM
CLIENT SATISFACTION	EFFICIENCY	VALUE CREATION	SIMPLICITY	PARTNERSHIP
TEAM SPIRIT	FIGHTING SPIRIT	EXCELLENCE	OPEN COMMUNICATION	AVAILABILITY
RESPECT	OPENNESS	SUCCESS	CLAIRVOYANCE	PERSONAL DEVELOPMENT
QUALITY	PLEASURE	ADAPTABILITY	AUTHENTICITY	SAVOIR-FAIRE
ENTREPRENEURIAL SPIRIT	COMPETITIVENESS	CONFIDENCE	TALENT	PLURALISM
RESPONSIBILITY	PASSION	PROXIMITY	PRIDE	COURAGE
FREEDOM	AMBITION	INVENTIVENESS	WELLNESS	INITIATIVE
PROFESSIONALISM	HUMILITY	SOCIAL RESPONSIBILITY	THOUGHTFULNESS	TRADITION
ACCESSIBILITY	SUSTAINABILITY	EQUALITY	DETERMINATION	CONFIDENTIALITY

#3: Promises

Your vision statement should also express the promises you'd like to make to your organization's stakeholders. What are your big plans? Your most significant ambitions? What do you hope to achieve, and over what time period? Progressive, the Fortune 500 automobile insurance company, says its vision is "to reduce the human trauma and economic costs associated with automobile accidents. We do this by providing our customers with services designed to help them get their lives back in order again as quickly as possible."[9] General Motors provides a very specific promise: "Over the past 100 years, GM has been a leader in the global automotive industry. And the next 100 years will be no different. GM is committed to leading the industry in alternative fuel propulsion."

You'll know you have a good strategic vision if it:

- *Changes the way that you and your colleagues perceive your organization.* For example, Sony's vision statement was once famously: "Become the company most known for changing the worldwide poor-quality image of Japanese products." It imagined a clear break from the past, a clear "before" and "after."

- *Is easy to understand, evocative, credible, and feasible.* 3M's vision statement is "To solve unsolved problems innovatively."

- *Is easy to share among those it impacts, and motivates key stakeholders.* Microsoft's original vision statement, for example, was "A computer on every desk in every home." That is far superior to such statements as "We want to be the #1 shoe company in the world" or "We will always work to be first in the nationwide business of wallboard manufacturing." Microsoft was very specific about what it hoped to achieve (and offered a vivid image to reflect it). Being #1 (or #2, for that matter) is open to interpretation and is ambiguous since it hinges on the verb "to be." What, exactly, does it mean to "be" #1 or #2? Does it entail a certain level of annual revenues? Market share? We encourage companies to use action verbs in their vision statements to make it absolutely clear what it is they want to accomplish.

- *Differentiates the organization from its competitors in specific ways.* Ben & Jerry's has a "product mission" about top-quality ice cream made using wholesome ingredients, as well as an "economic mission" focused on sustainable, profitable growth with expanding opportunities for employees, but it is most differentiated by its "social mission" to initiate innovative ways to improve the quality of life locally, nationally, and internationally.

- *Contains qualitative elements, and success criteria that go beyond traditional ways of measuring.* For example, not just "double our market share" or "hit $1 billion in revenues." Sony's historic vision statement was particularly persuasive in this regard: Rather than simply setting a financial benchmark, the company offered the remarkably bold and unusual promise of changing the world's perceptions of the quality of Japanese-made products.

- *Can be validated by key stakeholders.* For example, it is ethically acceptable, actionable, economically viable, and helps unite and inspire everyone involved, building on your core values. As emphasized throughout this book, a new box, if you get it right, can help bring people together both within and outside your organization, unifying their outlook around a common theme, idea, or sense of purpose and possibility.

Forging a collective vision is a huge challenge because it requires not only creativity but also great discipline and detailed thinking. When you and your group embark on this process, the destination is unknown. The process may be particularly difficult for those people within organizations who are customarily (or always) focused on the deductive, the logical, the "provable." As we've seen, the priority that many organizations place on the short term often creates incentives that significantly favor such highly analytical, convergent thinking. But developing a vision for your organization requires you to use both induction and deduction, to adopt a prospective mindset, focusing on longer-term possibilities to ponder not just what the future might hold for you and your colleagues, but how you can shape the future yourselves.*

Think about what matters to you most; the problems you want to help solve; the ones *only* you can solve. Consider exactly where you want to go, and what you want to do when you get there.

---

* For more on strategic vision, see de Brabandere, *The Forgotten Half of Change.*

NINE

Imagining the Future

□□□□□□□□□□□□□□□□□□□□□□□□□□□□□□□□□□□□□□

Today's science fiction is often tomorrow's fact.
> —STEPHEN HAWKING, renowned physicist, author, and cosmologist

CENARIOS ARE an elegant and powerful application of the thinking in new boxes process we have explored. Their fantastic potential for improving strategic thinking and long-range planning is generally acknowledged—but they remain greatly underused. In this chapter we will explain what we mean by "scenarios," since it's a term we've seen many people in business use differently than we do, and then explain how to marshal the five steps to create and use scenarios, and thus be better prepared for what you cannot predict.

HOW TO IMAGINE MULTIPLE POSSIBLE FUTURES

Imagine you are a top executive at AMC Theatres huddling with your colleagues in a plush office at the company's headquarters in Kansas City, Missouri, for an all-day workshop on the future of the movies. The tectonic changes in moviegoing habits are raising concerns about the company's revenues. Millions of people who used to go to the local megaplex are now staying home, paying for a single "ticket" using services like Netflix. Imagine that by the end of this all-day workshop, your team must have three or four scenarios—alternate possible but unlikely futures—pertaining to what the moviegoing experience could be like in the year 2025!

Much like the films that AMC screens, each scenario has to tell a unique story and offer a wildly different view of the future. At the end of your workshop, one of the scenarios you develop is called "Fit Family World," envisioning a future in which keeping the whole family buff and illness-free is paramount. Under this scenario, "going to the movies" might no longer be a sedentary popcorn-bingeing activity but might instead offer robust fitness and health benefits for the whole family. Another scenario is called "Custom Leisure World" because it contemplates a new realm of entertainment where everything is customized to satisfy individual tastes and desires. Under this scenario, perhaps AMC offers personalized multisensory filmgoing experiences that, though retrofit to each moviegoer's individual tastes and interests, still take place in a communal space. Moviegoers see the film of their choice without having to agree upon it with friends and families (and maybe without having to worry about babysitting). Perhaps each audience member has personalized virtual reality headsets (and other new sensory equipment yet to be invented) to select and enjoy individual, highly customized audiovisual experiences. Small children are supervised by employees to free up parents, and the start and finish times of each personal experience in each theater is engineered so families arrive and leave the megaplex at the same time.

Take a moment to consider what other scenarios would be possible for the moviegoing experience, circa 2025. Can you come up with one or two additional far-fetched yet still plausible ones?

This is the sort of scenario-thinking that is one of the most exciting and dynamic applications of our new boxes approach. It involves building new boxes (or reinforcing existing ones) to prepare for the future. People are often eager to know: "Where is the next crisis going to come from? How can I get ready for it?" They want to understand where the markets relevant to their organization are headed, but they don't know how to develop a broad range of hypotheses. "Is my future only in emerging markets? Is there still potential for my organization at home?"

In those situations, we often do scenario-planning exercises, using "what if" and "but if" scenarios—versions of the future based on far-out hypotheses—to shape new boxes and stress-test current ones. We all will face unexpected and even strange developments in the future, so the most robust new boxes must be able to help companies survive—and thrive—in highly unpredictable conditions. Exposing new boxes to the broadest possible range of events that could occur allows you to make them stronger for both the present and the future.

For example, when the terrorist attacks of September 11, 2001, disrupted the airline industry, several major airlines had very little room to maneuver—US Airways went into bankruptcy in 2002 after having low interest-coverage ratios, and others eventually followed. But Southwest had low debt levels and significant cash on hand, making it more "prepared" for the unexpected shifts in demand and fuel prices that occurred. Put differently, it doubted, it was ready to reevaluate, and as a result, it remained profitable during 2001–2003 and grew its presence nationwide. Scenarios are a tool that can help any organization be better prepared.

A set of scenarios usually includes three or four very discrete and distinct scenarios. None of the scenarios is likely to happen in all its detail—indeed the "real" future is likely to contain elements of all of them. Still, each one is plausible, so you can try to envision how things might change for you and your organization under each scenario. And each one provokes different thoughts, and suggests different opportunities and threats. By considering this range of possible futures, your sense of what could happen will become much broader, richer, and more imaginative. By creating such scenarios—each of which can be seen as a new "box"—you can help your organization make better and more robust decisions. Scenarios also enable you to develop a shared language and perspective with your colleagues, a more expansive common "box" regarding what to consider together when talking about and planning for the future.

Once you've focused on a few scenarios, you can guide your organization's strategy—and become vastly better prepared for future events—by discussing and devising the various ways your organization might react to and take advantage of each potential scenario. For instance, for Fit Family World, you might develop architectural plans for movie theaters featuring stationary bikes instead of seats. Or you might seek out food vendors that offer healthy organic vegan delicacies in lieu of fat-filled junk food. Or maybe you devise an enormous stadium with an outdoor running track surrounded by screens projecting a film that runners can watch as they jog around the track.

In our parlance, a scenario refers to a new box, or mental model, that relates to a distinct and often "far-out" future. A scenario is a broadly imagined future, along with the story that evokes how you went from today to that future, not a particular solution or outcome. But individuals, businesses, and others can make very practical valuable use of such scenarios, relying upon them as frameworks and reference points from which to develop specific new strategies, products, approaches, and other such innovations. So whereas Fit Family World is the scenario—the new box—the stationary bikes, organic food offerings, and revolutionary running/film-watching stadium are examples of how one organization (in our example, AMC Theatres) might decide to respond to and take advantage of it. And as we emphasized above, you will likely find yourself using (and rejecting) various pieces from each of the scenarios you created. As an executive at AMC, you might decide to design a future moviegoing experience relying on aspects, for instance, of two (or more) distinct scenarios. You might recommend making healthy organic foods available for every audience member in all theaters (in light of Fit Family World), while also encouraging the development of highly personalized virtual reality experiences for each individual moviegoer (inspired by Custom Leisure World).

Given how complex the modern world tends to be, and given all the combinations of trends that can occur to provoke constant new changes and challenges, scenarios often provide a welcome sense of simplicity and clarity. It is very difficult to keep track of, say, twenty or thirty trends at the same time, and then have to try to imagine all the various outcomes that could occur depending on which trends end up being the most influential and important. By contrast, scenarios, as you'll see, "bake in" the key trends that you have already decided are the most urgent as well as your analysis pertaining to some of the most extreme possibilities that could impact how those trends play out over the next several years. And ultimately, each scenario tells a unique *story* regarding what steps had to occur to make the new universe that it envisions actually become possible. The Fit Family World scenario, for example, might be based on your analysis of such trends as urbanization, childhood obesity, and green technologies and some of the wild if unlikely events that could occur in light of such trends. And the story or "backstory" behind Fit Family World might read as follows: "Cities everywhere draw more and more people away from the suburbs (to dwell or simply to enjoy entertainment and other experiences in the evening and weekends). As the crisis of childhood obesity deepens, families increasingly seek out opportunities to eat healthy meals and exercise *together*. Increasing risks regarding air, water, and ground pollution push people to seek out green solutions to everything they do, leading to new environmentally conscious restaurants, sports arenas, and movie theaters."

In a nutshell, a scenario describes a future as well as the steps required to get there.

THE WORLD (AND HISTORY) OF SCENARIOS

The use of scenarios, which has a long history in the military, was introduced to the business world by Pierre Wack at Royal Dutch/Shell in the 1970s. Shell, like many of its competitors, had been surprised by the rise in power of the OPEC cartel, and the first wave of environmentalism. Shell was eager to generate a range of strategic options, and by using scenarios (for instance, to foresee an overcapacity in the tanker business), executives at Shell for years were consistently better prepared to respond to ongoing shifts in their market than their counterparts.

Over time, a range of other organizations, from General Electric to various consultancies, have implemented various scenarios into their businesses. Automakers imagined ranges of results of car crashes. Jet engine manufacturers probed the efficacy of their products in the face of all sorts of risks: water, wind, flocks of seagulls. Perfume companies have placed human subjects in testing rooms that replicate the climates of places like Siberia, the Amazon jungle, and the Sahara, all in order to see how various scents hold up. Many businesses conducted elaborate "scenario planning" exercises involving weeks if not months of detailed research and number crunching.

For a host of reasons, however, we still believe scenario exercises are underused. Some executives believe that it takes too much time and money. Others argue that markets change too quickly for such scenarios to be of much help. Some claim that the use of the term *planning* in "scenario planning" itself puts too much emphasis on the deductive, when the role of scenarios is to stretch our thinking. Beyond all of those reasons, however, we believe many leaders are uncomfortable with the exploratory and provocative nature of scenarios—some people don't want their perceptions to be stretched. And even for those who are open to it, another core concern is the uncertainty inherent in the use of scenarios, the fact that it is an art more than a science. You can't deductively *prove* the accuracy or value of a scenario. You can't know in advance what its real impact will be, or whether one scenario will end up being better than another. Time has to pass before you can see its actual implications.

But when it comes to thinking in new boxes, we believe that the fanciful, indeterminate scenarios we will teach you to create will almost always be of tremendous value. You will not only come to feel comfortable with their more fuzzy attributes, you'll be enthusiastic about them, seeing them as a key to unlocking a range of new boxes, and new opportunities. The scenarios you imagine will permeate your mind and the strategies you pursue, helping you make better collective decisions overall. We have seen many companies become vastly better prepared for the future by creating, pondering, and responding to even the most far-fetched scenarios. To be clear, it is the very act of raising questions, exploring effective responses, and being better prepared for whatever the future may bring, the "scenario thinking" and the link to *strategy*, that ultimately provides value, not the scenarios themselves.

The development of scenarios need not be a time-consuming undertaking. You'll need to prepare ahead of time, and then we recommend that you set aside at least a half day for the scenario exercises described in this chapter, with follow-up required afterward as well. But our approach is a relatively efficient process.*

When developing scenarios, we encourage you to involve those individuals on your team, or in your organization, who have the responsibility and authority for making and executing key decisions, as opposed to a specialized team of scenario developers working in a separate atelier. We have found that by assembling the key people you will gain in impact what you might lose in rigor (that is, by not conducting the sort of intensive, time-gulping research and analysis associated with traditional scenario planning). If you and your colleagues develop the scenarios, your sense of ownership in them will increase dramatically. And this means that you, and they, will be that much more likely to derive practical value from them. We believe this is true across many types of organizations and institutions, such as the CEO and her executive team, managers of a business unit, or leaders of a small business or family enterprise.

With regard to the value of scenarios, be patient. We have found that the payoff is rarely either immediate or obvious; nor does it derive from any explicit prediction. Rather, the value of developing scenarios will come from what you learn during the process of developing them, and then from exploring the implications of them on your world. As U.S. Supreme Court justice Oliver Wendell Holmes, Jr., once said: "Man's mind, once stretched by a new idea, never regains its original dimensions."

There is one additional difference between most traditional approaches to scenarios and the thinking in new boxes approach: most classic approaches rely on megatrends and their analysis as the central

---

* There are several approaches to scenarios: for example, laying out specific axes of uncertainty and having scenarios emerge from the different quadrants, or a "morphological" approach involving laying out specific uncertainties and a range of possible outcomes for each. These approaches, well-known in scenario circles, differ from the approach we will lay out here, but we wholeheartedly advocate bringing creativity and expansive thinking to these approaches as well.

and most pivotal data points, whereas, in our approach, *wild cards* and extreme possibilities building on such megatrends are just as important. Consider, in this regard, the following question:

What is the probability that five years from now you will have to pay for a Google search?

"Zero," most people would say.

Now consider a variation on that question: Suppose that, five years from now, you *do* have to pay for Google searches. How did that happen? Those same people would quickly offer up a range of possibilities: Cash-starved governments were compelled to seek new tax sources; a global fuel shortage caused energy prices to skyrocket, forcing Google, with its massive server farms, to start charging for its services. Or perhaps a game-changing algorithm enabled Google to charge for premium search results.

In an instant, the impossible becomes reality. And if you ask the first question again, people's responses will have changed—scenario thinking stretches the boundaries of possibility in our minds.*

DEVELOP YOUR OWN SCENARIOS

To develop your own scenarios, you'll rely on the five-step process, and you'll end up going through several of the steps more than one time, both as you prepare for scenario development and as you actually churn out scenarios. You'll likely need a few days or perhaps a couple of weeks (or several months under certain circumstances) to conduct research and do some preliminary brainstorming.

There are four key building blocks for generating scenarios.

1. *Inputs, such as trends*—broad, major, highly likely-to-occur long-term trends affecting your industry, things like the rise in social

---

* This thought exercise also re-illustrates the predictive versus prospective distinction we explored earlier, in terms of deductive versus inductive ways of pondering the future.

networking and the digitization of information, the scarcity of certain natural resources, global warming, the expected exponential growth of the labor and consumer markets in countries like Brazil, Russia, India, and China. Some of these can also be informed by customer research, competitive intelligence, or other tools.

2. *Wild cards* or *extreme possibilities*—factors that, though highly unlikely, would have a significant impact upon the relevant trend: for example, the risk of a devastating nuclear accident, the possibility that the United States would split into two nations, the risk that the price of oil would escalate so high that all public transportation would rely on natural gas instead, the possibility that 75 percent of the most powerful corporate leaders in 2025 are women, the concept of a scientific breakthrough enabling everyone to live beyond age one hundred, the rise in Asian power leading to a world in which almost all global communication is done in Mandarin. Such wild cards are used, in essence, to "test" the importance and relevance of the megatrends you're considering.

3. *Variables*—imaginative real-life situations in which the critical megatrends would be likely to play out. For instance, if your organization is a national newspaper and some of the key megatrends are the ones mentioned in building block 1, above, one variable might be "Covering a White House Press Conference in 2025" whereas another one might be "Announcing the Daily Weather in 2025" or "Hiring Reporters and Correspondents in 2025."

4. *Hypotheses*—possibilities (based on brainstorming) as to what could happen and what could ensue in each of the various situations. For instance, for the "Announcing the Daily Weather in 2025" variable, one hypothesis might be referred to as "4-D Globe" and entail a multidimensional animated globe, a hologram, that jumps out from your iPad or other tablet, enabling you to see what the weather will be that day, anywhere on the globe, by moving your finger toward the place on the globe that interests you most. Perhaps the hologram would offer warning signals for dangerous weather patterns, and long-term risks like El Niño. We

generally encourage participants to come up with four hypotheses for each variable.

As you prepare to develop scenarios using the new boxes approach, you'll create a list of trends and wild cards, and you and/or a small core team of your colleagues will use these to draft a set of variables. You and any participants you involve will then develop a set of hypotheses pertaining to each variable and, after brainstorming and discussion, organize them into rough scenarios. Then you'll further polish the "raw materials" of the scenarios as needed, develop the full stories and communication materials, and identify the implications for your organization in terms of strategy and key decisions.

There is much flexibility in our model. You might decide it's necessary to spend several hours on just one part of the process or find ways of saving time in other areas. You might prepare with a couple of colleagues, and conduct a "scenarios workshop" with a small group of trusted colleagues, before exploring implications. Some clients choose to have a series of two, three, or even four workshops, for example, one to delve into the trends, another to develop the rough scenarios, and others to flesh out a view on the implications and actions to be taken. If you do have a workshop, identifying someone to facilitate the plenary discussions is important—this person should introduce the methodology and, later on, moderate the discussion when the scenarios are developed. The moderator should be familiar with the approach and the preparation that you've done. It should also be someone who is able to animate groups, and, ideally, is not associated with the project (for example, from another area of the company, or even from outside the company).

The key is to have the eventual users of the scenarios participate in actually developing them in some way, at a minimum in helping identify trends and explore implications, but ideally participating in the creative components of the effort, too.

SCENARIO PLANNING WITH UNIFE

In 2008 and early 2009, the financial crisis and subsequent recession put unprecedented stress on almost every business. Governments were changing, insurance companies were failing, and if you were in financial services, you might not have been sure if your company would exist a few weeks into the future. If you were involved in the train industry in Europe at this time, you would have seen leading newspapers reporting a 25 percent drop in freight volumes[1] and anticipating a drop in business travel of 10–20 percent.[2] More broadly, it seemed likely that trade patterns would be shifting, new competitors would be emerging, governments would be tightening regulations, discretionary consumer spending would become ever more stagnant. In short, it was a time to react and respond to a crisis with urgency and dispatch—but also to think creatively.

In the short run, you would work to increase passenger and freight rail traffic to mitigate the crisis. Thinking slightly longer term, you would be eager to understand the pivotal megatrends pertaining to the rail industry and how they might affect you. And over the long haul, you would really want to comprehend how the industry might continue developing through 2025—what could your world look like? For that, UNIFE, the association of the European rail industry, needed scenarios.

UNIFE represents European companies that design, manufacture, maintain, and refurbish rail transport systems and related equipment. Members include major private companies like Alstom, Bombardier, and Siemens, and many of the large national railway associations in Europe, such as the Fédération des Industries Ferroviaires (FIF) in France, ZVEI in Germany, and Swiss Federal Railways in Switzerland, are associate members.

UNIFE convened a small working group of executives from several of Europe's major rail companies. This group took four weeks to prepare for a one-day scenarios workshop, with us as facilitators. We worked with UNIFE by following the five New Box steps, as follows:

Step 1: Doubt Everything

In the world of rail travel, certainty is paramount. The trains should run on time, and nothing can be left to chance. In some ways, scenario planning offers the perfect counterpoint to this: It offers uncertainty, and encourages doubt.

As always, the first step of thinking in new boxes is to doubt everything—indeed, we believe that the willingness to embark upon the scenario-planning process already acknowledges some level of doubt. By thinking about what could happen in connection with multiple possible futures, you are essentially admitting that there are things you cannot forecast, but for which you'd still like to prepare; that your perception of the future is imperfect.

In working with UNIFE, we first conducted interviews with key stakeholders to understand their views of the future, and to begin to work through their existing boxes and constraints. We talked through the "new boxes" process, carefully explained our scenario-planning approach, and then used brainteasers, optical illusions, and other exercises to encourage participants to challenge their perceptions, and allow them to begin to "doubt." We then tried to "shock" the UNIFE participants. We asked them to consider a future world (say, by the year 2025) in which people everywhere refused to board trains! While most of the participants did not see this as a particularly likely situation, we used it to help "free up" their minds, analyzing how this might have come to be, and thinking about what it would mean for these executives and their companies.

Step 2: Probe the Possible

The main objective in this phase is to identify relevant megatrends, and to begin to think about "wild cards," that is, some of the more far-fetched, surprising factors that could influence how these trends might manifest themselves. Prior to the workshop, we encouraged UNIFE to identify a set of trends it believed had a relatively high degree of probability, were long-term in nature, and would have an impact on the whole social system. At the workshop, we asked the UNIFE participants to discuss the megatrends and their relative likely importance and impact (and then focus on a somewhat smaller set of them).

Some examples of key megatrends UNIFE considered most critical, given their links to the rail industry, included the following:

- Urbanization.
- Growth and aging of the population.
- Scarcity of fossil fuels.
- Increased mobility.
- Globalization and changes in trade barriers.
- Product personalization.
- Rise in power of India, China, and other rapidly developing economies.
- Boom in communication technology.
- Alternative energy.
- Increased focus on terrorism.

Why is identifying such trends so important for scenario development? Trends help ground the scenarios in reality, and spark additional thinking about a range of useful topics. Even an extensive set of trends, however, is not enough to build scenarios, as some aspect of the future is certain to escape us. Moreover, even if we did somehow have a "full" set of trends covering every eventuality, it would still be subject to our biases of perception and judgment. There can be no perfectly objective look at any trend in that set—we will always have to interpret.

Also, when developing scenarios, you need to allow for wild cards, extreme possibilities, and what we call "hypothetical breaks in continuity." These include, among other things:

- Risks of disruption such as new commercial alliances or a change in "the rules of the game."
- The impact of other related projects, such as the relocation of a competitor's manufacturing facilities to a low-cost country.
- Major uncertainties such as the emergence of new diseases, the possi-

bility of new and large-scale terrorist attacks, and the growing inci-
dence of tornadoes and floods.

Based on factors such as these, you can then begin to brainstorm in
an imaginative way about all sorts of situations that, though they have
a low probability, would have a big impact. You should also explore what
some of the boiling frogs (those slow-moving changes that are easily
ignored) or elephants in the room (the common-knowledge issues that
also get ignored) affecting your perceptions might be.

At UNIFE, participants considered several high-stakes wild cards
such as what could happen if cooperation among European Union
states faltered and individual countries grew in power again, or what
would take place if certain African countries adopted the Chinese yuan
given China's increasing influence there.

Once you've probed the possible, looking at numerous trends and
deciding which ones seem most significant, you can then move on to
Step 3. But we should stress that achieving consensus regarding exactly
which trends and wild cards your organization should focus on often
involves some complexity. Since people are likely to have differing perspectives, we often conduct surveys, or ask participants to vote on the
various trends, so that they can then be narrowed down to the ones that
seem the most important. You might also consider trying to identify
those megatrends that seem the most controversial, that is, where some
people strongly believe that they're extremely important but others
think that they are much less so. Indeed, in some instances, we have
polled decision makers regarding the trends and wild cards that they
think will have the most impact (or that they feel they and their organizations are the least well prepared to deal with), and then selected those
that were subjects of the greatest *disagreement* as the basis for Steps 3
and 4. Sometimes it is these highly debated trends that, though they
may seem very far-fetched and unlikely to occur, end up being the most
relevant when developing scenarios. To understand why, imagine how
helpful it might have been a few years ago if the top executives at the
major airlines, in a scenario-planning exercise, had pondered the possibility that volcanic ash clouds would disrupt air travel for weeks on

end. The idea of "reactivated volcanoes" as a critical trend probably would have seemed preposterous at the time. But of course, it's a wild card possibility that ended up actually occurring when in the spring of 2010 eruptions of Eyjafjallajökull in Iceland caused travel disruptions across western and northern Europe for more than a month. The airlines scrambled to create alternate routes and suffered significant financial losses.

Steps 3 and 4: Diverge and Converge

One key point of distinction in the scenarios application of the new boxes approach is that there are three distinct cycles of divergence and convergence. The first is to come up with variables, the second is to brainstorm on the variables and generate several hypotheses for each, and the third is to use these hypotheses to develop the scenarios themselves, as follows:

Diverge and Converge—Round I: Develop Variables

Variables are essential because the human imagination works best with images. And to spark creativity, it is essential to have specific images with clear constraints. Building on the work that you did researching trends and considering wild cards and extreme possibilities, you'll want to come up with variables that help you (and any other participants) visualize things, to imagine what things would be like in the situation evoked by that particular variable. For example, given current trends pertaining to urbanization, the aging population, and the growing importance of emerging markets, a variable we used with one client in a recent exercise was "a family lunch in Bangalore in 2020." This enabled discussion that clearly built upon the relevant megatrends, but also enabled workshop participants to visualize the family and imagine a range of possibilities for what they and their lunch together might really be like.

In our work with UNIFE, we began by looking at trends and topics relating to the broad global environment: the ways in which geopolitics, demographics, and economics would change. Then we looked at the overall shape of the transport industry. Finally, we explored the way in which suppliers of important products for the railway industry were organized and how healthy these businesses were. We developed ten to twelve candidates for variables (divergence) and eventually converged, agreeing upon four variables designed to spark creative thinking, which are shown in the exhibit on page 262.

For the broadest global environment/geopolitics factor, participants decided to ponder the variable of what the cover of the Christmas issue of *The Economist* would be in fifteen years. They also reflected upon what they thought it would be like to arrive at Penn Station in New York City on a Monday morning in 2025. To assess how the overall transport industry might change, they contemplated the variable of what shipping bananas from Harare, Zimbabwe, to Barcelona, Spain, would likely entail in 2025. And regarding changes specific to the rail industry, they considered the variable of what information and factors would likely be included in a tender document pertaining to a major new railway project to be launched in 2025. (In this context, a "tender" refers to an RFP or "request for proposal" document in which a rail company proposes and describes how it would complete the project, the fees, and other costs that it would need covered, the milestones for completion of the project, and so on).

In UNIFE's case, it would not have worked to have multiple variables all associated with the broader society (for example, the cover of *The Economist,* as in Variable 1 on page 262, along with a family lunch in Bangalore and what a general strike in Germany would have looked like). The reason is that the results of brainstorming on those variables would not have been relevant enough for UNIFE. It also would not have worked to have multiple variables associated with the transport industry (two of the four, as on page 262, is probably a good number), since the results would be too insular. We generally recommend one variable focused on the outer circle shown on page 262, the global environment; two focused on the industry; and one focused on the company/group in question, as in the UNIFE case. Finally, it would not have worked to have too many variables tied to the same set of trends (for example, all about demographics or alternative energy), since expo-

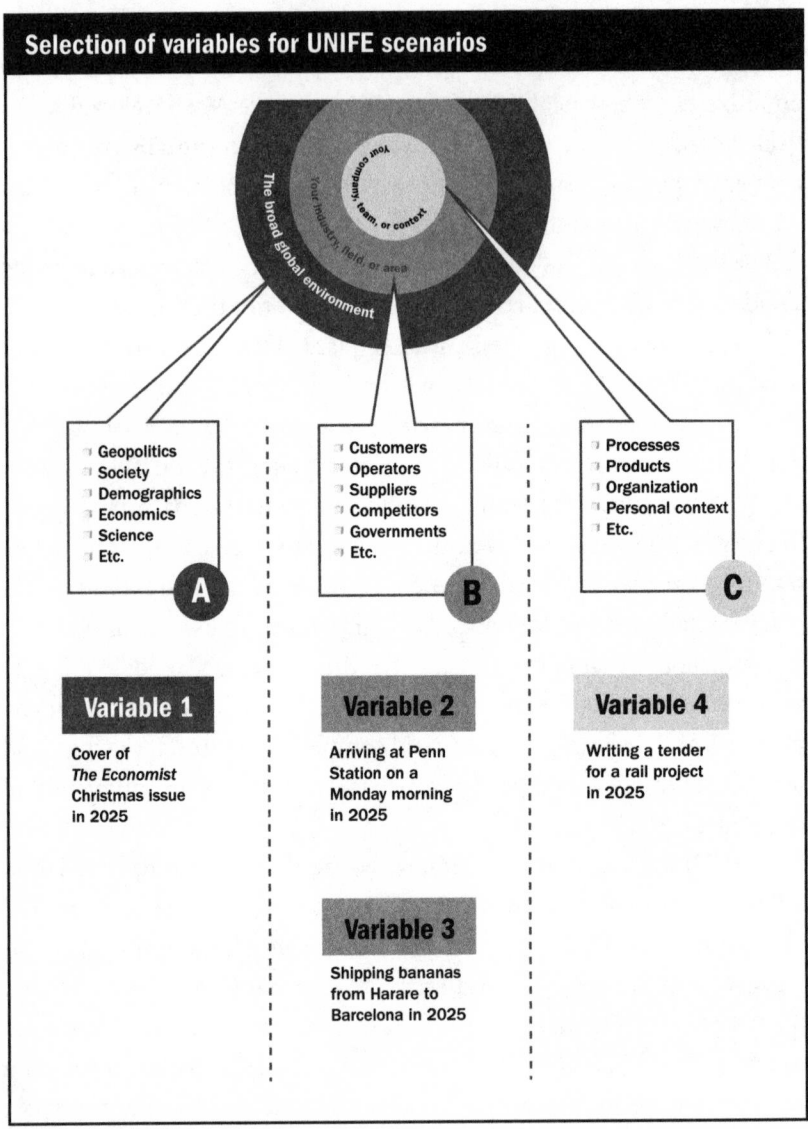

Selection of variables for UNIFE scenarios

Your company

Your company, team, or context

Your industry, field, or area

The broad global environment

A
- Geopolitics
- Society
- Demographics
- Economics
- Science
- Etc.

B
- Customers
- Operators
- Suppliers
- Competitors
- Governments
- Etc.

C
- Processes
- Products
- Organization
- Personal context
- Etc.

Variable 1

Cover of
The Economist
Christmas issue
in 2025

Variable 2

Arriving at Penn
Station on a
Monday morning
in 2025

Variable 4

Writing a tender
for a rail project
in 2025

Variable 3

Shipping bananas
from Harare to
Barcelona in 2025

sure to a broad and varied set of trends is key to expanding the realm of the possible.

The exhibit on page 263 shows some of the relevant trends associated with each of the UNIFE variables.

Four variables selected, building on trends and wild cards

Variable 1: Cover of *The Economist* Christmas issue in 2025

- Ecological awareness
- Urbanization
- Demography
- Shortage of engineering capacities
- Resource scarcity
- Geopolitics

Variable 2: Arriving at Penn Station on a Monday morning in 2025

- Intermodal cooperation
- Technological innovations
- Urbanization
- Demography (population aging/growing)

Variable 3: Shipping bananas from Harare to Barcelona in 2025

- Interoperability
- Intermodal competition
- Ecological awareness
- Geopolitics

Variable 4: Writing a tender for a rail project in 2025

- Customer profiles (government, private)
- Scope of offering/product/technology
- Contract types (build-operate-transfer, turnkey . . .)
- Price and financing options
- Regulation/standard
- Competition
- Process/organization

Diverge and Converge—Round II: Develop Hypotheses
About Each Variable

The second round of divergence and convergence entails brainstorming on the variables to refine or develop new "wild" hypotheses (which will ultimately lead to the scenarios).

Building on the preceding step, you'll want to subject each variable to bold hypotheses (H1, H2, H3, etc.), to reflect extreme limits, points of disruption, wishful thinking, chaos, booms, and so on. Each hypothesis must be plausible yet uncertain. An ideal list will be composed of varied and contrasting hypotheses.

For this part of the process, a group of three to six people should tackle each variable (or, depending on the number of people involved, have them do more than one variable each). Each group should discuss the relevant trends, coming up with a range of options (divergence), and then, after further discussion, decide upon four to five hypotheses for every variable (convergence). These hypotheses can then be shared with the broader group as appropriate.

For each variable, you'll want to raise all sorts of questions. For example, consider the second UNIFE variable—arriving at Penn Station on a Monday morning in 2025. What would the trains look like? How busy would the station be? What cities would be served? What modes of transport would connect to trains? What would the passengers be like, from a demographic perspective?

In our work with UNIFE, when we discussed the third variable— what it might be like to ship bananas across the globe—the group came up with several hypotheses. One entailed a boom in Africa encouraged by investment and trade with wealthier countries. Such a boom could lead to much better transportation, particularly rail, supported by low-cost Chinese technology. A different hypothesis was one in which low-cost air travel becomes even more common, displacing rail in many instances. Perhaps few people would even consider shipping a perishable good, like bananas, via comparably expensive rail in the future. Or, because of carbon emissions, perhaps air travel would be sharply limited; solar-powered trains could be the transport system of the future. Or maybe climate change would make banana cultivation more viable in Europe and then there would be little to no future demand for African bananas at all.

Once the hypotheses are developed, give them short, memorable names to help cement the images in participants' minds (at least temporarily). Below are the fanciful hypotheses UNIFE developed for each of the four variables it considered:

Variable 1: Cover of *The Economist* Christmas Issue in 2025

- *Virtual Christmas dinner.* Christmas dinner happens via webcam, with gifts exchanged online with virtual families. Everyone has a virtual identity along with a physical one.
- *Platinum age.* It is the golden age of unlimited green low-cost energy. Rechargeable low-cost batteries are used in transport and a new economic model is being developed as a result.
- *Beijing 1, New York 0.* China has become the world's preeminent economy, boasting 90 percent of the world's top managers, universities, and talent. Chinese engineers are preferred over cheaper engineers from California.
- *Last survivor.* The destruction of conditions enabling life on earth threatens the human race with extinction. Cities are being constructed underwater and in space.

Variable 2: Arriving at Penn Station on a Monday Morning in 2025

- *Easy rider.* Paperless tickets, complete interoperability of bus/train/ subway tickets, and faster rail travel mean a crowded station, yet one full of people moving efficiently.
- *Prison.* Security is an obsession. Transit is in sealed "tubes." Passengers enter at one end of the train and exit at the other. There are no services or stores in stations.
- *City peak.* The entire city is skyscrapers, with Penn Station an extension of some of them. Only long distances are covered by train.
- *Phantom.* Downtown is empty, Penn Station is abandoned, and New York is a "ghost town" with many suburbs but no real life in the center.

Variable 3: Shipping Bananas from Harare to Barcelona in 2025

- *Fair African banana boom.* Encouraged by a European sense of responsibility, fair trade creates wealth and opportunity in Africa. This leads to a boom in transport, particularly rail, supported by low-cost Chinese technology.
- *Fast bananas.* Consumers demand fast and fresh products at low prices. Low-cost and sustainable air travel and more air hubs displace rail.
- *Electric bananas.* To avoid increasing carbon emissions, trains powered by solar energy, including some high-speed trains, permeate Africa. A tunnel is created from Tangier to Gibraltar and this new, more dense rail network helps develop Africa.
- *Local food.* A desire for local consumption and improved confidence in local/regional products, along with protectionism and global warming enabling banana cultivation in Europe, means this type of shipping just doesn't happen. Overall, long-distance shipping declines dramatically.

Variable 4: Writing a Tender for a Rail Project in 2025

- *Click & buy.* Manufacturers offer standard trains for sale through catalogs, with a limited set of options. Clients buy them directly online.
- *Big elephant.* A pan-European mega-tender is conducted every ten years, covering the entire continent—winner takes all.
- *Complete mobility solution.* Train manufacturers offer a full-service solution, not only products and maintenance but also operation and infrastructure. They handle interfaces and links with other forms of transport, manage all risks, and remove responsibility from their clients.
- *Iron curtain.* A nationalist approach to tenders means local companies are prioritized, with engineering and manufacturing substantially local. Towns and regions get their share of local value-add, and contracts are in local languages.

Note the variety and range for each variable—the critical thing is to have wildly different, conceivable, but unlikely possibilities for each.

Diverge and Converge—Round III: Use the Hypotheses to Create Scenarios

The final round of divergence and convergence is about drafting the scenarios. The hypotheses should be presented in a visual matrix so that participants can see the common themes and begin to determine how, when intertwined, these hypotheses suggest distinct possible visions of the future. The hypotheses are the critical building blocks for scenarios, but this third session of divergence and convergence is important, too. As part of the plenary session, everyone needs to do a lot of diverging and discussing together, sharing thoughts and considering various theories as to what the future world could be like. Working together, you'll want to develop specific stories that link together a hypothesis (or several hypotheses) from each variable theme.

Each logical, coherent chain of hypotheses will thus become the raw material for a scenario.

The only way to convert various hypotheses into helpful, meaningful scenarios is to simply jump in and start—someone needs to propose a first thought, a coherent story that links several hypotheses together. It can then get adjusted via some divergent "yes, and . . ." conversation with the group, and eventually another completely different idea should be brought up. Ultimately the raw materials for approximately four scenarios should emerge and convergence can occur.

The chart on page 268 shows how UNIFE consolidated hypotheses into scenarios. As you can see, participants decided that the "easy rider" hypothesis, of modern, efficient rail travel at Penn Station, might happen in a world where the solar-powered trains were hard at work bringing bananas from Harare. The future in which Africa's economies had boomed might also be one in which New York was filled with many more skyscrapers. Some hypotheses were used twice, others not at all, and some were combined or adjusted. This sometimes seems counterintuitive but it's the scenarios that are the ultimate goal (the hypotheses and variables will soon be irrelevant). For example, under variable 2, "city peak" was used in two scenarios while "phantom" was not used, and "electric bananas"/"fast bananas" were combined under variable 3.

Once you decide upon scenarios, the next step is to give each scenario an imaginative and evocative title. It is also important to test each scenario. A good one needs to be colorful and surprising. It must be relevant, coherent, plausible, convincing, significant in terms of consequences, transparent, and easy to recount and even to illustrate.

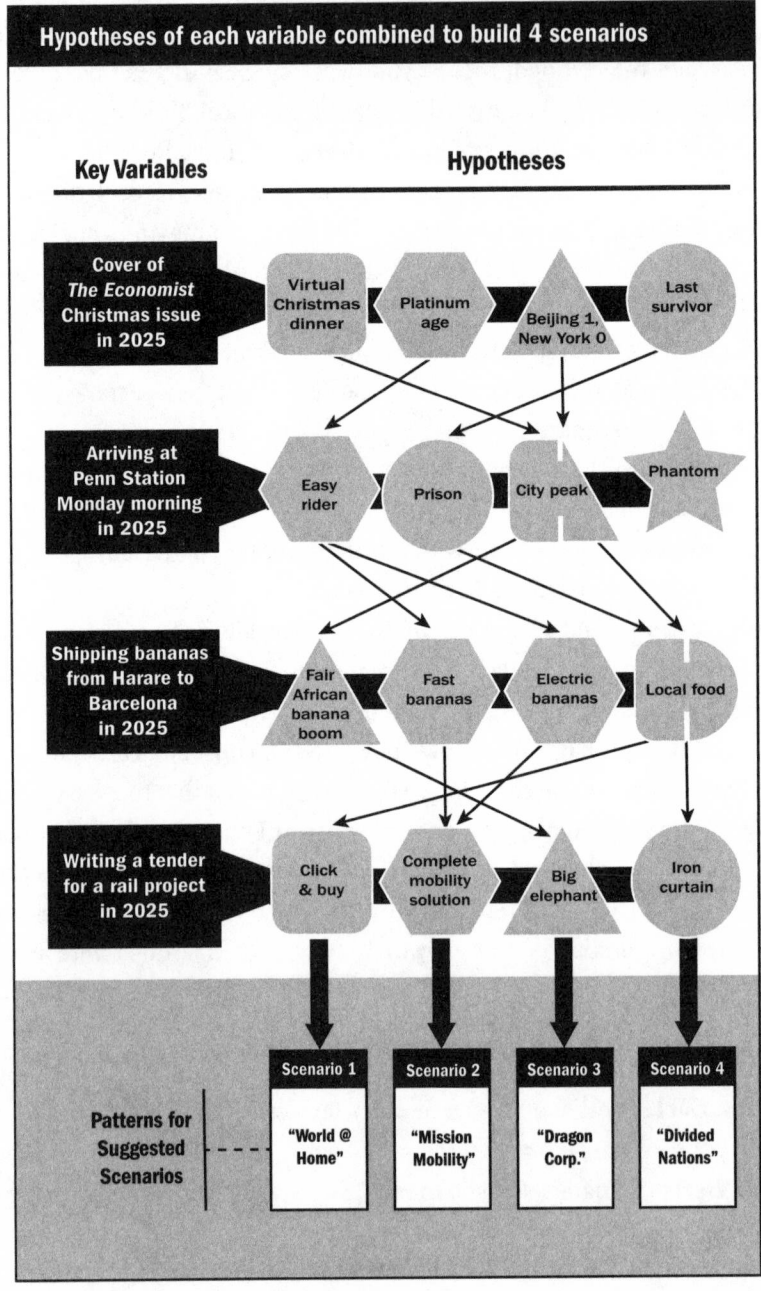

All of your creative juices as scenario builders should go into developing realistic and coherent scenarios derived from the imaginative combination of hypotheses.

The ideal set of scenarios has three or four narratives, structurally or qualitatively different, and not just simple variations of a scenario. The ideal set has to cover as many future alternatives as possible and vary the road maps that lead to these futures. It has to reveal the diverse problems and tensions, and present a range of projects.

In the case of UNIFE, participants developed the following four scenarios:

- *World @ Home.* After the financial crisis ebbs, the world experiences a boom in communication technology. The virtual universe is the backbone of society: We communicate virtually across the globe. We become a more urban society, and the contrast between rich cities and poorer agricultural regions intensifies. Mobility becomes less important for people; passenger transportation declines while transportation of goods increases. Yet transportation of some goods, like foodstuffs, decreases because we now, more than ever, "buy local."

- *Mission Mobility.* A major discovery in the science of energy enables a "clean tech" revolution, which in turn ends the financial crisis. Unlimited recourse to green energy leads to the intensive development of green transportation technology. Cars and even planes become green, and the mobility of people and goods increases worldwide. The rail industry changes: There is now strong competition with other modes of transport; operators develop and combine air, car, and rail options; rail vies with air and auto to become faster, cheaper, and more convenient.

- *Dragon Corp.* As the West experiences decades of stagnant growth, China dominates the world's economy, industry, and financial markets. The country attracts the best minds and has the world's best universities; it operates huge companies, exploiting the resources of Africa and South America; and its government acquires large companies with the enormous cash stockpiles China's booming economy has generated. Chinese rail enterprises lead the world; Western

companies fight to survive by cutting prices and offering more services.
• *Divided Nations.* Several decades of low growth cause a rise in protec-
tionist spirit in many parts of the world. Economic factors cause the
demise of both the European Union and the International Monetary
Fund; nationalism becomes the dominant political ideology worldwide, with economies reorganizing at the local and national levels.
The disparity between the global rich and poor intensifies. Transport
is largely local, given new barriers between nations. There is minimal
international traffic and no interoperability; suppliers are local and
benefit from subsidies.

Once you've come up with a title and summary for each scenario, the
raw materials for scenarios will be clear (if not, some additional iteration and tweaking may be required). After that, you'll augment and
enrich each scenario, each new box, to flesh out the story and its potential implications. As you do so, explore the global context in which this
scenario evolves, and how each scenario links with anticipated megatrends. Try to understand what the impact of each scenario would be on
the different areas of your organization, and what can be concluded in
terms of each scenario's potential opportunities, benefits, and advantages as opposed to its possible challenges, risks, and disadvantages.
What can be added to the story to make the scenario even more convincing? What is the "trigger" (which could be a black swan or some
more natural evolution of events) that would lead to this scenario actually happening? Use your imagination to help you visualize the situations, events, and settings that could potentially cause one or more of
the scenarios to materialize.

In our work with UNIFE, for each scenario we fleshed out the stories
and the triggers that could set them in motion.

• *World @ Home.* The story focuses on a major European city, hyper-
connected and full of skyscrapers, with a detailed description of life-
styles in 2025. The trigger: eBay buys Wal-Mart.
• *Mission Mobility.* The story focuses on a U.S. university campus that is

"plugged in" to the green and "alternative energy" cultures. The trigger: Engineers finalize a new low-cost green battery.

- *Dragon Corp.* Looking primarily at Africa, where the Chinese are omnipresent, this story illustrates the new economic forces affecting the world. The trigger: China passes Intel in the production of electronic goods.
- *Divided Nations.* The story explores three major European capitals, primarily Brussels, where politicians debate the future of the EU and multilateralism. The trigger: Three regions within different European nations simultaneously declare their independence.

The complete story for each scenario could even include thousands of words. But, as the adage goes, less is often more. Following the development of scenarios, it is of critical importance to communicate them succinctly and use them effectively and compellingly, since circulating a detailed four-thousand-word treatise describing them is not useful within most modern organizations (indeed, such overkill is perhaps one of the reasons why classic scenario planning is underused). Clear, fun, easy-to-grasp communication of the scenarios is a much more effective way of allowing everyone not directly involved in the exercise to benefit from the effort expended. The final UNIFE scenarios, with brief descriptions and implications for different stakeholders in the rail industry, as well as cartoons appealing to the "right brain," are included on pages 272–275.

These diagrams represent just one possible approach to expressing scenarios. UNIFE ended up including the scenarios in its annual report, while others keep them confidential but use made-up 2020 newspapers and the like to communicate them internally. No matter what approach you take, it is critically important that, once you've come up with the scenarios, you focus on how you're going to communicate and implement them. Remember that a scenario is not an action plan. The scenarios should be tools for promoting constructive, timely, and often urgently needed thought processes within your organization. Ideally, they become an invaluable reference point for everyone, at every level of the organization, any time there is a question about the future, or about

- Communication technologies boomed after the financial crisis to improve cost efficiency and environmental friendliness
- Virtual worlds become the backbone of society: Communities develop, meet, and live via the Web
- High degree of urbanization increases contrast between city centers and rural agricultural areas
- Higher sensitivity to environmental concerns and nutrition quality, increasing demand for local products
- People mobility is secondary, only goods are moving

Key implications for rail

Consumers	Virtual communities are central to day-to-day life: People travel much less but home delivery of goods is expected Strong "green awareness," desire for local food
Authorities	Decreased government support of rail, as it doesn't gain votes Only financially viable routes survive
Operators	Passenger: small market, premium segment Freight: very high speed, urban and underground services Large intermodal players and flexible last-mile specialists
Suppliers	Overall market drop accelerates consolidation Chinese players prosper in large domestic market Standardization is key, trains are commodities sold online
Technology	Integrated communication systems Automation systems in all rail segments R&D focus is on freight: speed, efficiency, cost, "green"
Business models	Super-efficient supply chain Economies of scale and scope drive consolidations Information and intermodal management essential

- A discovery in energy science led to a "clean-tech revolution," which helped overcome the financial crisis
- Strong development of "green transport" (particularly automotive) due to the new "green energy"
- People and goods mobility is increasing: Complete and intermodal services are expected
- Rail industry is challenged:
  - strong competition with other transport modes
  - operators expanding and combining different transportation modes (air, road, rail)
  - increased pressure for differentiation in speed, service quality, price

Key implications for rail

Consumers	Passengers want integrated and customized solutions; full-mobility services combining all transportation modes Strong competition between rail and other modes
Authorities	Less incentive for governments to support rail versus other modes of transport: no CO_2 issues anymore Overall, minimal government implications
Operators	Freight: international and intermodal consolidation Increasing pressure on suppliers to improve interoperability, speed, quality, cost position
Suppliers	Western suppliers have first-mover advantage in intermodality until China develops disruptive concepts, leading to a new advantage
Technology	Open source, interoperability, convergence across modes, integrated software for scheduling Very rapid innovations: Capacity to innovate quickly is key
Business models	New players, even from other industries, enter at every level Capacity to integrate several transportation modes is key

Scenario 3: Dragon Corp.

- The planet has organized into regions, with Western countries getting poorer and China taking the lead
  - domination economically, financially, and industrially
  - leveraging resources from Africa and South America and huge cash reserve
  - "brain domination" with the best universities
  - Chinese players acquire companies worldwide
- Chinese companies are global leaders in rail
  - large Chinese market, with latest technologies
  - cost and technology leadership
  - Western markets stagnating

Key implications for rail

Consumers	Demand for low-cost solutions for freight and passengers Commoditization of offering, limited customization, and low level of service
Authorities	Strong liberalization and competition among operators Low-cost and standardized solutions increase profitability Governments' financial support is decreasing
Operators	New players with commoditized basic transport service Global operators leverage scale on the basis of standardization Freight decrease in developed countries
Suppliers	Chinese suppliers produce low-cost rolling stock Chinese mergers and acquisitions in the West exacerbate competition The few Western players focus on service and quality
Technology	Chinese suppliers access high-end technologies via mergers and acquisitions China develops new technologies and sets standards, but generally decreases level of innovation
Business models	Chinese companies in every segment of the value chain (rail supply, operations) and buying existing assets Low-cost trains enable development of leasing services

Scenario 4: Divided Nations

- EU and IMF have broken down, regional trade blocs no longer exist, decrease in international trade
- Protectionism and insecurity spread as the financial crisis continues to affect Western countries
- Nationalism becomes the predominant political approach in all regions
- Transport is mostly local (urban, mass transit, regional) because of high barriers between countries and regions
  - no interoperability, little international traffic
  - less international harmonization and liberalization
  - local suppliers with local subsidies

Key implications for rail

Consumers	Demand for local and regional mobility, not international
	Demand for security in transport and public areas
	Wealth and demand gap in mature versus poor countries
Authorities	Less liberalization, rise of protectionist initiatives
	Governments support local and public rail industry
	Authorities deal with security issues in transport
Operators	Decrease in global expansion; less long-distance freight
	Back to era of local incumbents, with one operator for each segment
Suppliers	Local footprint required, for protectionist reasons
	Global players succeed only by acquiring local companies
	High costs/inefficiencies due to local standards
Technology	Strong differentiation across countries on technology
	Decrease in innovation overall (no incentives)
	Development of technologies to address security issues
Business models	More local players and pressure to have local content
	Only national protected players survive
	Slow growth for industry overall

what might happen. They can help test management methods, challenge perceptions, ensure the strategic vision is as robust as possible, and evaluate the soundness of strategies as they apply to completely different situations, even exceptional ones.

As you work to understand the practical implications of any scenario, you and your other decision makers should consider such questions as:

- If you knew this scenario was going to occur, what opportunities and threats would you face?
- What strategies would you implement, and how would it change your current approach?
- What signposts or leading indicators would alert you if this scenario were going to occur?
- What would be needed to perform successfully in this environment? What would be the impact on each part of your organization? On your customers? On your competitors?
- *What do you need to do today to prepare?*

To build upon those questions, you can use techniques we've discussed in this book. For example, you can take the perspective of different stakeholders (competitors, customers, regulators, etc.) to understand how each of these groups might potentially react to each scenario. You could enter a new divergence phase, for example using the "joint ventures" exercise to list potential new product or service opportunities that would arise in each potential future.

As you begin to apply the scenarios as meaningful new "boxes," your organization's vulnerability to surprises will be reduced; you will become more adaptive. You'll be more likely to experience *Eureka* than *Caramba*. The organization will have its mental models stretched and understand the environment in a much more comprehensive way. And there will be a common language available for you and your colleagues to use whenever you're trying to anticipate and address the uncertain future.

UNIFE members found the scenarios provocative and practical as they grappled with a changing world. As a result of the scenarios, UNIFE developed "deep-dive" analyses into six topics: the rise of rapidly developing competitors such as China, the future of government regulation, new and disruptive technologies, the changing landscape for operators, potential changes to the business model, and the demand for integrated and customized transportation services. Individual members were able to look into their own business opportunities differently and more deeply as a result, as the scenarios and deep dives became valuable inputs to their strategies—they are now focusing on segments with higher barriers to entry for emerging-market players, increasing the scope of their maintenance offering, adapting their R&D process to reduce time-to-market, and more. At the end of the exercise, there was a major conference in Warsaw where the twenty people who had participated in the scenario workshop shared the scenarios and the deep-dive analyses with almost two hundred leaders from across the industry, including most of the CEOs.

Juergen Meyer, the director of strategy in Siemens's Rail Systems division, notes that "we still use the scenarios when doing strategic planning, and also in our daily business to see if there is something we are missing, and how each scenario is evolving. It's clear that it changed the way we think about the future."

Step 5: Reevaluate Relentlessly

Like any box, even the most brilliant, forward-looking scenario will not be valid forever. During the UNIFE exercise, participants generally felt that the Dragon Corp. scenario was too extreme. The detailed description stated that "Chinese rail enterprises lead the world, attracting the greatest markets with cutting-edge technology, along with commanding economies of scale. Western companies fight to survive by offering services." The scenario was still helpful for European rail companies, however, as they planned for how they would address a changing world—after our workshop together, many were no longer ignoring Chinese advances into their backyards as unimportant and irrelevant.

Indeed, after the UNIFE scenario exercises, reality bore out many elements of Dragon Corp. China recently invested more than $300 billion to create a high-speed "bullet" train network that promises to cut travel times between cities across China by as much as half. Expectations are that making such transport easier and quicker will encourage trade and stimulate such industries as construction, commodities, and tourism.[3] China already has a line connecting Shanghai and Beijing making the 820-mile trip in five hours (it would take eighteen hours on railways in many other countries); estimates suggest the project will be completed by the year 2020.[4] China is now helping construct high-speed rail routes in Turkey, Venezuela, and Saudi Arabia and exploring projects in seven other countries, including the United States.[5] As U.S. leaders envision the construction of high-speed train corridors in Texas, Florida, and California, several of the members of UNIFE are keenly interested in the lucrative contracts to help supply the key technologies required to build and run them. And yet, much as Dragon Corp. envisioned, Chinese high-speed train producers are formidable contenders that may very well offer steep competition to UNIFE members from Europe.

Still, as much as Dragon Corp. could be seen to be coming true in some ways, our advice to UNIFE's members—and to you as you develop various scenarios to help your organization—is to remain ever vigilant. Each scenario you develop, like any other box, is at risk of becoming outdated, incomplete, or simply obsolete. Step 5 asks you to reevaluate your current boxes relentlessly, and to keep an eye on the evolution of trends, any elephants in the room and boiling frogs, or other radical new future shifts or changes.

Be careful: Don't fail to concede *Caramba* if it has, in fact, occurred. For instance, if Boeing creates "train jets"—inexpensive, efficient, superfast airplanes that attach to railroad lines and soar at speeds competitive with or better than those of current bullet trains—and if this new dazzling technology leads Boeing to own and control 75 percent of the long-distance mass transit industry in China and other countries previously dominated by high-speed rail, it would be time to replace Dragon Corp. with a new set of more specific scenarios.

Look, too, for paradoxes. UNIFE members might currently be well-advised to ask themselves, Are more and more people in China and elsewhere flying on inexpensive airlines despite the construction of new high-speed rail networks? Are the tickets for high-speed trains too expensive for many customers, thus causing a boom in traditional (low-speed) rail travel and alternate transportation such as express buses?

In addition, try not to lose sight of "weak signals" that the current scenarios you're relying upon may need to be tuned up or replaced. For instance, as much as China has evinced tremendous early success in setting up its high-speed rail network, the project has not been without its share of problems, all of which could properly be seen as just the sort of "weak signals" suggesting that Dragon Corp. could soon become less important to UNIFE members than other new possible scenarios. In addition to the massive, difficult-to-recoup cost of building the new rail networks in China, there have already been numerous third-party reports alleging government corruption in connection with the project, problems with the quality of the technologies, and serious concerns about how safe they are for travelers. These issues all could be seen as signals that Dragon Corp. is, after all, just a box, a mental model that at some point will become less apt and helpful than other new scenarios.

Indeed, as the world evolves, you may come to feel uncertain about the megatrends you recently thought important and relevant, as well as the scenarios you developed in response to them. One way of coping with such uncertainty is to discard your current scenarios and replace them with new ones. But another approach is to take one existing scenario and to spin off several more specific ones based on it that help illuminate things even more clearly. For example, the rail companies that are members of UNIFE now know much more about China's rail industry than they did when Dragon Corp. was first developed. Some of them may now be finding that referring to Dragon Corp. is not itself enough; instead, they may need to begin drilling down on specific aspects of how China's ascendancy in this area is likely to affect them. By developing additional scenario "boxes" building exclusively on Dragon Corp., they could generate three or four new, highly focused scenarios that offer a much more granular and specific set of insights.

You'll also want to keep a close eye on the nuances of your organization's performance metrics. As you're piloting your metaphorical helicopter, are numerous key dials beginning to augur danger ahead? If you are an executive working for a high-speed rail business that is a member of UNIFE, you might want to closely monitor such metrics as:

- Your company's respective share of the overall international market for high-speed rail construction projects.
- Shifts in the decision-making of key customers in the nations that are most keen on building high-speed-rail networks (are these nations increasingly acquiring whole new sets of third-party products and technologies rather than those of your company?).
- Capital and other costs that are significantly increasing or that remain remarkably high for your company as compared with those being incurred by your competitors.

If several of these "dials" are simultaneously askew, you might decide that it is time to replace Dragon Corp. with an entirely new box.

Finally, even if all the signals in front of you look wonderfully positive, we hope you will not become complacent! Even if your scenarios currently strike you as perfectly on target, you must continue monitoring them very closely, shaping them to meet change as it occurs. Remember, "no idea is good forever."

LISTEN TO EINSTEIN'S COUNSEL: DON'T OVERDO IT!

One question our clients ask us when preparing scenario exercises is how exactly Shell *knew* about overcapacity in the tanker business, or how UNIFE members *knew* China would "double down" in rail. The answer, in both cases, is that they didn't. Rather, they used scenarios as models to better prepare for what they could not forecast in detail. Scenario planning is never a magic way to *know* the future. It's important to embrace ambiguity, or at a minimum, accept it, and recognize that your boxes (in this case, scenarios) represent an inductive response to this ambiguity.

The following diagram (building on the one at the end of chapter 4) shows how, by following the five steps in the scenario-planning process, you are repeatedly inducing from what is "in front of you," to converge upon constructs that are "within you":

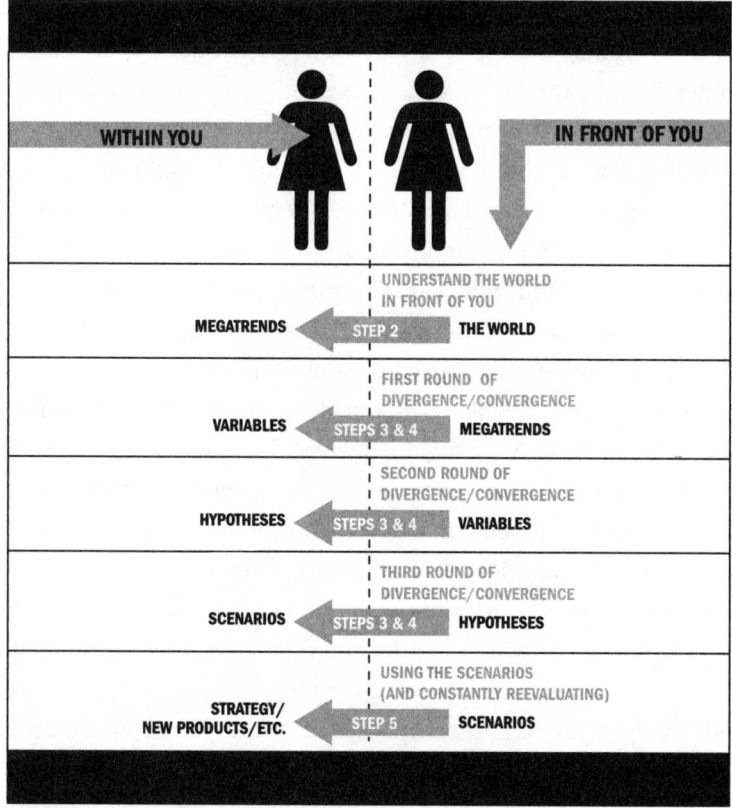

Optimally, this process is a simple one: You do your best to flow from megatrends, to variables, to hypotheses about those variables, to scenarios, and then on to creating your new strategies, products, ideas, models, and other boxes. You're not trying to find "the" one answer; you're developing broad, open, flexible mental models, guiding ideas that can later be interpreted, refined, and made practical. Or, as we like to say, you're creating boxes that you'll subsequently "fill in."

Still, we realize that some minds gravitate toward detailed nuances and complexity. We often collaborate with clients who are highly analytical and find it difficult to become comfortable with the ambiguity inherent in simplifying things, in using only *some* megatrends, variables, hypotheses, and scenarios. Even when their organization is committed to a scenario exercise, these individuals try to impose order wherever they can. They often feel compelled to spend a huge amount of time on trends, listing hundreds of trends in dozens of categories, with detail and backup for each. This can be useful, though there is a point of diminishing returns, especially given the inevitability of "unknown unknowns" that make identifying "all the right trends" futile. In the divergence phase, when they are required to develop variables, rather than recognizing the ambiguity inherent in narrowing down their list of trends and "wild cards," sometimes these individuals try to rank their extensive list, and develop "the best variables" that way. This is often time-consuming and inefficient, although it will tend to produce a good set of variables. During the subsequent rounds of divergence, when they're working to develop hypotheses and ultimately scenarios, their fear of missing something important often leads to a form of paralysis wherein they become afraid to commit to any set of hypotheses and scenarios. As a result, they often end up with a large number of scenarios (for example, six to ten instead of three or four), which can make it much harder for them to focus, especially when trying to determine what their strategy or other practical response should be with respect to each scenario. To be clear: Even coming up with more than four scenarios can still be valuable—and we believe that doing so is much better than *not* completing a scenario exercise at all.

But as a general matter, we encourage you not to overdo things. The human mind and memory cannot process eight scenarios all at once, and we find that developing around three or four is generally the most sound and effective approach. Trying to be sure you have the best possible scenarios out of all the many possibilities is like trying to prove that seven is a better answer than eight when asked how many colors are in the rainbow. You may be sweating too much without reaping any additional benefit. Scenario planning should help you come to embrace ambiguity and uncertainty, rather than stress about their existence. We subscribe to Albert Einstein's famous quote: "Everything should be made as simple as possible, but not simpler." In other words, when you're engaged in the scenario-planning process, you'll want to keep things as simple as possible without losing the critical detail. Appropriate simplifying means keeping complexity that is absolutely necessary, while allowing that you'll cut other corners: letting certain very good ideas drop away, for instance.

In the end, the impact and value of scenarios are not in their perfection. The benefit lies in how you interpret the scenarios, the extent to which you and your colleagues are able to rely upon them to be creative, pragmatic, and productive in coping with change and dealing with all the exciting risks and opportunities that lie ahead.

We see our new boxes approach to scenarios as a powerful way of stretching, challenging, and enriching your strategies. Developing scenarios is not a high-cost process seeking precision and finality. Rather, it is a relatively low-cost but high-return way to expand your perception of the possible, to break free from the constraints of how you've routinely handled things in the past, and to cultivate instead highly creative, entrepreneurial, resilient new ways of planning for potential threats and seizing upon emerging opportunities.

TEN

A New Beginning: How to Custom-Fit the Five Steps to Your Situation

□ □

OW THAT YOU KNOW the five steps and understand the breadth of potential applications, we would like to offer a few practical suggestions regarding how to apply our approach in your situation. Although there is not a one-size-fits-all methodology to which you must adhere, below are some general guidelines.

YOU CAN USE THE PROCESS BY YOURSELF BUT GENERALLY WILL WANT TO INCLUDE OTHERS IN SOME WAY

We realize that you may be getting ready for a solo session—and, indeed, you can sit down and use any of the creative techniques we recommend in this book on your own. Doing such independent work may be particularly helpful if you're trying to come up with ideas regarding a personal problem, such as dealing with a difficult boss or coping with some other specific situation primarily affecting you as an individual rather than your organization as a whole. But even in such personal situations, you will probably be able to generate the best solutions if you ask for some help "diverging" with a small number of friends or colleagues. We often run workshops for our clients with large numbers of people, but we have seen amazing things happen with small groups of three to four as well. There is really no minimum; it's simply that by bringing people together, you'll capture the power of multiple minds to produce as wide a range of ideas as possible. Since one of the most significant prerequisites to sustainable creativity is the constant generation of lots of new ideas—or new perspectives on old ideas—we would recommend that you generally try to implement the five steps with others.

DIVERSITY AND OPEN COMMUNICATION ARE KEY

When organizing a creativity session using our approach, or just trying some exercises with a couple of friends, you'll be well advised to do your utmost to include a mix of people with different backgrounds and perspectives. A diversity of experience and individual outlooks (people from different levels and in different roles within your company, people of different genders, ages, and educational backgrounds) will lead to a greater number and range of ideas and thus to greater overall imaginativeness and productivity. Your spouse or your closest friends may be helpful, but they may also be too close to your own outlook. And at work, just because there is an existing "leadership team" for the business, or just because Tristan is the head of R&D and Chelsea is the head of HR, it doesn't mean they are necessarily the right or the best people to come up with new ideas.

Cultivating open communication in the interest of creativity means setting a tone that allows everyone, no matter what their status or station within the group you've engaged, to speak up and be heard. If you're doing a formal workshop-type session, beware of including too many people in the same reporting line in the room: If there is hierarchy present, it can stifle idea generation unless you shatter all the pretenses and empower all members to give their uninhibited feedback. This is best done thoughtfully and deliberately through some form of warm-up or icebreaker-type exercise. Indeed, in the early part of your workshop, we'd encourage you to state directly to all participants (or have the most senior person state) that during the workshop, they should try to put aside the differences of seniority and status among them, give everyone the same chance to participate, and respect and embrace all the ideas that people offer up.

In addition, including senior leaders in whatever ways you can is a good idea whenever possible. If your organization is small, you might even want everyone, or nearly everyone, to come together and participate, but in all cases, from a change management perspective, when the decision makers are involved in the development of ideas, those ideas are more likely to come to fruition.

PREPARE BY AGREEING UPON YOUR OBJECTIVES AHEAD OF TIME— AND ASK A GOOD QUESTION

As a simple existential matter, if you don't know your overall destination, you won't possibly be able to navigate the various pathways for getting there. Before you even step into the actual creative process, one of the most important prerequisites is to agree ahead of time as to what exactly your specific objectives are going to be. To do so, you can think carefully using a blank sheet of paper, or conduct interviews with key people at your organization and circulate a "statement of purpose" so that they can refine it according to their best thinking. You may then opt to share a summary of the interviews, or of research done in the "explore" step, or even a set of questions to ponder, as a pre-read for anyone who will be joining you. Whatever approach you take, the key is clarity on what exactly you most hope to achieve.

In terms of *output,* are you trying to get a long list of ideas that can then be prioritized later, or is it critical to whittle the output down to your top five ideas (that is, to do divergence and then convergence within the same workshop)?

In terms of *topic,* are you trying to find new product ideas, a replacement for a specific product, or a new vision for the company? Are you hoping to improve your organization's operations, its productivity, your overall business model?

Put another way, before launching into the creative process in earnest, you will want to know what questions you're really trying to answer and make sure that you've framed them (as we've seen throughout this book) in a way that will help provoke a maximum of ideas. For instance, if executives at BIC approached a divergence session thinking that the key question was "How should we come up with more ideas for pens?" they would have probably come up with just that (pens with special features, in different colors, of various shapes and sizes, and so on). But the outcome would probably have been quite different if the questions they posed instead were "What do we actually do at BIC?" and then "How could we change or redefine what we do at BIC so that five years from now, our products are in every grocery store, pharmacy, tobacco shop, and newspaper kiosk the world over?" These sorts of questions would invite the kind of prospective thinking that very well could have led the company to shift its paradigm from the relatively limited one of a "low-cost disposable pen company" to the much more expansive (and as it turns out, profitable) one of a "company that makes low-cost disposable products of all kinds."

Being as clear and specific as possible about what you're after, having a clear view of key constraints and relevant criteria, and deciding together ahead of time "what success would look like" in as much detail as you can will be helpful in determining your agenda and how to proceed. Keep asking yourself and anyone joining you on the adventure, "Are we asking the right questions?" Even the most brilliant and creative ideation sessions, with huge amounts of preparation done in advance, will probably have little impact if they're generating lots of new ideas, strategies, or approaches for a problem, or a question, that isn't actually pertinent or important, or that's keeping you trapped in an outdated and increasingly irrelevant old box.

CREATE THE RIGHT PHYSICAL ENVIRONMENT

The ideal environment to foster the development of new boxes is usually somewhere off-site, comfortable, and as unfamiliar to you and anyone joining you as possible. A new environment provides a new perspective and thus helps stimulate new thinking. If resources allow, you might meet at a boutique hotel somewhere fun and interesting, at a "retreat" in a verdant natural setting, in a private space at a sports venue, or simply at a nice local restaurant. We have run workshops in the wilderness in Botswana, in the mountains of Pakistan, at ski lodges on snowy hillsides, and at numerous less glamorous places (as well as in our offices, which at least provide a fresh perspective for our clients). If resources are more limited, as will often be the case, that needn't stop you from working somewhere unfamiliar—you might meet together in a quiet spot within a local park or garden, at someone's house, in a different, unexpected part of your offices, or perhaps in an interesting space within a local art museum.

Allowing people to escape their usual surroundings and "get away from it all" will often help nourish their imaginations.

Moreover, these days it's not just a question of physically getting away from the day-to-day: If there's any way of enforcing a ban on electronic devices and phone calls, so much the better. The more you're able to help people separate from quotidian pressures, obligations, and distractions, the better.

MASTERMIND THE LOGISTICS

If you're with a group, try to think through the logistical aspects ahead of time. Two key considerations: First, as people share ideas, you'll want to record them in a way that enables those participating to observe and think about them as you proceed. You might want Post-it notes and markers (for everyone to put their own individual ideas on the wall), whiteboards that can be erased and reused, laptops or iPads or some other container for the ideas. Second, we'd encourage you to try to take various approaches and use materials that will help remove participants from their everyday conventions and expectations, and even maybe shock them a bit! For instance, when presenting basic information, instead of using diagrams and memoranda that look and feel just like the ones they're used to seeing at your organization on a daily basis, you might instead present the same information as a comic strip, a self-published book with photographs of all the participants, or as a dramatic play performed by you and a few other courageous colleagues.

When we are running a session, we love having flip charts (to explain concepts and track ideas) as well as PowerPoint and a projector (to show images, remind the group of key inputs such as trends, display interim output, and illustrate the group's consensus around various ideas during convergence). All of the suggestions in this section build on our general advice to make things visual, the better to affect what happens in our minds as we develop new boxes.

ALLOW SUFFICIENT TIME

When it comes to deciding how much time to allot for the process, our essential advice is to avoid rushing things. Some of the best ideas often arise toward the end of such creativity sessions, and sometimes spending, say, thirty or forty-five minutes on one issue generates a lot more helpful ideas than if you allocate only ten minutes to it. These things being said, we've seen effective two-hour sessions as well as wonderful weeklong sessions. It is also fine to let things "percolate" within you over the course of weeks, if you aren't bound by specific workshop dates or personal timelines.

In general, most of our clients who take the workshop route spend a full day on the first four steps of the process, allowing at least three hours for divergence, and one to two hours for convergence (which will often continue after the workshop ends). When in doubt, give yourself at least half a day (or a full day if resources permit) in order to dig as deeply into the creative process as possible and provide everyone sufficient time to generate all sorts of ideas on all the key issues and problems you're addressing.

One of the key reasons you will want to allocate a fair amount of time to the process—and especially to divergence—is this: In the corporate setting, participants generally begin the process with their backs up. They tend to feel a bit constrained, as though maintaining the status quo would be the most effective and sensible way of handling things. Everyone has been through workshops or brainstorms that don't work—usually, in our view, because the "doubt" phase is skipped, which means people aren't primed enough to understand and then challenge their mental models. As time passes, however, people relax and begin to see things they may not have noticed before. They let their guards down. They free up. Before long, ideas are flowing.

THE NEW PARADIGM—AND YOUR CHALLENGE

Thinking in new boxes is about changing the way you think, or, more precisely, increasing your awareness of how we all create and use mental boxes. It is a new paradigm for creativity, by virtue of the focus on interplay between the broad new boxes and smaller ones that fill them. There is no limit to the power of the five steps we have presented, or to what you can accomplish with them.

And so as we leave you, your challenge is this: To open yourself up to the unexpected, to astonishment, and to surprise. To challenge yourself to take creative risks and allow others you interact with, at work or at home, to do so, too. To free yourself from the shackles of your existing boxes, and foster an environment where your mental models are constantly being thoughtfully reevaluated, where a healthy dose of doubt allows new possibilities to take root. And if you succeed for a while, that's great, but you'll still need to reevaluate relentlessly, to make sure that you continue to do so.

We began with Sartre the dog and his quest for freedom—and we will end with a quote from the philosopher Sartre, who famously said that "freedom is what you do with what's been done to you." There is no shortage of issues facing our world today: from climate change and government deficits to cancer and the common cold, from combating doping in sports to finding ways to argue less with your life partner, or striving to make your first (or next) million. Whatever your goal is, it is your mind and your boxes that will take you there. And the most wonderful thing about that is that it means you have the opportunity, indeed the freedom, to shape the future, for yourself, your company, and the world, by breaking constraints and looking at the world in front of you in new ways.

What are the challenges you face? And how will you change the world in front of you, using the power of the boxes within you? What will your contribution be?

We hope that you will take every possible opportunity to think in new boxes, and we challenge you to change the world while doing so. And in the spirit of reevaluating our own boxes, we will always be grateful and happy to hear from you at TINBcomments.com.

Acknowledgments

□ □

E ARE GRATEFUL to The Boston Consulting Group: As an institution, it has been our professional home for many years. With that said, BCG is in essence a collection of amazing individuals, and we are particularly indebted to many of them.

First, Matthew Clark has served for years as our guide to anything related to marketing and publications, from our very first *Thinking in New Boxes* perspective to reading early drafts of every chapter of this book. His comments were sometimes tough but always thoughtful, and without his guidance the end product would not be nearly as good.

We are also especially grateful to Mike Deimler and Lisa Ellis, who as the leader and manager of BCG's Strategy practice, respectively, made so much happen in our worlds, and to Knut Haanaes, Mike's successor, who has continued to do so.

Simon Targett, as BCG's editor in chief, has been a longtime proponent of our ideas, a reader of our drafts, and a friend of creativity.

Many other individuals have graciously served as our thought partners for particular topics or stories in this book, and we are no less grateful to those who shared ideas or vignettes that did not end up making it into the final version. These people, generous with their time in the true BCG spirit, include Agnès Audier, Wendi Backler, Aaron Brown, Guillaume Charlin, Olavo Cunha, Filiep Deforche, Philip Evans, Thomas Gaissmaier, Jean-Christophe Gard, Marin Gjaja, Aurélie Granger, Michael Greenway, Gabrielle Halpern, Emmanuel Huet, Ashish Iyer, Nicolas Kachaner, Simon Kennedy, Matt Krentz, Florian Kuehnle, Zhenya Lindgardt, Claire Love, Hubertus Meinecke, Antonella Mei-Pochtler, Crista Merendino, Mark Ostermann, Kes Puckorius, Deepak Ravindran, Martin Reeves, Nneka Rimmer, Enrique Rueda-Sabater,

Alison Sander, Mark Shaner, Larry Shulman, Abheek Singhi, George Stalk, Andrew Taylor, Brenda Thickett, Jorge Tomaz, and Doug Woods.

Other mentors and helpful guides along the way have included Karen Gordon, Antoine Gourevitch, Nicolas Harlé, Beth Hoffman, Chris Howe, Rich Lesser, and Amyn Merchant.

We are also thankful for the many people who help make things happen behind the scenes at BCG. This group includes Katherine Andrews, Gary Callahan, Dan Coyne, and Gerry Hill for their help with our BCG-published pieces; Beth Gillett, Eric Gregoire, and Corrie Maguire for anything relating to book promotion and marketing; Dave Fondiller, Lexie Corriveau, and Madeleine Desmond in media relations; Kelley Kossakoski for coaching Alan on Twitter and social media; Deborah English and Jennifer Marden of the Strategy practice; and David Littleton from our design team, who was instrumental in the preparation of all the exhibits in the book. We are also grateful to Dave Cutler for his original cover concept.

We are grateful to all of the partners and consultants with whom we've collaborated at a wide range of clients, and to all of the clients we have served, especially those mentioned in this book—thank you for giving us these opportunities. We hope that we haven't forgotten to mention any of you individually above; we are grateful to all of you.

Outside of BCG, we are most indebted to Todd Shuster and Esmond Harmsworth, of the Zachary Shuster Harmsworth literary agency. They both started out as invaluable guides to the world of book publishing, helping us develop a book proposal that impressed Random House and challenging us to shift our own mindset based on what the typical reader would require. Todd subsequently served as a thought partner and collaborator throughout the process of developing a manuscript, helping us draft each story and chapter in as compelling a way as possible, and becoming a trusted friend at the same time. Bob Roe also helped us edit our early manuscript, bringing a fresh perspective (and the willingness to cut dramatically) when we needed it most, and Catherine Cuddihee made a range of last-minute corrections and improvements as well. Tonu, of CartoonBase, created the fantastic cartoon in Chapter 1, along with the four illustrating the UNIFE scenarios.

And last but far from least, we are deeply indebted to Will Murphy and the entire team at Random House for being excited at the potential they saw in our book proposal, for thoughtfully sharing their comments, and for the terrific marketing, promotion, and publicity teams we have only started to see in action as of this writing. Will is a brilliantly insightful person, an incisive editor, and a fiercely enthusiastic advocate. Our heartfelt thanks go to Ben Steinberg on the editing side, as well as to production editor Steve Messina, and Susan Kamil, Tom Perry, Theresa Zoro, Sally Marvin, Leigh Marchant, Erika Greber, Kate Childs, Maria Braeckel, and Melissa Milsten, among others, on the marketing and publicity side. As authors, we have witnessed just how excited Random House is to think in new boxes—and in these challenging days of book publishing, that is more important than ever. We are deeply grateful to have such a creative, powerful, and visionary publisher behind this book.

□□□□□□□□□□□□□□□□□□□□□□□□□□□□□□□□□□□□□□

T his glossary is neither a comprehensive nor an alphabetical list of all the terminology you will find in this book. Instead, it defines a set of key concepts the book explores, and is grouped thematically. In this way it can serve as a simple "toolbox" for your efforts to think in new boxes.

I. The Theory of the Box: The Quest to Understand the Mental Models Within You and Interaction with the World in Front of You

Box: In this book, a box is a mental model.

Mental model: A construction that exists purely "within you," that is, in your mind, in which the reality in front of you is simplified in order to be apprehended in a useful way, according to a given objective. It allows you to think, and subsequently to act. It is an abstraction from the present and a base to build the future. Examples include concepts, stereotypes, categories, ideas, frameworks, and paradigms.

Thinking: Thinking is done within you, and is about organizing facts, data, and observations from the world in front of you by introducing links—and then using this information. This first type of thinking (induction) creates a form, a pattern with some meaning, a box, which is then used to return to the world in front of you, where it is confirmed, refuted, or modified (deduction).

Induction: Induction is a form of thinking involving moving from fragmentary details (particulars) observed in the world in front of you to a connected view of a situation, a binding principle, which eventually forms a theory, a working hypothesis, a box. Analogies provide one of the most classic ways to induce.

Deduction: Deduction is a form of thinking involving the application of an existing box, such as a framework, say, to details observed in the world in front of you, testing the box's capacity to interpret them. Logic is the science of deduction.

Concept: A concept is a box formed via a mental integration of several elements. This abstraction and generalization is built on common observed characteristics, neglecting differences and quantitative measures (for example, the concept "square" is a two-dimensional shape with four segments of the same length joined at right angles).

Judgment: A judgment is a box that simplifies a piece of reality into a few words, generally "A is B." It can be a factual judgment (it is below freezing) or a value judgment colored by one's perceptions of reality (for example, it is very cold, Canadians are nice). A stereotype is a type of value judgment.

Paradigm: One of the most robust and complex forms of boxes, a paradigm is a theory that is relatively broad and widely shared, within which many other theories and frameworks can fit (for example, relativity or democracy).

Eureka: A *Eureka* moment is when you suddenly realize a possible way to move forward in a timely manner—you shift your perception and come up with a new box in a timely way.

Caramba: A *Caramba* moment is when you suddenly realize that one or more of your boxes are out of date, and hence you're in trouble. It's an acknowledgment that the world has changed around you—change is happening to you rather than through you—and you then have to cope by catching up.

II. THE FIVE STEPS: OUR APPROACH TO *THINKING IN NEW BOXES*

Perception: Perception is trying to match some elements of the observed reality with one or more of your existing boxes.

Cognitive bias: A cognitive bias is something that distorts your thinking (in either inductive or deductive mode). It can be seen as a lens or prism that complicates your path from the world in front of you to the boxes within you (induction), or the path to using those boxes to address the world in front of you (deduction).

Doubt: For our purposes, doubt means remembering that all your boxes are working hypotheses, that they represent the world in front of you but are not "true" or "real."

Ambiguity: Ambiguity is the feeling that you have when you cannot choose between a range of possible boxes that could help you understand or address elements of the world in front of you. Ambiguity is not the exception, it's the rule. Contrary to what is commonly heard, a situation is never ambiguous. A situation is what it is—and our inductive interpretation of it is always subject to ambiguity.

Paradox: Paradoxes appear when there is no box available that fits with a given situation in the world in front of you. To process this situation, you need to either create a new box or modify one or more existing boxes. As with ambiguity, a situation is never paradoxical—it is what it is; the paradox is within you.

Divergence: Divergence is the step in the creative process of coming up with a wide range of concepts, ideas, and possibilities in order to find potential new boxes to achieve your organization's specific goals/vision/objectives. Having a large quantity is helpful, and hence withholding judgment is key—selecting the "good" ideas can happen later.

Convergence: Convergence is about applying your skills of reasoning and judgment, focusing in, winnowing down, and, in the end, making decisions about which boxes to take forward based upon agreed constraints and criteria.

Constraint: A firm and specific limit or restriction on potential boxes. In the context of divergence and especially convergence, it is a means to bound your results (for example, "we cannot spend more than $1,000").

Criteria: A set of guidelines to help make a decision, or principles by which to evaluate new boxes. These can be quantitative (such as using cost as a criterion to determine which materials to use in your factory) or a qualitative means to add rigor without figures (for example, including personal preference as a criterion to decide whether to bid on a painting at auction).

III. APPLICATIONS TO BUSINESS

Megatrend: A megatrend is a sweeping but relatively predictable change that is expected to affect the world in front of you (usually your customers, competition, market, etc.). It happens independent of your company and your issues. Megatrends can serve as sources of ideas in the search for new boxes.

Scenario: A scenario is a story about a possible future; it is a box consisting of the description of an end state, a related interpretation of current reality, and an account of how the world gets from one state to the other. A set of scenarios is used to stretch executives' perceptions about alternative future environments in which their decisions might be played out; to better prepare for what cannot be predicted.

Strategic vision: An ambitious image or box relating to the future that is radically preferable (or a necessary alternative) to the current box, according to those who develop it. It is a box that becomes a reference for a company, and thus serves as a guide allowing each employee to approach work more effectively.

Value: An idea or box that expresses the way you feel about the way something should be, for example, "honesty" or "teamwork."

Uncertainty: Thinking about uncertainty is a state of doubt about the world in front of you. Ignoring or underestimating the range of uncertainty in the world is often the reason existing boxes become a limitation or even lead you to *Caramba* moments. One possible categorization of different types of uncertainty is as follows: 1) Known unknowns are things you are aware of that you cannot predict with certainty (for example, the outcome of a sports match, or the possibility of an accident at a busy intersection while crossing against the light); 2) unknown unknowns are things you are not aware of until they happen, such as an earthquake (an example of a black swan or wild card) or a surprise announcement by your competitor (which could be an example of a *Caramba* moment). Dealing with uncertainty is a key component of management and leadership in business.

Black swan/wild card: A black swan or wild card is an event with three characteristics: It is unpredictable, it has a significant impact, and, after the fact, an explanation is readily available that makes it appear less random and more predictable than it was.

Creativity: Creativity can be defined as individuals' ability to change their perception of reality; by so doing they can create new boxes of varying types and sizes. It is possible to have creativity without innovation (for example, an idea that goes nowhere).

Innovation: Innovation can be defined as a change in reality, that is, taking a new box (such as a new product, service, or business model idea) and turning it into reality (for example, revenues, profit, market share). It is possible to have innovation without creativity (for example, copying someone else's idea).

Notes

CHAPTER ONE: NEW BOXES FOR A NEW REALITY

1. Genesis 1:26.
2. Sources regarding the concept "thinking outside the box" include http://en.wikipedia.org/wiki/Thinking_outside_the_box, www.phrases.org.uk/meanings/think-outside-the-box.htm, and John Butman.

CHAPTER TWO: HOW TO CREATE AND USE BOXES

1. Sources for the presentation of double-entry bookkeeping include Michael Chatfield, *A History of Accounting Thought* (New York: Dryden Press, 1977); http://en.wikipedia.org/wiki/Double-entry_bookkeeping_system; and Regina Libina, "The Development of Double-Entry Bookkeeping and Its Relevance in Today's Business Environment" (Honors College Thesis, Pace University, 2005).
2. Yoshinori Fujikawa, "Case Study: Kumon Institute of Education," *Korea Times,* July 31, 2011, http://www.koreatimes.co.kr/www/news/bizfocus/2011/08/342_91956.html. Kumon currently boasts some 1,400 sites in the United States alone that offer keen competition to such established North American supplementary education companies as Sylvan Learning Centers and Huntington Learning Center. Missy Sullivan, "Behind America's Tutor Boom," *Smart Money,* October 20, 2011, http://www.smartmoney.com/spend/family-money/behind-americas-tutor-boom-1318016970246/.
3. Syed Muazzem Ali, "Rise of Sir Fazle Hasan Abed," *Daily Star,* January 6, 2010, http://www.thedailystar.net/newDesign/news-details.php?nid=120600.

4. This story on Rothberg is largely based on an interview with him and on Kevin Davies, *The $1,000 Genome: The Revolution in DNA Sequencing and the New Era of Personalized Medicine* (New York: Free Press, 2010), p. 17.

5. Davies, *The $1,000 Genome*, citing Anita Hamilton, "The Retail DNA Test," *Time*, October 29, 2008, http://www.time.com/time/specials /packages/article/0.28804.1852747_1854493_1854113.00.html.

6. Davies, *The $1,000 Genome*. See also Jonathan Rothberg et al., "An Integrated Semiconductor Device Enabling Non-optical Genome Sequencing," *Nature* 474 (July 21, 2011): 348–53.

7. For more details on the science see Andrew Pollack, "Taking DNA Sequencing to the Masses," *New York Times*, January 4, 2011, http://www .nytimes.com/2011/01/05/health/05gene.html?pagewanted=all, and the following information from Ion Torrent's website (http://community .topcoder.com/lifetech-network/life-technologies/). "Up to now scientists have had to go through an intermediary, such as light, to translate chemical data into digital data. That approach requires proprietary chemistry and optics, like cameras, lasers and scanners. As a result sequencing is complex, slow, and hugely expensive, making it accessible only to the biggest research labs. By contrast, Ion Torrent sequencing technology requires no proprietary chemistries or optics because it's based on a well-characterized biochemical process. When a nucleotide is incorporated into a strand of DNA by a polymerase, a hydrogen ion is released as a byproduct. That hydrogen ion carries a charge that our proprietary ion sensor can detect. If a nucleotide, for example a C, is added to a DNA template and a signal is detected, you know that nucleotide was incorporated. Our sequencer—essentially the world's smallest solid-state pH meter—has called the base, going directly from chemical information to digital information. Because this is direct detection, each nucleotide incorporation is recorded in seconds and you can do an entire run in about an hour."

8. Pollack, "Taking DNA Sequencing to the Masses."

9. Ibid.

10. http://ir.lifetechnologies.com/releasedetail.cfm?releaseid=519891.

CHAPTER THREE: DOUBT EVERYTHING

1. Peter Abailard, *Sic et Non* (1122), ed. Blanche Boyer and Richard McKeon (Chicago: University of Chicago Press, 1977), p. 103.

2. Oliver Wendell Holmes, Jr., "Ideals and Doubts," *Illinois Law Review* 10, no. 3 (May 1915).

3. Gary Wolf, "Steve Jobs: The Next Insanely Great Thing," *Wired*, February 1996.

4. Sources for the story of the Fosbury flop include the International Olympic Committee website at http://www.olympic.org/richard-douglas-fosbury, http://en.wikipedia.org/wiki/Dick_Fosbury, and *The Guardian*'s excellent article "50 Stunning Olympic Moments #28: Dick Fosbury Introduces 'the Flop,'" by Simon Burnton, May 8, 2012, for all Fosbury quotes and other journalist quotes.

5. Rod Nordland, "In Reaction to Two Incidents, a U.S.-Afghan Disconnect," *New York Times*, March 14, 2012, http://www.nytimes.com/2012/03/15/world/asia/disconnect-clear-in-us-bafflement-over-2-afghan-responses.html?ref=rodnordland.

6. See Edward Stein, *Without Good Reason: The Rationality Debate in Philosophy and Cognitive Science* (Oxford: Oxford University Press, 1996).

7. J. M. Henslin, "Craps and Magic," *American Journal of Sociology* 73 (1967): 316–30.

8. Ye Li, Eric J. Johnson, and Lisa Zaval, "Local Warming: Daily Temperature Change Influences Belief in Global Warming," *Psychological Science* 22 (2011): 454.

9. Amos Tversky and Daniel Kahneman, "Extensional Versus Intuitive Reasoning: The Conjunction Fallacy in Probability Judgment," *Psychological Review* 90 (October 1983): 293–315; and Tversky and Kahneman, "Judgment under Uncertainty: Heuristics and Biases," *Science*, New Series 185, no. 4157 (September 27, 1974): 1124–31.

10. Wikipedia, "Monty Hall Problem," http://en.wikipedia.org/wiki/Monty_Hall_problem.

11. Matthew Carlton, "Pedigrees, Prizes, and Prisoners: The Misuse of Conditional Probability," *Journal of Statistics Education* 13, no. 2 (2005), http://www.amstat.org/publications/jse/v13n2/carlton.html.

12. Based on a blog post about anchoring by David McRamey, which built once again on the work of Tversky and Kahneman: http://youarenotsosmart.com/2010/07/27/anchoring-effect/.

13. This experiment was done in 1960 by English psychologist Peter

Wason, who did extensive work exploring the confirmation bias and how we test our hypotheses.

14. Troy A. Paredes, "Too Much Pay, Too Much Deference: Behavioral Corporate Finance, CEOs, and Corporate Governance," *Florida State University Law Review* 32 (2005): 690, in which the author states: "Studies of annual reports have found evidence of such self-serving tendencies among managers, although the findings might reflect a form of impression management, in addition to cognitive bias." Paredes cites James R. Bettman and Barton A. Weitz, "Attributions in the Board Room: Causal Reasoning in Corporate Annual Reports," *Administrative Science Quarterly* 28, no. 165 (1983); Stephen E. Clapham and Charles R. Schwenk, "Self-Serving Attributions, Managerial Cognition, and Company Performance," *Strategic Management Journal* 12, no. 219 (1991); Gerald R. Salancik and James R. Meindl, "Corporate Attributions as Strategic Illusions of Management Control," *Administrative Science Quarterly* 29, no. 238 (1984); Barry M. Staw et al., "The Justification of Organizational Performance," *Administrative Science Quarterly* 28, no. 582 (1983). "In general," writes Paredes, "it is difficult to distinguish self-attribution as a cognitive bias from self-attribution as an impression management strategy."

15. Paredes, "Too Much Pay, Too Much Deference."

16. Richard Thaler, *The Winner's Curse: Paradoxes and Anomalies of Economic Life* (New York: Free Press, 1991), pp. 63–78.

17. Ibid.

18. George E. P. Box and Norman R. Draper, *Empirical Model-Building and Response Surfaces* (New York: Wiley, 1987), p. 424.

19. Felix Gillette, "Ryanair's O'Leary: The Duke of Discomfort," *Bloomberg Businessweek*, September 2, 2010, http://www.businessweek.com /magazine/content/10_37/b4194058006755.html.

CHAPTER FOUR: PROBE THE POSSIBLE

1. http://jacksonville.com/opinion/blog/423471/gary-mills/2012-04-02 /burger-king-launches-new-menu-including-salads-smoothies.

2. This data is from the Entertainment Software Association's 2011 study, carried out by Ipsos MediaCT.

3. PepsiCo's website states: "Our mission is to be the world's premier con-

sumer products company focused on convenient foods and beverages." It also states: "PepsiCo's responsibility is to continually improve all aspects of the world in which we operate—environment, social, economic—creating a better tomorrow than today." http://www.pepsico .com/Company/Our-Mission-and-Vision.html.

4. Rob Walker, "How a New Camera Will Revolutionize Photography," *Atlantic*, December 2011, p. 36; Kim Eaton, "Lytro: The $50 Million Technology That May Change Photography Forever," *Fast Company*, June 20, 2011, http://www.fastcompany.com/1762270/harry-potter-esque -photos-worth-50-million-lytro. For one journalist's review of the new technology, see http://www.youtube.com/watch?v=JDyRSYGcFVM.

5. U.S. Energy Information Administration, *International Energy Outlook 2011*, http://www.eia.gov/forecasts/ieo/pdf/0484(2011).pdf.

6. UN Department of Economic and Social Affairs, Population Division website, World Urbanization Prospect.

7. Ibid.

8. http://en.wikipedia.org/wiki/2010%E2%80%932011_Belgian _government_formation.

9. http://en.wikipedia.org/wiki/Boiling_frog.

10. Philips Company annual report 2011. Home Healthcare Solutions is 14 percent of Philips Healthcare, which is 8.852 billion euros, out of a 22.579 billion euros total. Of note, Home Healthcare Solutions is only one part of Philips's healthcare business, which also includes Imaging Systems and Patient Care and Clinical Informatics.

11. http://www.gmaonline.org/file-manager/Sustainability/Environmental _Success_Stories.pdf, General Mills 2011 Corporate Social Responsibility report.

12. Interviews with Philips executives, Wikipedia, http://www.usa.philips .com/c/airfloss/287417/cat/en/, http://www.waterpik.com/oral-health /videos.html.

13. Interviews with Philips executives, plus article and short video at http:// www.dailymail.co.uk/sciencetech/article-1310446/The-Airfryer-The -frying-machine-gives-perfect-chips--oil.html.

14. Various sources (including Dwayne Spradlin, "Are You Solving the Right Problem?" *Harvard Business Review*, September 2012) attribute this quote to Einstein, some with fifty-five minutes instead of fifty-nine. But he is a person to whom quotes are regularly misattributed, and we have been unable to find the root source.

CHAPTER FIVE: DIVERGE

1. Mars Pathfinder Landing Press Kit, July 1997, NASA.
2. Nineteen ninety-seven is indicated in Wikipedia as the Mars Pathfinder landing date.
3. See "Mars Pathfinder Air Bag Landing Tests," www.nasa.gov/centers /glenn/about/history/marspbag_prt.htm.
4. All facts taken from Wikipedia and Linux.com.
5. Sources for the low-cost hospital pieces include http://online.wsj.com /article/NA_WSJ_PUB:SB125875892887958111.html, http://hbswk.hbs .edu/item/4585.html, and the Aravind Eye Hospital website.
6. There are numerous possible exercises along these lines; we first came across this one in Micael Dahlén, *Creativity Unlimited* (New York: Wiley, 2008).
7. Ibid.
8. From an interview with Vern Burkhardt on IdeaConnection.com, January 28, 2012.
9. As quoted in Jeff Himmelman, "The Secret to Solar Power," *New York Times*, August 12, 2012.

CHAPTER SIX: CONVERGE

1. This quote appears on numerous websites, including thinkexist.com and goodreads.com. Original source unknown.
2. Malcolm Gladwell, "Creation Myth: Xerox PARC, Apple, and the Truth About Innovation," *New Yorker*, May 16, 2011, http://www.newyorker .com/reporting/2011/05/16/110516fa_fact_gladwell#ixzz1Zdlrs6KV.
3. Ibid.
4. Source for this is the first few paragraphs of Wikipedia's entry on "attention deficit hyperactivity disorder," http://en.wikipedia.org/wiki /Attention_deficit_hyperactivity_disorder.

CHAPTER SEVEN: REEVALUATE RELENTLESSLY

1. Oliver Wendell Holmes, Jr., "Ideals and Doubts," *Illinois Law Review* 10, no. 3 (May 1915).

2. "Will the Latest Corporate Shakeup Be the Last for Thomson Reuters?" http://techbytes4lawyers.wordpress.com/2011/12/08/will-the-latest-corporate-shakeup-be-the-last-for-thomson-reuters/; Edmund Lee, "Thomson Reuters CEO Glocer Steps Down as Smith Takes Over," *BusinessWeek*, December 5, 2011, http://www.businessweek.com/news/2011-12-05/thomson-reuters-ceo-glocer-steps-down-as-smith-takes-over.html; Amy Chozick, "Glocer, Chief Exec of Thomson Reuters, is Being Replaced," *New York Times*, December 5, 2011, http://mediadecoder.blogs.nytimes.com/2011/12/01/glocer-head-of-thomson-reuters-is-being-replaced/?ref=media.

3. Nick Wingfield and Brian Stelter, "How Netflix Lost 800,000 Members and Good Will," *New York Times*, October 24, 2011.

4. Email quoted in Nick Greene, "Netflix Fee Increase: Humanity's Most Trying Moment," *Village Voice*, July 15, 2011, http://blogs.villagevoice.com/runninscared/2011/07/netflix_fee_increase.php.

5. Ibid.

6. Compustat U.S. public company data, BCG Strategy Institute analysis.

7. Patrick J. Sauer, "The Mother of Reinvention," *Inc.*, April 27, 2009.

8. "A Timeline of Ford Motor Company," NPR, January 23, 2006, www.npr.org/templates/story/story.php?storyID=5168769.

9. Sauer, "The Mother of Reinvention."

10. Ibid.

11. "A Timeline of Ford Motor Company."

12. All details about Henry Ford's failure to move beyond the Model T are taken from Richard S. Tedlow, *Denial: Why Business Leaders Fail to Look Facts in the Face—and What to Do About It* (New York: Portfolio, 2010).

13. Ibid., pp. 17–19.

14. All facts pertaining to Gelb and the Metropolitan Opera are taken from Gelb's biography posted on http://www.metoperafamily.org, and an interview in March 2012.

15. Interviews with Philips executives, and http://www.uselog.com/2010/03/senseo-real-story-behind-coffee.html.

16. See http://www.senseo.com.

17. Most facts, CEO and other executive quotes, and other assertions about HLL and Nirma come from the case study "Hindustan Lever Limited: Levers for Change," INSEAD-EAC, Fontainebleau, France, 2002. This quote, however, is from the case study "Hindustan Lever Re-invents the Wheel," IESE–International Graduate School of Management, 2003.

18. See Marcel Planellas and Silviya Svejenova, "Creativity: Ferran Adrià," ESADE Business School, May 2006.

19. Julia Hanna, "Customer Feedback Not on elBulli's Menu," *Working Knowledge*, Harvard Business School, November 18, 2009.

20. Ibid.

21. M.S., "Creativity and Business Studies: From Liquid Raviolis to Illiquid Businesses," *Economist*, October 27, 2011.

22. Lisa Abend, "What Will the World's Best Restaurant Become Next?" *Time*, February 18, 2010.

23. Lisa Abend, "The Night elBulli Danced: The World's Most Influential Restaurant Shuts Down," *Time*, August 1, 2011.

24. M.S., "Creativity and Business Studies: From Liquid Raviolis to Illiquid Businesses."

25. Ibid.

26. http://www.pepsico.com/PressRelease/PepsiCo-and-Worlds-Greatest -Chef-Announce-New-Innovation-Partnership06162011.html.

27. Sue Shellenberger, "Better Ideas Through Failure," *Wall Street Journal*, September 27, 2011.

CHAPTER EIGHT: FROM INSPIRATION TO INNOVATION: BUILDING BOLD NEW BOXES—AND THEN FILLING THEM IN

1. All details on Läng's jump are taken from "Remo Laeng, Swiss Base Jumper, Becomes First Ever to Cross a Mountain Range in a Free Fall," *Global Post*, March 10, 2012, http://www.globalpost.com/dispatch /news/regions/europe/120310/remo-laeng-swiss-base-jumper-becomes -first-ever-cross-mountain-r; and "Swiss 'Birdman' Flies Across Alps in Free Fall," Reuters, March 10, 2012, http://uk.reuters.com/article /2012/03/10/us-swiss-freefall-idUKBRE8290FJ20120310.

2. Steve Jobs, "Apple's One-Dollar-a-Year Man," *Fortune*, January 24, 2000, http://money.cnn.com/magazines/fortune/fortune_archive/2000/24 /272277/.

3. http://en.wikipedia.org/wiki/Jean-Fran%C3%A7ois_Champollion and http://en.wikipedia.org/wiki/Rosetta_Stone.

4. http://www.greenstar.org/butterflies/Hole-in-the-Wall.htm and http:// www.bbc.co.uk/news/technology-10663353.

5. http://www.corp.att.com/attlabs/about/mission.html.

6. Sooksan Kantabutra, "What Do We Know About Vision?" *Journal of Applied Business Research* 24, no. 2 (2008), citing J. C. Collins and J. I. Porras, *Built to Last: Successful Habits of Visionary Companies* (London: Century, 1994).

7. http://www.avisbudgetgroup.com/company-information/our-mission-vision-and-values/.

8. http://www.landolakesinc.com/company/philosophy/default.aspx.

9. http://www.progressive.com/progressive-insurance/core-values.aspx.

CHAPTER NINE: IMAGINING THE FUTURE

1. Fabrice Amedeo, "Le fret ferroviaire s'effondre," *Le Figaro*, February 18, 2009.

2. Christopher Hinton, "Drop in Business Travel Slams Airlines, Hotels," Market Watch, April 16, 2009, http://articles.marketwatch.com/2009-04-16/news/30778714_1_high-end-hotels-iata-business-travelers.

3. Brian Spegele and Bob Davis, "High-Speed Train Links Beijing, Shanghai," *Wall Street Journal*, June 29, 2011.

4. Keith Bradsher, "High-Speed Rail Poised to Alter China," *New York Times*, June 22, 2011.

5. Keith Bradsher, "China Is Eager to Bring High-Speed Rail Expertise to the U.S.," *New York Times*, April 7, 2010.

Index

Page numbers beginning with 303 refer to endnotes.

About the Authors

Luc de Brabandere is a fellow and a senior advisor with The Boston Consulting Group. He leads strategic seminars with boards, senior executives, and managers from a wide range of companies looking to develop new visions, new products and services, and long-term scenarios to prepare for the future. He also teaches at the Louvain School of Management, and at the École Centrale in Paris. He is the author or co-author of a wide range of books in French, and of *The Forgotten Half of Change: Achieving Greater Creativity Through Changes in Perception.* He is a regular columnist for various newspapers in France and Belgium, and prior to joining BCG he was the general manager of the Brussels Stock Exchange.

Alan Iny is the senior specialist for creativity and scenarios at The Boston Consulting Group. He has trained thousands of executives and BCG consultants, runs a wide range of workshops across industries, and speaks around the world about coming up with product, service, and other ideas, developing a new strategic vision, and thinking creatively about the future. Before joining BCG in 2003, he earned an MBA from Columbia Business School and an honors BSc from McGill University in mathematics and management. Iny lives in New York with his wife and daughter.

ALAN INY is available for select readings and lectures. To inquire about a possible appearance, please contact the Random House Speakers Bureau at 212-572-2013 or rhspeakers@randomhouse .com.

About the Type

□□□

This book was set in Scala, a typeface designed by Martin Majoor in 1991. It was originally designed for a music company in the Netherlands and then was published by the international type house FSI FontShop. Its distinctive extended serifs add to the articulation of the letterforms to make it a very readable typeface.